Sacramental Commons

Nature's Meaning

**Series Editor: Roger S. Gottlieb, Professor of Philosophy,
Worcester Polytechnic Institute**

Each title in Nature's Meaning is created to have the personal stamp of a passionate and articulate spokesperson for environmental sanity. Intended to be engagingly written by experienced thinkers in their field, these books express the comprehensive and personal vision of the topic by an author who has devoted years to studying, teaching, writing about, and often being actively involved with the environmental movement. The books will be intended primarily as college texts, and as beautifully produced volumes, they will also appeal to a wide audience of environmentally concerned readers.

Integrating Ecofeminism, Globalization, and World Religions,
by Rosemary Radford Ruether

Environmental Ethics for a Postcolonial World,
by Deane Curtin

The Ecological Life: Discovering Citizenship and a Sense of Humanity,
by Jeremy Bendik-Keymer

Sacramental Commons: Christian Ecological Ethics,
by John Hart

Sacramental Commons

Christian Ecological Ethics

John Hart

ROWMAN & LITTLEFIELD PUBLISHERS, INC.
Lanham • Boulder • New York • Toronto • Oxford

ROWMAN & LITTLEFIELD PUBLISHERS, INC.

Published in the United States of America
by Rowman & Littlefield Publishers, Inc.
A wholly owned subsidiary of The Rowman & Littlefield Publishing Group, Inc.
4501 Forbes Boulevard, Suite 200, Lanham, Maryland 20706
www.rowmanlittlefield.com

PO Box 317
Oxford
OX2 9RU, UK

British Library Cataloguing in Publication Information Available

Library of Congress Cataloging-in-Publication Data

Hart, John, 1943–
   Sacramental commons : Christian ecological ethics / John Hart.
      p.   cm.— (Nature's meaning)
   Includes bibliographical references (p.) and index.
   ISBN-13: 978-0-7425-4599-1 (cloth : alk. paper)
   ISBN-10: 0-7425-4599-7 (cloth : alk. paper)
   ISBN-13: 978-0-7425-4605-9 (pbk. : alk. paper)
   ISBN-10: 0-7425-4605-5 (pbk. : alk. paper)
   1. Human ecology—Religious aspects—Christianity.   2. Nature—Religious
aspects—Christianity.   3. Sacraments.   4. Sacred space.   5. Stewardship,
Christian.   I. Title.   II. Series.
   BT695.5.H36   2006
   241′.691—dc22   2006004816

Printed in the United States of America

♾ ™ The paper used in this publication meets the minimum requirements of American
National Standard for Information Sciences—Permanence of Paper for Printed Library
Materials, ANSI/NISO Z39.48-1992.

To friends
who have engaged the Spirit in creation
and
who have worked in complementary ways
for the good of the commons
and
for the common good—
Daniel Berrigan
mentor, activist priest, poet, and peacemaker;
Dorothy Day
suffering servant of and with the poor, worker for justice;
Phillip Deere
Muskogee elder, spiritual grandfather, healer,
and human rights activist;
Gustavo Gutiérrez
mentor, priest, liberation theologian, and social activist;
Dorothee Soelle
innovative and compassionate scholar, teacher, and social activist;
David Sohappy Sr.
Wanapum elder, spiritual grandfather, healer,
and human rights activist

Contents

Foreword

$\mathcal{T}$his work by John Hart is very unique. It discusses a traditional theme in Christian theology—the sacramental world—but in an original and surprising way. It recovers a sense of the sacramental through the new perception of the world that comes to us from the new cosmology, from ecology, and from cosmic spirituality, all in permanent dialogue with the great tradition and with indigenous traditions. The universe is sacramental because it is full of messages and meanings that can be appropriated by the human being who is sensitive to the spiritual dimension of the world. The world is not just transcendent and immanent. It is transparent to the presence of the Spirit who actuates it in the evolutionary process and in all the movements of nature and history. We form, truly, an immense cosmic, biotic, and human community.

This vision is inherent in indigenous cultures and was attested to in an exemplary way by St. Francis of Assisi, who saw in every being a brother and a sister and a sign of the presence of God. It is not without reason that John Hart begins analyzing the significance of the experience of St. Francis for today, especially, in a world that orients itself more by objects, functions, and structures than by symbols and natural and existential sacraments.

The importance of John Hart's contribution is that he recovers natural sacraments and joins them to social sacraments. He does this exemplarily with the sacramental significance of water, considered not as a commodity but as a natural and common good, vital and irreplaceable, the real great sacrament of life in all its forms. He does something similar with the salmon, which the Wanapum Indians see as the thread that ties the human world to the rest of the biotic community.

Why is it important to recover the sacramental vision in these times? Because it is precisely the countries with a Christian tradition that have the greatest violations of the dignity of nature. Christians are the ones who most pollute, contaminate the soil, and cause global warming. Recovering the sacramental dimension, whether with the doctrinal patrimony of the Christian tradition or with the new vision of Earth as Gaia, a living superorganism, fills us with veneration and respect and puts brakes on our voracity to dominate and consume everything.

Discussing a sacramental vision of the world as John Hart does helps to create a new spirituality—that is, a new experience of the Spirit acting within everything. At the same time, he offers a valuable contribution for a culture to appreciate the sacrality of creation and to learn to respect it and care for it as it is in itself and as it is in communion with us.

—Leonardo Boff
Petrópolis, Rio de Janeiro, Brazil
February 15, 2006

Leonardo Boff (1938–) is a native of Brazil and one of the founders of the theology of liberation. He is also a community activist and former university professor. He has more than seventy books published, including *Ecology and Liberation: A New Paradigm* (1995) and *Cry of the Earth, Cry of the Poor* (1997) linking theology, ecology, and social justice. He works for ecojustice by promoting the *Earth Charter* while serving as a member of the Earth Charter Commission.

Acknowledgments

𝒞ritical thought emerges in context. It builds upon foundations provided by previous scholarship and reflection. It contributes to the development of new insights through its integration of words and work, of reflective theory based on practical experience. People who consider traditional ideas or new insights will utilize or modify what they encounter after evaluating it on the basis of their own education and experience. Intellectual constructs should be dynamic. They should be intended to be clarified and strengthened, to be related to and altered by new data and understandings, and to be reformulated. They mediate tradition, embody transition, and could promote spiritual, social, and intellectual transformation.

I am especially grateful for the insights and ideas of the friends to whom I have dedicated this book. Phillip Deere and David Sohappy became friends through my human rights work with the International Indian Treaty Council, a nongovernmental organization accredited to the United Nations; each recorded insights for me from their respective traditions. Daniel Berrigan has been for almost four decades my friend and brother, a fellow worker for peace. Gustavo Gutiérrez and I have been friends since I wrote about his work in my doctoral dissertation, and I served as his tutor (teaching assistant) at Union Theological Seminary in New York almost thirty years ago. While at Union, I volunteered periodically at the Catholic Worker because I shared its ideals, expressed so well by Dorothy Day in her life and writings. I participated in a peace walk with her, and shared lunch with her and with another mentor and friend, Dorothee Soelle, whom I had taken to the Catholic Worker so that she might meet Dorothy Day. I am grateful to these friends for their influences on my life and work.

Sacramental Commons has been in process periodically for seven years. Consequently, earlier conceptual expressions of several chapters have been published. Segments of "Salmon and Social Ethics—Relational Consciousness in the Web of Life," published in the *Journal of the Society of Christian*

Ethics (2002), are incorporated in "Species Survival" and "Commons Commitments: Ecological Ethics." Sections of "Living Water: A Sacramental Commons," published in *Catholic Rural Life* (Spring 2003), are retained in modified form in "Living Water." Similarly, "A Jubilee for a New Millennium: Justice for Earth and for Peoples of the Land," from *Catholic Rural Life* (Spring 2001), is reconstituted and elaborated as "Jubilee in the Commons." Segments of "Sustaining the Sacramental Commons" in *Dialog—A Journal of Theology* (Fall 2003) appear in "Spirit, Commons, and Community." Permission to use previously published material is gratefully acknowledged.

I thank the editor of the series Nature's Meaning, Roger Gottlieb, for his friendship; his commitments to justice, creation, and community; and his patience. I thank Brian Romer, editor at Rowman & Littlefield, for his encouragement, his interest in my work, and his dedication to ecological concerns.

I greatly appreciate the loving encouragement and support of my wife, Jane Morell-Hart, and of our children, Shanti and Daniel.

Introduction

Sacramental Creation

$\mathscr{A}$ *sacred* place is a place made holy by an active and relational divine presence. Creation is sacred because it is the dynamic realization of divine imagination and the locus of divine immanence. A *sacramental* place is a place that reveals signs of the transcendent and immanent creating Spirit. People who are open spiritually (consciously or unconsciously) are able to see these signs, are drawn into a conscious experience of divine presence, and are inspired to walk in creation in a new way. It is a mode of consciousness and a way of conduct in which they care for Earth and all life, and are compassionate toward all people.

All places are sacred because all creation is present in and to the Creator. Since the transcendent-immanent Spirit simultaneously is in creation and is not limited by space or time, every place is a sacred place. But the sacrality of a place is visible only to those who use their physical and spiritual eyes to see beyond the immediately apparent. Then they participate in all of reality in its spiritual, social, and personal dimensions. Spiritual vision enables people to experience the sacred presence of the immanent-transcendent Spirit who permeates Earth and the cosmos at large. Creation mediates the Creator. The eyes of the human spirit, when open to the divine Spirit, see signs and symbols of the Spirit in the cosmos and the commons, in nature and in human communities. While creation mediates—reveals—the Creator in different dimensions of reality, spiritual vision provides a deeper encounter with the Spirit than physiological vision.

All places can become sacramental to people who see signs of the Spirit in them. When they see these signs, people experience sacramental moments. These are times in which they become immersed in divine Spirit, are conscious of divine creativity, and are in union with divinized creation—in itself and as infused with divine presence. A sacramental experience is a place, a moment, a prayer, or an event that is graced by and revelatory of, and provides relational engagement with, divine presence.

Sacramental places are not located just in pristine nature; nor are sacramental moments limited to church, synagogue, or temple, or to experiences in only one sacred tradition. Cities and farms, airplanes and highways, markets and concert halls can be sacramental places. The joys and tragedies of human existence can be sacramental moments. The presence and experience of God are found in different ways and places: in the religious rituals of all cultures and faiths, in the cries of the hungry and the tortured, in tears of joy over the birth of a child or tears of grief over the loss of a loved one.

In the twenty-first century, people are ever more aware of ecological crises and their political and economic causes. Individuals and communities might be conscious simultaneously of religious perspectives that challenge the current state of affairs and deplore the desecration of creation, the extinction of species, and the political, ethnic, racial, sexual, and economic oppression of people and peoples that causes them physical, social, and spiritual suffering. Awareness of creation as a sacramental commons can help people to work toward the alleviation and elimination of human-caused misery and to live with the natural, if disruptive and at times harmful, events and processes of the dynamic universe. Creation is in process: cosmic dynamics are ongoing; biological evolution continues; intercultural exchanges of insights occur; human consciousness and conscience develop.

SACRAMENT

Sacraments are signs of the creating Spirit that draw people into grace-filled moments permeated by a heightened awareness of divine presence and engagement with divine Being.

A *natural sacrament* is a place, event, or creature in nature that, as a sign of Spirit's immanence and presence, draws people toward the Spirit and simultaneously invites them to relate not only to the Spirit but to all living and nonliving creation. A natural sacrament, then, can be an occasion of grace, a moment of encounter with Spirit. It can be both a sign and a stimulus: a sign of a relational divine presence and ongoing divine creativity; a stimulus to explore more fully the intricacies of the universe, Earth, and living communities and to seek more in-depth relational bonds: spirit and Spirit, human being and divine Being; human experience and divine Becoming; spirit and spirit; individuals and species.

In Christian churches, sacraments ordinarily have been understood to be religious rituals, usually led by a member of the clergy in a dedicated, human-constructed sacred space. They are viewed as visible signs or symbols of an invisible experience of God's "grace" (divine presence expressed in relational love) in a special way. Outside such church settings, pristine places came to be viewed as *sacramental* because they reveal the Spirit's loving creativity in their biodiversity, textured topography, and provision of food, water, and shelter for their inhabitants; or, because they have been the locus of memorable encounters with the Spirit. The former are remembered in stories, poetry, and song. The latter are commemorated by the construction of altars, temples, or churches, and remembered or reenacted in rituals overseen by designated clergy; or they are left in relatively pristine condition, visited occasionally by devout pilgrims or by seekers of similar or complementary experiences.

In earliest Christianity, *sacrament* referred to numerous distinct religious ceremonies and practices. Later, Augustine (354–430) defined sacraments as "visible forms of invisible grace," which allowed for an almost unlimited variety of mediations and experiences of the sacred in creation. This implied that rituals led by ordained clergy were not necessary, since all creation could be sacramental to the spiritually observant person. Hugh of St. Victor (twelfth century) reduced the number of sacraments to thirty. In the Catholic Church, seven church rituals that were derived from teachings and actions of Jesus were officially designated sacraments by the Council of Trent (1547–1563). Previously, Martin Luther (1483–1546) and other Protestant reformers had limited the sacraments to two, baptism and holy communion, which seemed to them to be the only ones that had a scriptural justification in the words and work of Jesus.

There have been exceptions, in recent Catholic Christian thought, to a ritually reserved use of the term *sacrament*. The document *Lumen Gentium* from the Second Vatican Council (1962–1965) of the Catholic Church called the church a "sacrament." Edward Schillebeeckx, a Dutch priest and theologian, called Jesus Christ "the sacrament of the encounter with God," a phrase helpful to people in the Christian faith. In Medellín, Colombia, in 1968, Pope Paul VI declared, in the spirit of the Last Judgment story in the gospel of Matthew (25:31–46), that "the poor are a sacrament of Christ";[1] that is, the poor concretize theologically the teaching that Jesus as the divine judge— the Son of Man—dwells among the poor and will judge people of all nations and grant them a blessed afterlife on the basis of their practical works of compassion toward the poor. These works include feeding the hungry, giving drink to the thirsty, clothing the naked, sheltering the homeless, visiting the sick, and visiting the imprisoned.

Linked together, the implications of these teachings are that Christians seeking to encounter God might work with the poor, who reveal Christ (who he is, what he teaches), who in turn reveals God (and God's attributes and expectations). In the Bible, compassion for the poor and oppressed is present in the life and teachings of Jesus and the Hebrew prophets. Understandings from the Christian tradition complement other religions' insights that link belief in a divine Spirit with doctrines about the Spirit's love for all peoples, not just for adherents of a particular faith, and complement others' ethical principles advocating justice for the economically, politically, and ethnically oppressed.

Places and people can be sacraments. People become spiritually immersed in places where in the past extraordinary events occurred or extraordinary people lived. People become spiritually engaged in places where dramatic visions or experiences of flowing energy occur in the present. These are sacramental places and moments today for those who experience such phenomena and for those who acknowledge that the experience occurred, and appreciate that such moments will occur again. People walking with the Spirit in the way of the Spirit express their spirituality by doing the work of the Spirit, and so they are sacramental. People who care for creation and are compassionate toward creatures reveal the Spirit's love for and relationship with all being, and so they are sacramental. People who are suffering mediate to others the Spirit's call to alleviate their pain, and so they are sacramental.

In the Christian tradition, Jesus is the Word of God "in the beginning" as the mediation of the Creator Spirit's creative imagination emanating into the concrete material forms and energy flows of the universe. The Word made flesh is the mediation of the Spirit's liberating presence in history. The church's sacraments, instituted by Jesus, the historical Word, are signs of the Spirit's loving presence expressed in ritual form. Creation's sacraments are signs of the eternal Word's cosmic creative presence, activity, and guidance.

The Word remains in creation as its activating presence, principle, and power. Thus, for Christians, the work of Christ Jesus, God and Man, is sacramentally twofold. First, through the church, the community of believers, which is called to live and proclaim a Spirit-presenced integral relational community, a "reign of God," evidenced by a creation commons community, so that humankind will strive to ensure that God's will be done on Earth as it is in heaven; this effort was initiated by the Word made flesh. Second, through creation, which carries the creative activity of the Word begun prior to incarnation in the historical Jesus into creating activity, the dynamic evolutionary processes of the integration of matter and energy that reveal the interaction of cosmic constructs and chaotic contingents.

What do the ideas and ideals of "sacramental creation" and "sacramental commons" have to do with the everyday life of people (and how will they impact Earth and the entire biotic community)? What do they mean for, and how will they affect the lives of, poor people, blue-collar working people, hungry people, and office workers? How will they ameliorate the conditions of those who are politically, economically, ethnically, racially, and sexually oppressed? How will they help to alter periodic or continual occurrences of individual and structural social sin? How will they avoid being the esoteric possession of a few, or just another individualistic, self-satisfying, self-aggrandizing, "feel good," conscience-quieting, individual or group superiority-affirming form of escapism (the temptation and result of some "New Age" movements, fundamentalist religions, and humanist ideologies)?

COMMONS

The diverse but complementary meanings of *commons* provide initial answers to the queries just expressed. A *school commons* in a dining hall is a common table from which students obtain food for nourishment; it is a microcosm of a village commons and the Earth commons. A *village commons* is a shared place, often at the village center, where people derive some individual and community benefit, including bodily nourishment—it can be a grazing place for cattle that provide milk or meat (limited in number so that one person's animals would not consume all the available grass) or a source of community water; social nourishment—it can serve as a gathering place for community meetings and celebrations; and bodily and social nourishment—it can be the site of a marketplace that provides livelihood for some, needed goods, such as food, for others, and community interactions for all, in the form of conversation or social events. A *bioregional commons* is a part of Earth where diverse species in their individual members live integrated, interdependent lives in a fixed or fluid, expanding or contracting ecosystem. The *Earth commons* is Earth as a whole, in which ecosystems are globally related and integrated. Earth has integrity in itself, in the integrated workings of its basic elements and events, and Earth is a commons for others as it nourishes all peoples and all living creatures.

SACRAMENTAL UNIVERSE AND
SACRAMENTAL COMMONS

Appropriation of the depths of meaning present in the concepts of sacramental universe and sacramental commons, and the consequent development of a creation-centered consciousness, enable people to appreciate personal and community well-being derived from their relationships with Earth, with all life, and with the Spirit immanent in all of these.

Sacramental universe and *sacramental commons* express complementary perceptions of divine immanence in, and engagement with humanity through, the created cosmos. A *sacramental universe* is the totality of creation infused with the visionary, loving, creative, and active power of the Spirit's transcendent-immanent and creating presence. A *sacramental commons* is creation as a moment and locus of human participation in the interactive presence and caring compassion of the Spirit who is immanent and participates in a complex cosmic dance of energies, elements, entities, and events. It is a place in which people in historical time integrate the spiritual meaning of *sacramental* with the social meaning of *commons*, and consequently is characterized by a sacramental community consciousness that stimulates involvement in concrete efforts to restore and conserve ecosystems. People in the sacramental commons who have a sacramental consciousness care about and for creation as a whole; care about and for members of the biotic community; and care about and for members of the human community who are denied needed goods of creation.

A sacramental consciousness is a creation-centered consciousness; it sees signs of the Creator in creation. The creation-centered consciousness integrates creation spirituality and creation ecology. *Creation* implies the activity of a Creator, and expresses the consequences of the Creator's creativity. A creation-centered consciousness recognizes that all creatures emerge from the dynamic cosmic processes and the evolutionary biological process set in motion at the origins of the universe, and brought to fruition over time in the interplay of cosmic laws and contingent events. A creation-centered consciousness recognizes as well human responsibilities to respect those laws and to live in harmony with them and with the biotic community while meeting human needs.

In the current historical context of ecological devastation, political domination, wartime destruction, and economic deprivation, the understanding of a sacramental commons stimulates exploration of the revelatory, prophetic, communal, and ecological dimensions of Christianity (and of other faith traditions).

TRANSCENDENCE AND IMMANENCE

Spiritual, religious, and theological perspectives have had a tendency to focus on transcending and transcendent experience. Often such understandings are vestiges of a worldview that believed divine being to be primarily if not exclusively encountered in a spiritual dimension of reality; people looked beyond Earth to a better, immortal life beyond "mere" material existence. Today, for example, some Christians focus on a "personal relationship with Jesus" and ignore the social implications of his life and teachings for their daily lives in community. They limit "salvation" to a future, heavenly realm. They set transcending experience completely beyond Earth existence. In a parallel way, some members of more "mainstream" churches limit transcendence to an end in itself, an experience encountered in "spiritual" practices of prayer and meditation, often in personally isolated moments of solitude.

While the preceding understandings might be personally beneficial, they are socially meaningless if they remain at that stage. However, those people whose prayer goes outward, whose life, even in monastic settings, includes prayer for the well-being of others, including for the promotion of social justice, peace, healing, and care for Earth, complement the struggles of people working for a better world, including those who endure oppressive social conditions. The complementarity of roles unites transcendent and immanent immersions of distinct ways of life.

Social activism without a spiritual base of some kind can drain the energy and discourage the engagement of committed people. Spiritual asceticism without a social involvement of some kind can divert attention from, and distract commitment to, the interrelationship of transcendence and immanence, the spiritual and the social, the pneumatic and the prophetic. The union of the two overcomes the dangers of prayer without commitment, and of commitment without prayer. Transcendence in such a context has several meanings and implications. It need not be reserved as a term for "otherworldly" engagement. Transcendence might be nonworldly to some extent in that it is, in part, experience of divine being in a spiritual dimension, and momentary intellectual separation from the physical limitations of a particular place and the ideological limitations of a particular (sub)culture.

Transcendence means to be independent of, not limited by, and to be free(d) from, not constrained by, exigencies of the moment such as financial pressures, oppressive structures, or authoritarian people. It is to be engaged with and in and within, but not limited by, current social and corporeal reality. It surpasses that reality at least in thought while experiencing divine-human engagement and, possibly, if the context is appropriate, in action also. It means being within yet distinct from and outside a social context, even while being part of that context and seemingly bound by its conditions and circumstances; it is to be simultaneously immersed in and separated from, and personalized, socialized, and individuated (not "individualized") within, that context.

Transcendence means that human transcending is not corporeally separated from, but neither is limited by, material reality. Transcendence means to be engaged simultaneously with more than one dimension of reality. Transcendence means to be "in the world (in both senses of "world": a mind-set; material existence) but not of it." Transcendence means, for humans, that they intellectually and spiritually go beyond, become beyond, are beyond, and are in more than one dimension of reality; they are not bound or limited by their contextual, historical, cultural, religious, political, economic, class, or physical conditions, even while being physically still present and immersed in them, and constrained physically or mentally to some extent by them, until the transcending vision is *act*ualized (acted upon) and *reali*zed (made real) in concrete historical context(s). Individuals and communities can be transcendent from the material while immersed in it: engaged with but not enchained by corporality, historicity, and contextuality, nor by text or tradition.

Immanence means that human material or social experiences are not materially separated from, nor limited by, spiritual reality. Immanence means engagement with distinct but related dimensions of reality. Immanence means that people are not absorbed by spiritual dimensions of reality, even while engaged with them. Immanence means that people recognize that the spiritual dimension, even while experienced, does not represent the totality of reality; people resist the temptation to regard it as such, to be self-absorbed in it while claiming to be divinely absorbed, and work to enable other people to have the time and place to have similar experiences unencumbered by exigencies of material and social survival.

Divine transcendence-immanence means that the Spirit-transcendent is not limited by the Spirit-immanent, nor is the Spirit-immanent limited by the Spirit-transcendent. The Spirit retains a divine identity or "personness" in both ways of being, and is Spirit-transcendent-immanent or Spirit-immanent-transcendent, depending on the direction and experience of the Creator-creation-creature engagement with divine Being-Becoming.[2]

The insight of Rabbi Abraham Heschel is helpful here: "the divine pathos is the unity of the eternal and the temporal, of meaning and mystery, of the metaphysical and the historical. It is the real basis of the relation between God and [humanity], of the correlation of Creator and creation."[3]

RELATIONAL CONSCIOUSNESS

A *relational consciousness* integrates the transcendent and the immanent. It has two aspects: relational transcendence and relational immanence.

Relational *transcendence* means that while people transcend their social condition—either to analyze it critically and propose alternative contexts for themselves and their community, or to be drawn intimately into union with the Spirit—they are still united with and engaged by it. They remain material beings, and they will become immersed consciously in the world (physical, ideological, structural) again when the transcendent moment is over. Relational *immanence* means that while people are immersed in their social condition, they remain connected to and engaged with the spiritual and analytical dimensions of reality. Their awareness and intellectual and spiritual acceptance of the reality that Spirit-transcendent is Spirit-immanent can help people to understand how relational consciousness brings them into this integrated mode of being, thinking, and acting. In this relational consciousness mode, Spirit, nature, and community are engaged together.

This perception is illustrated to some extent in the Korean Mask Dance, described in *minjung* theology. This traditional dance is an annual event in which community members portray the interplay of their controlled roles in life with the freedom and authority of those who control them: political rulers, economic overlords, and traditional religious leaders. The dance gives them an opportunity to ridicule somewhat those who exercise power over them and to poke fun at themselves at the same time. As the dance ends, the audience participates in the event by dancing with the actors. After the dance, community members usually resign themselves to their social station and status.[4]

Hyun Young-hak describes the "critical transcendence" experienced by some dancers. The *minjung*, who are the oppressed common people, lament their lot in life but regard it with a certain rueful humor, thereby transcending it to some extent. They are able to envision a different social reality from this transcendent place where they understand and analyze their social position. They come to this moment and position on their own, based on their contextual experience; they do not rely on the pronouncements of rulers or the teachings of religious leaders. The acting and dancing provide an outlet for suppressed feelings and ideas, and enable people to reflect more seriously on their social position and suffering, and consider possibilities for altering this reality. Their new ways of thinking result not from formal study or religious instructions but from their own life experiences, from their shared social biography.[5]

In relational transcendence—relational immanence a moment arrives when people analyze their social conditions and formulate a vision to stimulate projects to alter them. It is a "relational" transcendence, rather than the "critical" transcendence suggested by *minjung* theologians from their cultural context, because people would not be critical of the Spirit with whom they are engaged (except, perhaps, to lament and question, as did Job and the prophets of old, the apparent divine distancing from oppressive conditions afflicting people).

People who link the transcendent and the immanent in their lives experience sacramental moments. Such moments are times and places in which people recognize and experience the fullness of the reality in which they live. The corporeal and spiritual dimensions of reality are known simultaneously. The subsistence, social, and spiritual aspects of human existence blend into one. Such moments, rarely experienced, are both transcending and immanentizing. They link people with the spiritual and catalyze them to engage the social. They occur when people have a heightened consciousness of the divine presence that is always immanent in the cosmos and the commons; seek or are open to divine-human engagement; and have a willingness to live and act according to the insights received through their experience. These revelatory moments can occur in pristine nature or in the presence of the suffering poor; in human-constructed places of worship, or amid God-created settings; while hearing beautiful music or enjoying a child's laughter; while conversing with a close friend or while reading a novel; at work or at play.

People are called, in their individual and community lives and contexts, to integrate the *personal spiritual* (their individual engagement with the Spirit), the *social spiritual* (their communal engagement with the Spirit in communities of faith, religious institutions, organized prayers and rituals), and the *universal spiritual* (their sense of the sacred that is not limited by personal experience or religious doctrines; spiritual experiences and understandings shared transculturally). When people of distinct faiths acknowledge the personal spirituality of each other, and when they acknowledge that each faith from its own cultural base expresses a sense of the same Spirit, however religiously and culturally defined, and acknowledge further that they share in divine being in complementary ways with mutual but sometimes unexpressed or undefinable understandings, then the Earth commons becomes a shared revelatory commons. People develop an integral relational consciousness and are part of an integral relational community, that is, in Christian terms, they participate in the relational community ("reign of God") advocated by Jesus.

Sacramental Commons explores present and prospective understandings of "sacramental universe" and "sacramental commons," discusses creation as a "mediation of the Spirit," offers ways to care about and take care of creation, and reflects on implications of these themes for people of faith in the third millennium. Although the title emerges from concepts formulated in the Christian tradition, the ideas presented are not limited to, or intended to be limited by, that tradition. Other faith traditions provide complementary insights into the relationship between Creator and creation, and express those insights in doctrines, ethics, and rituals that use their own symbols and beliefs. Humanists have similar perspectives, even if they are not expressed in religious or spiritual terms. The book develops Christian *ecological* ethics. Some writers use the words *environment* and *ecology* interchangeably, but they do have distinct meanings. An *environment* is the context and conditions in which biota exist, their habitat. *Ecology* is about relationships among organisms and between organisms and the context(s) of their existence.

Since the book emerges from the Christian tradition, perspectives from the Bible engage ideas in the text. There is, of course, a danger in citing biblical texts: the *eisegesis* that uses biblical quotations as "proof texts" to support an idea or view. In the present work, biblical citations are intended to be illustrative, not supportive or normative. Reflection on contexts, for a Christian, include consideration of biblical teachings that relate to them: How has the tradition considered this particular idea or situation, or something analogous to it? How do biblical texts and norms converse with, not coerce, considerations of contemporary concerns? Biblical verses are used here because they are pertinent to, not proofs of, what is expressed. In the imagery of Gustavo Gutiérrez, reflection on biblical texts comes "at sundown," to provide insights into what transpired during a day of engagement with issues in context.

In the pages that follow, Part I, "Creation," discusses divine creativity and people's response to it and to divine immanence. "Sacramental Universe" explores the revelatory nature of creation as a whole. "The Spirit of St. Francis" draws insights from Francis of Assisi, for people of all times and cultures, about human relationships with sacramental Earth, communion with and concern for other species, and compassion for human outcasts. "Native Spirits" links Francis to kindred spirits: the Lakota elder and healer Black Elk, and the Muskogee elder and healer Phillip Deere.

Part II, "Commons," discusses creation as the context of the interdependent and interrelated lives of members of the biotic community. "Sacramental Commons" focuses on Earth as a place on which and in which all life in its personal and communal manifestations strives to find its place and meet its needs, while interacting in integrated ecosystems with other individuals and species. It discusses how the life and ideas of naturalist John Muir evidence his sense of the revelatory aspect of creation and his regard for Earth and all life, effectively expressing a perspective that is complementary to and at times congruent with consciousness of a sacramental commons. "Living Water" discusses water privatization and pollution, and water's availability, abundance, and accessibility; and it explores water's sacramental nature while suggesting that it be recognized as a human right and a natural right. "Species Survival" uses the plight of salmon and of the Wanapum people on the Columbia–Snake rivers system in the northwestern United States to focus on the interaction and interdependence of humankind and biokind as a whole, through discussion of salmon extinctions and their impact on native peoples, particularly on the River People represented in the life and actions of the Wanapum elder and Washat healer David Sohappy.

Part III, "Community," discusses relationships within the human community, between the human community and the rest of the biotic community, and between creation and Creator. "Nature's Natural Rights" explores extending the concept and practice of "natural rights" to all nature, beyond the customary anthropocentric limitation of natural rights solely to members of the human species. This chapter relates this proposal to recognition that individuals and species have an intrinsic value that precedes, endures through, and is greater than their instrumental value; and proposes that relationships among species should be, to the extent possible, primordially "I-Thou" and not primarily "I-It," to borrow Martin Buber's terminology. "Commons Good, Common Good, and Common Goods" advocates concern and care for the Earth commons shared by all life; regard for the needs of all life; an equitable distribution of Earth goods among members of the biotic community, who live at times in predator-prey relationships; and the relationship of commons understandings to principles expressed in the *Earth Charter*. "Job, Injustice, and Dynamic Nature" reflects on the relationship of religious faith, the goodness of creation, and experiences of suffering, through a discussion of natural disasters, human evil, evolution, and divine *kenosis*, using the story of Job as a foundation.

Part IV, "Common Ground," focuses on human responsibility toward other created beings at their places of interaction. "Jubilee in the Commons" discusses the biblical Jubilee Year and suggests contemporary ways to implement Jubilee provisions: rest for the land, release of slaves, remission of debts, and redistribution of land. "Commons Commitments: Ecological Ethics" suggests guiding principles for concrete social projects that flow from understandings of sacramental creation and community. "Spirit, Commons, and Community" discusses nature as the locus of engagement with divine being, and the implications of that engagement for human individuals and communities. It incorporates insights from the four parts of the book: to use present people's memories of the past, experiences and insights from the present, and visions for the future to stimulate development of a sacramental commons that would be the new reality for Earth and for all the biotic community.

The book explores nature's meaning from a faith perspective that is based on biblical teachings, the Christian tradition, and native people's insights. It discusses human-divine engagement in complementary dimensions of Earth existence: the subsistence (material), the social, and the spiritual. The book offers a glimpse of the present moment of an evolving exploration. It is offered for consideration and further development. The relational consciousness and social vision presented invite people to deliberate them, debate them, and develop them dynamically, as needed in distinct times and places, to renew Earth and to revitalize Earth communities. The book emerges from the author's interaction with text (particularly the Bible and extrabiblical religious and ecological thought) and context (experiences with the struggles of oppressed people, with free members of the biotic community, with Earth, and with the Spirit-transcendent-immanent. It is an ethical reflection that emerges from social commitment and ecological engagement.

The Bible teaches that without a vision, people will perish. In troubled times today and into tomorrow, visions of a sacramental commons and a sacramental commons community can draw people away from spiritual and social ennui or despair, immerse them in creation and community, instill hope in them, and inspire them to work to realize a utopian vision.

NOTES

1. This phrase of Paul VI is cited in Peruvian Bishops' Commission for Social Action, *Between Honesty and Hope*, trans. John Drury (Maryknoll, N.Y.: Maryknoll, 1970), 226.

2. Arthur Peacocke discusses the concept of God Being and Becoming in *Theology for a Scientific Age: Being and Becoming—Natural, Divine and Human* (London: SCM, 1993). I came to appreciate this phrasing through his lectures and writings while I participated in the "Oxford Seminars in Science and Christianity," 1999–2001.

3. Abraham J. Heschel, *The Prophets: An Introduction* (New York: Harper Torchbooks, 1969,) 2 vols., II: 11.

4. See the essays in Commission on Theological Concerns of the Christian Conference of Asia, ed., *Minjung Theology: People as the Subjects of History* (Maryknoll, N.Y.: Orbis, 1981). In the Middle Ages, a similar event called the "Feast of Fools" was held in Europe. It is described by Harvey Cox in a book of the same name. At the festival, commoners ridiculed the nobility and church leaders. Eventually, as their words became more pointed, and suggested that political change might result from their personal and communal resentment, the feast was stopped by the nobility. Stripped of its overt political and social commentary, it continues today in costumed Halloween celebrations.

5. Commission on Theological Concerns, *Minjung Theology*, 50–52.

I

CREATION

Cosmos-chaos-cosmos is brought into being by and reveals the creating Spirit-transcendent. Perceptive people from distinct cultures have seen signs of the Creator in creation throughout history and in diverse places. The encounter has changed their consciousness and conduct and inspired them to see living creatures in a new way, as relatives in creation. Their spiritual experiences have stimulated people to share their insights with others and to seek the well-being of Earth, of all peoples, and of the extended community of all life.

Sacramental Universe

$\mathcal{T}$he universe flows from the dynamic imagination of the Creator Spirit. Since its primordial flaring forth some fifteen billion years ago, the universe as a whole and in its myriad parts has been gradually self-organizing within the parameters imposed by laws of physics, chemistry, and biology. Its increasingly complex formation is periodically stimulated and enhanced by contingent events or by the Spirit's creative power. When cosmic time and finite being began with the exploding singularity, then cosmic history, stellar history, geologic history, biotic history, and cultural history emerged in turn and became dynamic aspects of a creation in a continuous state of being and becoming.

The Spirit permeates creation and makes all space sacred space. Creation is born continually from the divine vision and fashioned by the creative power of the Spirit. Creation is sacred because the transcendent-immanent Creator Spirit dwells in it. Creation is sacred because the Spirit experiences material reality and consciousness intimately within it rather than apart from it. Creation is sacred because it is guided continually by the Spirit's creativity and loving power. Creation is experienced as sacred when the Spirit who permeates it is encountered as a distinct and divine presence.

The Spirit is distinct from, but permeates, the cosmos and the commons. The primary human contact with the Spirit is with divine becoming, with the Spirit immanent who is absorbing the processes, events, and life stories of creation and being affected by them. Human contact with the Spirit in nature is an experience of sacred Being mediated by the sacred commons (the localized sacred cosmos).

Creation is sacred. Churches and synagogues, mosques and temples, all of which have been constructed by human hands, are considered "sacred" because they have been dedicated to the service and worship of a Spirit (or spirits, in some traditions), and they are regarded as places where divine being dwells in some way. Creation is even more notably sacred, since it results from divine creativity, remains engaged with its Creator, and is presenced by the Spirit-immanent.

While all places are sacred, sometimes people distinguish human-designated and human-constructed "sacred" space from "profane" space. In human understandings, a natural (unaltered by humans) place might become sacred space because a particular special event—an individual's or a community's encounter with the divine—occurred there. Often the encounter involved some form of divine communication with an especially revered leader. In some such places, a simple shrine or a more elaborate building was constructed to mark the spot of encounter. Eventually, people of that faith community became accustomed to confining their worship to places where such events had occurred or to other specific sites where religious officials constructed a building to host religious rituals. Ordinary people came to be regarded as laity who depended on ordained clergy to designate not only places of worship but how that worship was to be conducted and what beliefs were to be associated with it. People lost, to some extent and often voluntarily, the freedom and desire to encounter the Spirit-immanent in all moments and places.

The Spirit transcendent-immanent encountered by people open to engagement with divine being is a Spirit Being-Becoming who intentionally in Spirits ("incorporates") within the divine self the dynamic cosmos and evolutionary commons in all their diversity and complexity. The Spirit transcendent-immanent voluntarily relinquishes power over the dynamic cosmos and evolutionary commons in a divine *kenosis*, an emptying of divine control over the course of cosmic events and the direction of cosmic development. The Spirit enables cosmic and commons freedom while engaging with humans and other creatures in revelatory moments and personal relationships. The Spirit creates indirectly within the parameters of cosmic laws as they interact with contingent and apparently chance or chaotic events. These interactions stimulate fulfillment of a divine vision for the dynamic universe.

The universe as a whole and in its parts reveals the presence of its Creator. Historically, Christian churches have focused on the Spirit-transcendent. Recently, Christians have become more conscious of the Spirit-immanent. When Christians regard *creation* as sacramental, as revelatory of the Spirit, then their understandings of the transcendence and immanence of God are integrated, and they have an enlightened commitment to care for the Spirit's creation in its local manifestation, the commons in which they live and work. When Christians regard the *commons* as sacramental, and consequently care for and about it as sacramental, they become involved in practical projects to provide for the well-being of the commons and of the community of all life, and to ensure a just distribution among people of commons goods needed by all humankind.

Similarly, when people of other faith traditions regard and care for the commons as revelatory of, blessed by, or formed through divine creativity (or as sacred and nurturing in itself, as, e.g., Mother Earth), they will care about and for it. When people of no faith tradition value the commons intrinsically, value it instrumentally because it provides human habitat and needed natural goods ("resources"), or value it for its instrumental value as an integrated ecosystem of interdependent beings, they will care about and for it.

The universe and Earth are signs and loci of God's presence. Earth is the context of the biotic community as a whole and of the human community within it, and the sacred space where people live in divine presence, immersed in divine being. Earth is a natural "sacrament" for humanity and a "commons" habitat for all creatures. Since the earliest human spiritual stirrings, the grandeur of the universe and the wonders of Earth's community of life have served a sacramental role—though not usually expressed as such—for reflective people.

SPIRITUAL SAGES IN SACRED SPACE

In the course of human history, religious visionaries usually encountered the Spirit and engaged the sacred during sojourns in wilderness areas, not in a building dedicated to divine worship. The Spirit was not confined to a particular site for these people, however dramatic their encounter with the divine had been in special places; any of Earth's pristine places could be, and many were, the locus of revelation and instruction. Although some prophets, such as Isaiah, received their call through a vision in a temple (Isaiah 6), most defining religious experiences occurred away from human structures, however holy these edifices might have been perceived to be. People's encounters with the Spirit present in pristine places, and their consequent understanding that this presence makes nature sacred space, are described in distinct spiritual traditions.

In the Bible, Moses converses with God by a burning bush (Exodus 3); Elijah speaks with God outside a cave on Mount Sinai (1 Kings 19); Ezekiel has visions by the river Chebar in Babylon (Ezekiel 1); Jesus encounters demonic spirits and angelic spirits in the process of overcoming temptations in the wilderness (Matthew 4); Jesus is transfigured on an unnamed mountain (Mark 9); Paul's conversion occurs on the road to Damascus (Acts 9). In other religious traditions, Buddha receives enlightenment and encouragement beneath a tree; Muhammad is instructed and inspired in a cave. The presence of the Spirit in pristine places, making them sacred space, is recounted also in native peoples' spiritual traditions. In (American) Indian peoples' traditions and practices, for example, mountains, forests, riverbanks, and prairies are usually the places where the Spirit's call is heard, and where the one called receives spiritual teachings and a special identity. Black Elk's Great Vision occurred on a prairie, and in it he is taken to the clouds nestled on top of a mountain.

In the Hebrew Scriptures, Solomon's temple dedication prayer recognizes that Yahweh is not just in one place, and cautions against limiting God to a sacred structure: "Even heaven and the highest heaven cannot contain you, much less this house that I have built!" (1 Kings 8:27).[1] Similarly, in the Christian scriptures, Paul in Athens says of God, "In him we live and move and have our being" (Acts 17:28). God is not just in specific sites but can be encountered everywhere. God is not aloof from humans but engaged with them and with all creation, whose individuality and interrelatedness God called "very good" (Genesis 1:31). Yahweh affirmed creatures' diversity and complexity in the biblical flood story (Genesis 6–9) by instructing Noah to preserve all creatures, not just humans, and by establishing with all creatures an Earth covenant, whose sign is the rainbow.

Similarly throughout religious history, the perspective and practice of human responsibility for creation have been promoted in diverse traditions. In Judaism and Christianity, this responsibility has been understood to be grounded in awe of and obedience to the power and requirements of the Creator who brought and brings the universe into being. In native peoples' traditions from the Americas, care for nature flows from a loving regard for Earth, who is understood to be a nurturing entity, Mother Earth. In Christian stories such as those about the Irish hermit St. Brendan and the mendicant friar St. Francis of Assisi, different but related types of creation consciousness are evident: awareness of the presence of God in pristine nature; affection for and relatedness to other living creatures. In the Orthodox Church, where ritual and reality, Creator and creation are inextricably intertwined, the Ecumenical Patriarch Bartholomew I declares that humans and the environment form a "seamless garment of existence" created by God.[2] People's use of the world's goods is a way in which they relate to God, and "the world incarnates the word of the Creator just as any other creation embodies the word of its artist. The objects of natural reality bear the seal of their divine Creator's wisdom and love."[3]

The goodness and perfection of creation are not complete. In the Catholic tradition, the *Catholic Catechism* states that "Creation has its own goodness and proper perfection, but it did not spring forth complete from the hands of the Creator. The universe was created 'in a state of journeying' (*in statu viae*) toward an ultimate perfection yet to be attained."[4] It might be added that creation is not only good and unfolding toward "perfection" but also sacred because it did "spring forth" from God, and because God is involved with it during its journey and has granted it a share of the complementary divine attributes of freedom, spontaneity, relational engagement, personal commitment, order, and innovation and of the integrated divine states of being and becoming. All time, space, and history in the universe have been presenced by divine consciousness, creativity, and compassion and are continually absorbed into divine being and assumed into divine becoming. The Spirit who is love experiences the pains and sorrows of a universe still being born, allows it freedom to unfold while communing with it, and inspires or guides it toward the fulfillment of its greatest potential.

The Creator Spirit did not immediately concretize or realize (make real) in extradivine form what was already real in divine imagination, all aspects of divine vision for the cosmos. The creating Word—Logos—expressed the guiding laws and brought into being both the initial expression of their eventual embodiment and time, which would both complement their development and enable it to occur. The Creator Spirit did not release from divine mind and imagination and engagement the initial results and ongoing processes and new products, and then move on to other novelties. The Spirit is immanent in the creation and, paradoxically, perhaps, both guiding and setting free its developing manifestations of divine imagination. Divine guidance is not divine control; it is not a continuous manipulation of freed creation to ensure that it emerges according to some divine "design" or "intelligent design." It is the granting of freedom with the possibility that the Spirit will inspire a new direction or understanding, or engage directly the process of creation, when the primary virtue of love, a virtue superior to freedom, requires such guidance or engagement to benefit, not order, a dynamic cosmos.

There would, then, be no instability in creation, or "violence" done to the ongoing cosmic dynamics, or a curtailment of freedom for the universe, if the Spirit were to decide, for a moment in time, to temporarily work with and integrate natural laws or cosmic process in creative ways (and perhaps make the creative new integration permanent, in this or other existing universes); or, Spirit might creatively and positively alter an entity, form of energy, or event. For compelling reasons of divine love and in the interests of the holistic well-being of the universe and its component beings, the Spirit might intervene in cosmic time and place to guide creation's process or its biotic participants. The Spirit might creatively integrate and use existing and not-yet-existing, known and unknown, and developed, developing, and to-be-developed natural laws of cosmos and commons in a new way, to affect creation and to effect novelty in creation, to continue creating without negatively impacting the integrity of creation. The Spirit would be anticipating human discoveries or chance correlations of new products or processes that result from new combinations of matter and energy. A parallel is evident in scientific discoveries about DNA. It has the potential for a variety of possible combinations, some of which will occur only when the environmental conditions are appropriate for such innovations. A concerned and immanent divine Spirit with knowledge of the properties of specific aspects of creation and the laws that govern them, could anticipate their future development and accelerate a future eventuality for its needed and helpful use in the present. Moments of intervention might include responding to native healers who call on the spirits in creation to help their medicinal herbs and prayers to be efficacious in healing people's illnesses, or inspiring a scientist to explore a new way to develop an herbal "cocktail" to eliminate or ameliorate suffering caused by intrusive microorganisms.

In the Christian tradition, this dynamic interaction between Creator and creation has been expressed since early Christianity in understandings of the Logos, the Word as creative manifestation of divine being. The dialogic relationship is presented in perspectives on Logos cosmogony and Logos incarnation.

Divine cosmogenic activity is expressed biblically in, among other places, the first chapter of the first book. Genesis declares, anthropomorphically, that Yahweh creates by speaking: "God said, 'Let there be . . . .'" The gospel of John takes up this theme, its opening chapter formulated to continue, parallel, and complement the Genesis understandings of God "speaking." For John, the "spoken" word is the Word, the creative aspect of divinity, and more: it is the incarnate aspect of divinity, for "the Word became flesh" to live on Earth among creatures as a creature, and to teach people about God by Word, word, and deed in Christ Jesus. The covenant between Spirit and creation noted in the Noah story is renewed, and affirmed in a particular way, in the relationship between Spirit and all people and peoples that is brought to an enhanced state in the person of Jesus.

Incarnational divine activity affirming the sacramentality of creation is taught in Christian stories—and in their interpretation—about church sacraments established by Jesus. Sacramentality is taught also in the teaching that Jesus himself is a "sacrament," a revelation or mediation of divine being and presence. The creating Logos resides in and is revealed through Jesus, and initiates a new kind of creation, a community of love, through the work of Jesus. The Logos/Word, then, is revealed in and mediated by church sacraments and creation sacraments. In some Christian traditions, the dialogic relationship is heightened in the sacrament of the Eucharist or Holy Communion, particularly where there is present some understanding of the transformation of Earth elements into incarnational bread and wine. In one sense, this would not actually be something extraordinary in that the Logos/Word is always incarnate in creation, which is the concretization of divine thought and the locus, or cosmic temple, of divine immanence. Complementarily, however, the Logos incarnation in Jesus would be extraordinary in that it becomes bonded in some way with a reflective creature's consciousness and voluntary activity. The materially invisible Creator of the cosmos becomes materially visible, in a sense, through Jesus. The followers of Jesus, to the extent they are faithful to his message and do his work, carry him and his teachings within them and pass them on intergenerationally and intertemporally, in a way that complements his sacramental presence in church rituals.

In the years of patristic Christianity, the monk, mystic, and martyr St. Maximus the Confessor (580–662) described the interaction between the creative divine *Logos* and the *logoi*, the words of the divine that flowed from the Spirit in the creative process and remain within each part of creation. Maximus taught that a *dialogos*, a dialogue between Creator and creation, continues through time as the *Logos* and the *logoi* interact. Maximus viewed creation as the context and revelation of God, and referred to it as a cloak worn by the creating Word (an image complemented in the twentieth century by Sallie McFague's metaphor that creation is the "body of God"). The creating *Logos* continues a work as yet incomplete, a work still becoming even while it is being. Maximus again: "The author of existence gives himself to be beheld through visible things,"[5] which recalls biblical passages already cited. He questioned how anyone who has seen creation's beauty and greatness could not perceive that God brought it all into existence. He taught that people integrate the visible and invisible realities. The human being "unites the created nature with the uncreated through love . . . showing them to be one and the same through the possession of grace, the whole [creation] wholly interpenetrated by God."[6]

Centuries after Maximus, the visions and writings of the great twelfth-century mystic, musician, pharmacologist, poet, and writer Hildegard von Bingen (1098–1179) complemented his teachings. In her *Book of Divine Works*, which describes her visions and her interpretations of their meanings, Hildegard quotes God as saying, "I, the highest and fiery power, have kindled every spark of life. . . . I remain hidden in every kind of reality as a fiery power."[7] She reflects that when humans were created, they were illuminated with the "living breath of the spirit," and they emerged "as both fire and flame: The fire was in the human soul, and the flame flaring up out of the soul was in our reason."[8] Maximus's vision of the interplay of divine words, *Logos* and *logoi*, is complemented in these passages. In this vein also, Hildegard declares that "the word of God has penetrated everything in creation."[9] The eternal Word of God "awakened all creation by the resonance of God's voice," "called creation to himself," "led all creatures to the light," and "committed himself to all of creation"; and "when the Word of God resounded, this Word appeared in every creature and this Word was sound in every creature."[10] Hildegard declares that human beings, through faith, know God in every creature and in the whole creation.[11] Although Hildegard does not use the phrase, she conveys the essential meanings of sacramental universe and sacramental commons.

Hildegard is also a child of her historical moment and place, with its understandings or beliefs about the human in the universe. She expresses an anthropocentric view when she states that all of nature should be at humanity's service,[12] because people are more important than every other creature (even though she notes that people cannot survive without other creatures) and are created in God's likeness.[13] Hildegard had no knowledge of cosmic and biotic dynamics such as stellar and species evolution and extinction, and tectonic plate movement. Consequently, in commenting on the divine origins of creation, she declares, in a literal reading of Genesis 1, that humankind was created last so that everything people needed would be ready for them.[14] She interprets the Bible's second creation story and flood story literally and, interestingly, includes as a reason for the flood that the descendants of Adam and Eve had harmed nature. Hildegard understood the spinning wheel in one of her visions to mean that the created world is unchanging, being neither aged nor augmented through time. Yet, in what might be a pre-Darwinian nod to evolution, as perceived in her visions, she also states that creation had to provide for creatures' needs and "had to guarantee the fullness of developmental possibilities along with the capacity to grow."[15] When interpreting her vision of the spinning wheel, Hildegard also expresses what would be called "panentheism" a thousand years later. She observes that God encloses all creation within divine being, and is greater than all creatures.[16]

St. Francis of Assisi (1182–1226), whose lifetime overlapped Hildegard's, complemented her writings as he celebrated the wonders and vitality of creation. He also hinted at insights of Maximus when he preached to the birds and called on all creatures to praise God in his *Canticle of Creation*. In this song, whose words Francis wrote to the melody of a romantic ballad of his time, the community of creation is presented as sharing in divine communion. His words celebrated the familial character of inanimate being, while the melody's original verses celebrated animate being. The *Canticle* calls on all creation to praise God, exulting in the interaction of what today would be called abiotic creation, the biotic community and the Creator-creation relationship.

What might be derived from these Christian mystics is that in the sacramental universe there is an engagement and union of an emanant divine fire and respondent divine sparks within creatures. Flame is attracted to and intertwined with flame; the sparks that leap out from the Spirit in moments of dynamic creation and inhere in all creatures, dialogically are drawn back into the Spirit, intensified in energy, and released again. Humans consciously enter into this engagement and relationship when they are open to the divine flame reaching out toward them and respond to its touch.

REVELATION

Christians and adherents of some other faith traditions regard creation as one of two "books"—the other being the Bible—that reveal the Creator to the discerning believer, and are thereby sacramental. Peoples of faith are called to "read" it carefully—observe it, study it, analyze it—so as not to have misunderstandings about God. The "book of nature," like the "book of Scripture," must be read exegetically, not eisegetically, to understand the insights it contains, which are revealed through and in its visible appearance, its material being. Just as biblical scholars, two thousand years after the writing of the Christian Scriptures and more than three thousand years after the first oral formulations of the Hebrew Scriptures, try to discern their meanings for a new time, place, and culture, so, too, do scientists and others try, fifteen billion years into stellar, planetary, and biological evolution, to discern the workings of the universe. The possibility of doing so to any great extent is contingent on the degree of openness people bring with them when reading either book. If their minds are made up about conclusions, little will be learned; if they read with a true scientific spirit, open to new data and insights and wonder, they will learn much, and if they read also with a spiritual openness, their understanding will be enhanced even more.

People should not read "into" creation, but read "from" creation. Open to its mysteries and aware of the goods and harms that result from contacts with its various aspects and events and constituent parts, they should strive to see what it reveals about itself and its Creator, not glossing over or ignoring or rejecting something not congruent with the beliefs, theories, and apparently complete data that they had when they began to study the universe and its processes and inhabitants. They must recognize and acknowledge their personal and professional limitations of education and experience, of knowledge and skills. They must acknowledge the current, ever evolving, incomplete state of scientific development (and of technology and expertise in its use) in their area (place and profession) and era. No less than with the study of Scripture, the study of nature must not deteriorate into "eisegesis," the "proof texting" in Christianity that is the recurring temptation of those who want to justify their prior understandings by an appeal to selected biblical texts extracted from their contexts or by what they encounter in nature but do not examine in depth. Rather, people must learn from these two teaching texts by letting them speak for themselves, by allowing them to reveal the insights they contain—to the extent these can be seen or understood in a given historical moment.

Similarly, theoretical scientists should avoid appeal to ambiguous data, speculative science, or metaphysical arguments to "prove" their previously developed theory or ideology or their views of material realities.

The Spirit's power is ongoing and engaged. It is not limited to inspiring the Bible, nor has its exercise been restricted to events described in the Bible, nor is it reserved to guiding and caring for only those people who embrace the Bible as their sacred scriptures. God is "with us always," Jesus taught. Similarly, the Spirit's creative power was not exhausted by primordially bringing into being the dynamic cosmos and the evolving commons. The Spirit's creative power continues in the dynamics of the universe itself that unfolds freely through the interaction of law, chance, and time, and in God's relationship with humans and with all creation. Human power will never equal divine power, however much it seeks to replicate or replace it. Humans will not be "like God," no matter the extent to which they mimic, manipulate, or manage the products of ongoing divine creativity and activity.

A SACRAMENTAL UNIVERSE

The universe is *sacramental*. It is a revelation of the Spirit's ongoing creativity and a place of interaction and relationship between the human and the divine. The holistic universe and its local places are sacramental. The cosmos as an integrated whole and in each of its parts can be a sign and experience of divine creativity and a revelation of Spirit's presence; an occasion of grace and a conveyor of blessing; and a bearer of sacred creatures, all called "very good" by their Creator.

Human consciousness of the relationship of human care for creation to divine creativity and presence in creation prompted use of the phrase "sacramental universe" to express the Creator Spirit's cosmic engagement with creation. People had discerned the Spirit's active presence in the commons through their openness to invisible reality revealed in visible reality.

In Christian traditions whose religious practice includes ritual *sacraments*—signs of God's granting of grace to their recipients—the universe itself can be viewed as *sacramental*. The beauty, diversity, and complexity of the created world can stimulate people, if they are open to the encounter, to become aware of the divine presence immanent in Earth. *Ecclesial* sacraments, particular rituals ordinarily mediated by a member of the clergy or by a designated church representative, are distinct from but complementary to *universal* sacraments, mediated by creation as a whole or in part. The *universal sacrament of creation*, then, can offer moments of grace, of personal or communal engagement with the Spirit, who is *transcendent* to creation (distinct from creation) and yet *immanent* in creation (permeating creation).

The concept of a "sacramental universe" probably was expressed first by the Anglican theologian and archbishop William Temple in his book *Nature, Man and God* (1934). The contemporary priest-chemist-theologian Arthur Peacocke notes Temple's contribution, and observes that church sacraments have both an instrumental function, whereby God "effects changes within the participant(s)," and a symbolic function, whereby God "signifies particular features" of God's "ongoing relation to human beings transformed by the Christ event."[17] Peacocke relates cosmic "entities, structures and processes," the instruments by which God effects divine purposes and the symbols of God's nature, to the functions of church sacraments. An elaboration of Peacocke's insights would be that creation sacraments—virtually limitless—and church sacraments—usually taught to be between two and seven in number—have complementary roles in effecting changes in people and in signifying the relation of the Spirit to the cosmos. The concepts expressed earlier of a transcendent Logos creating, an incarnate Logos teaching, and an ongoing Logos-logoi dialogue through both dynamics describe sacramental moments in which Spirit power becomes evident and spirit empowering. The Ecumenical Patriarch Bartholomew I declares that the world is "a sacrament of communion with God and neighbor."[18]

All creation, from the grandeur of the stars to the life of creatures of the air, land, and waters, all the energies, elements, events, and entities of the extensive sacramental universe and its localized sacramental commons, stimulate Creator-consciousness and creation-consciousness, creation care and community care. This results in conscious immersion in creation communion, and conscientious concern and care for, and commitment to, the human family as a whole and the biotic community that is its extended family.

The created universe is dynamic, not static. When people are open to the presence of Spirit in creation, they can experience the creative power of God at work and believe that the universe is evolving, meaningful, and ultimately good. When they view creation as sacramental, people become conscious not only of who they are and what and where their place (their role and their location) is in it but also of their integral ecological relationship with their regional biotic community and with the character and rhythms of the Earth they share as their common home.

In the Hebrew Scriptures, Wisdom, Sirach, and Isaiah state that people can perceive signs of the Creator in creation. In the Christian Scriptures, this understanding is complemented by Paul's statement that "Ever since the creation of the world, [God's] eternal power and divine nature, invisible though they are, have been understood and seen through the things [God] has made" (Romans 1:20). The created world reveals the Spirit's powerful creativity of thought and action, and inspires awareness of the Spirit's love for all creation. The universe is sacramental, revelatory of the presence of its Creator.

The book of Wisdom says of Yahweh that "you love all things that exist . . . your immortal spirit is in all things!" (11:24; 12:1). Because this divine presence permeates creation, "from the greatness and the beauty of created things comes a corresponding perception of their Creator" (13:5).

Sirach complements Wisdom when it proclaims, "How desirable are all [God's] works, and how sparkling they are to see! All these things live and remain forever; each creature is preserved to meet a particular need. All things come in pairs, one opposite the other, and [God] has made nothing incomplete. Each supplements the virtues of the other, who could ever tire of seeing [God's] glory?" (42:22–25). In this passage, written millennia before the concepts were formulated scientifically, the author expresses understandings of "biodiversity" and of ecosystemic integrity, interdependence, and interrelationship.

Isaiah offers a related perspective. He laments the fact that people worship gods whose images they make themselves, rather than the one God, a Spirit who cannot be seen but who has created what can be seen. Isaiah describes a carpenter who fells a tree that God provided for human need, then cuts from it sections of wood that will serve respectively to heat his food, warm him, and . . . be worshiped after he carves an idol from them. Rather than worship the God who made the tree, the carpenter worshiped the tree wood that he made into a god (44:13–17).

While Christians over the centuries had a sense of the presence of the Creator in creation, the advent of scientific discoveries and technological advancements in the twentieth century reinforced eighteenth-century Enlightenment thinking and nineteenth-century scientific ideas. In the new perspective, God was believed to be nonexistent or not involved; the universe and Earth were viewed in mechanistic terms; and people lost a sense of the spiritual dimension of nature. The poet John Keats (1795–1821), as he reflected in his poem "Lamia" on Isaac Newton's experiments with prisms that led to a scientific understanding of rainbows, lamented science's role of "unweaving the rainbow." He thought that people no longer would be able to appreciate a rainbow's beauty but would focus instead on the mechanics of its formation. Keats feared that this and other scientific discoveries would lead to a loss of an aesthetic (or spiritual) appreciation of nature. According to the British priest, physicist, and theologian Alister McGrath, this is precisely what has occurred. Nature has lost its "enchantment" because of a cultural overemphasis on science and a consequent acceptance of some scientists' metaphysical speculations on cosmic processes, which are usually mechanistic views masked as objective science. What the world needs today is a sense of divine immanence, which McGrath explores in *The Reenchantment of Nature.*

In their environmental pastoral letter *Renewing the Earth: An Invitation to Reflection and Action on Environment in Light of Catholic Social Teaching* (1991), the U.S. Catholic bishops spoke of a "sense of God's presence in nature" and observed that "through the created gifts of nature, men and women encounter their Creator." They taught that God's creation is a "sacramental universe," a "world that discloses the Creator's presence by visible and tangible signs."

In their descriptions of a sacramental universe, the bishops reflected Augustine's fifth-century teaching that there are uncountable sacraments in the world, "visible signs of invisible grace," that can draw people to God, their Creator. Augustine's understanding, for its part, related back to the biblical texts cited earlier from Wisdom, Sirach, and Isaiah, and later it was complemented by the insights of Maximus and Hildegard.

The bishops' teaching of a sacramental universe complements Catholic doctrine about the church's seven sacraments. Both teachings relate to church and biblical traditions. Sacramental rites and sacramental nature mediate the active, grace-giving presence of God. They are the means of communication from the spiritual dimension of reality to the social and personal dimensions of reality, all of which are one unified reality. Sacramental places, people, moments, and acts are mediations, the media through which and the occasions in which divine presence is experienced; they are permeated with possibilities of human-divine engagement. Church sacraments are symbols that signify their role of mediation in a special ritual way, ordinarily through the actions of a priest. The universe, the creation of God-transcendent permeated by God-immanent, provides countless means and moments of mediation when people reflectively commune with individual creatures or reflect on the beauty of Earth's vistas or other visible parts of the cosmos. The sacramental universe, as a whole and in each of its parts, in its natural state and when related to complementary symbolic religious rituals, can be a holistic and holy mediation of God's immanence, a revelation of the Spirit working in and through all being.

In the Catholic Church, sacraments instituted by Christ, the historical

Word, are signs of God's graceful presence. Creation is sacramental, a sign of the eternal Word's cosmic creative presence, activity, and guidance. The Word remains in creation as its activating principle and power. In the Christian view, the work of the Logos, God, and Man is expressed sacramentally in two ways. The *church*, in its teachings and practices, proclaims the message of Christ and carries on the grace-conferring activity of Jesus, the Word made flesh, through its seven sacraments. *Creation*, in its beauty and evolutionary processes, carries on and is revelatory of the creative activity of the Word begun prior to the Word's incarnation in the historical Jesus and continuing through time.

Through human history, people have encountered the Spirit in creation—on mountain summits and desert dunes, by cascading waterfalls and surging springs, in dense forests and rolling fields. People still sense, although for most in a diminished way, the Spirit's immanence in creation and the possibility of encountering it and being transformed by the experience to see in a new way themselves, other people and their needs and all creation in its intricacy, intimacy, and dynamism. The universe is simultaneously the Spirit's creation and the Spirit's temple. In it, people can encounter the Spirit in the Earth commons and in the community of life, and they experience and appreciate their sacramentality.

Peoples across cultures and through history have had a sense of the sacred. Sometimes, in an especially revelatory encounter, a sacramental engagement occurs. This is at once the experience of the immanence of God-transcendent and of the transcendence of God-immanent. It is a recognition of and engagement with the Spirit, inspired by a perception of signs of the divine in the vast universe and in a local place.

The terms *sacramental universe* and *sacramental commons*, which express a profound sense of divine immanence in, and divine engagement with, creation and creatures, articulate the special relationship of Creator and creation, as well as acknowledge awareness of the ongoing loving presence of the creative Word in all creation. When human consciousness reflects on these ideas, human conscience can prompt people to realize that, in the words of Pope John Paul II, their "responsibility within creation and their duty towards nature and the Creator are an *essential* part of their faith."[19] Similarly, Orthodox theologian John Chryssavgis, when presenting the ideas of the Ecumenical Patriarch Bartholomew I, notes that "a spirituality that is not involved with outward creation is not involved with the inward mystery either."[20] Caring for creation is not something added on to the identifying characteristics of a Christian, an option that might be selected or rejected; it is intrinsically part of a Christian identity. Such an understanding negates the sometime

Christian attitude of neglect or disparagement of this world in favor of the life to come.

CREATION-CENTERED CONSCIOUSNESS

A creation-centered or *creatiocentric* consciousness is a holistic understanding that the Creator, abiotic creation, and the biotic community are interrelated. Such a consciousness is not *cosmo*centric (universe centered), because it understands the complementary roles of cosmos and commons, and the latter as the locus of engagement with creation; or *geo*centric (Earth centered), since it goes beyond planetary concern (while including it in its purview); or *bio*centric (life centered), since it recognizes that life needs a habitat—provided by Earth—for survival; or *anthropo*centric (human centered), since it is aware that humans are but one part of the biotic community, with their specific (particular human, and human species) responsibilities, and not superior to or obedient to others, and live dependent on goods from abiotic creation in the Earth commons; or *andro*centric (male centered), since it recognizes the intrinsic equality and complementarity of men and women; or even *theo*centric (God centered), since it is oriented toward God as Creator and as a creating power, not in isolation from the fruits of divine creativity; and it is certainly not *ego*centric (self centered), although it is ego regarding (interested in the personal well-being of self and of others in the community). It is all of these (except androcentric and egocentric), in a sense, and more: these perspectives are bound together at the core of cosmic being. "Creation" implies Creator and creatures; to be creatiocentric is to recognize their interrelationship.

People with a creation-centered consciousness understand well that they live in a sacramental universe and that Earth is a sacramental commons. They recognize that all creatures flow from the evolutionary process set in motion at the origins of the universe, when divine *kenosis*—self-emptying—expressed divine freedom granted to creation, and divine love for creation. Kenosis does not imply divine desertion but rather a relinquishing of coercive power over the creatures that result from the interaction of law, contingency, and time (cf. Philippians 2:6–8).

A creatiocentric consciousness includes Earth awareness and engagement. People recognize their responsibilities not only to the Creator, but to each other, to all life, and to Earth. They take note of the inherent elegance, goodness, value, and dignity of creation. By centering Creator-creation in their consciousness, people mediate some of the Spirit's ongoing, loving, and good-forming creative power.

Human history is inextricably linked with evolutionary ecology. Humans emerged relatively recently in the approximately 3.5-billion-year history of life on Earth, and they are genetically tied to all life, across the globe and through time, in a web of relationships. Indeed, humans are tied to all the created universe, as complexified stardust whose origins lie in the singular point of cosmic emergence some fifteen billion years ago. Humans are an integral part of the biotic community, and provide cosmic self-consciousness in this part of the Milky Way galaxy and within the vast universe. Human lives on Earth and eventually into the broader universe participate in the interaction, interdependence, and interrelation of the biotic community and abiotic creation.

A creatiocentric focus inspires or even impels people to be committed to caring for and about the Spirit's unfolding creation, working with the Spirit and with cosmic rhythms and rules. It keeps people mindful that the Creator Spirit is a Creating Spirit, simultaneously God of nature and God of history, who initiated cosmic dynamics and granted cosmic freedom, the latter exercised in cosmic or coevolutionary conversation with the constraints of ongoing laws of the universe, but with openness to influences and changes caused by contingent events and apparently chaotic events in unanticipated moments.

The creatiocentric consciousness and mode of existence is, in the broadest sense of relationships (animate-to-inanimate; life-to-life; life-to-Spirit; creation-to-Creator), an ecocentric (interrelational) perspective. People are in some nondualistic, integrated way incarnated spirits, unions of the immortal and the mortal, the spiritual and the corporal, the immaterial and the material, the temporal and the eternal. Humans mediate between spiritual reality and physical reality, which are dimensions of one reality permeated by the Spirit immanent, whose presence can be discerned in creation. Humans are embodied spirits and enspirited bodies, in an integrated whole without division, an integration whose mystery still remains beyond human comprehension, where each flows through the other analogous to the flow on a closed Möbius strip, where two sides and two types of existence are bonded into one; or, analogous to electric transmission, where current flows on the outside of the wire, not through it: each needs the other to fulfill their respective roles in, but collective role of, providing energy.

THE SACRAMENTAL AND THE SOCIAL

The sacramental dimension of creation is complemented by its social dimension. Together they constitute the totality of created reality. In the Christian

Scriptures, Matthew 25:31–46 states that the criteria for entrance into divine presence (in a "last judgment" beyond any consideration of religious faith) will be practical works of compassion: feeding the hungry, giving drink to the thirsty, clothing the naked, sheltering the homeless, visiting the sick and imprisoned—to do these is to help out not only the person in need, but also the Son of Man among them, whose presence they mediate in their need. James 2:14–17 teaches that a person who sees someone in need and merely blesses them and prays for them is not fulfilling his responsibility to care for them, since "faith without works is dead." 1 John 3:17–18 questions how God's love could dwell in anyone who refuses to help a sister or brother in need when they have the goods needed to do so, and declares that love must be expressed not just in words, but also in practical works of compassion. The letter goes on to state that "God is love, and those who abide in love abide in God, and God abides in them" (4:16) followed shortly thereafter by the commandment that people should love brothers and sisters when they love God (4:21). The Johannine passages, when combined, link the social and the sacramental; the person who acts compassionately toward the needy can reveal God's love acting through themselves, and thereby reveal also God's presence within themselves. James links faith with compassion for the poor; 1 John links love with compassion for the poor. In all of these texts, Christians are taught to use creation goods for the common good, the well-being of the community. In doing so, they will combine faith and compassion, linking sacramental consciousness with social commitment.

In a similar vein, Patriarch Bartholomew I forcefully advocates care for creation and concern about social issues. He laments exorbitant military expenditures and the consolidation of wealth into a few hands while the poor majority suffers. The Orthodox tradition of *asceticism* is not self-denial for its own sake, he states, but rather self-sacrifice so that others might have a sufficiency of Earth's goods. Care for the environment and a proper distribution of Earth's goods are necessary for human well-being. Patriarch Bartholomew links the sacramental and the social by advocating care for creation and an asceticism that enables people in need to have a sufficiency of goods. He also declares, in strong theological terms not otherwise used in Christian discourse about environmental issues, that abuse of the environment is a *sin*. Sinful human abuses of creation include acts that cause species extinction; destruction of biological diversity; climate change; deforestation; wetlands destruction; diseases that injure humans; and contamination of Earth's waters, land, air, and life with poisonous substances.[21]

Bartholomew I's voice complements and reinforces one of Hildegard von Bingen's visions and warnings that a thousand years earlier linked the sacramental and the social, creation and community. Hildegard described an end time when "the greening power of life on Earth was reduced in every seed because the upper region of the air was altered in a way contrary to its first destiny. Summer now became subject to a contradictory chill while winter often experienced a paradoxical warmth. There occurred on Earth times of drought and dampness." During this period, "evil moneychangers came, scattering my children in their greed," acting like "evil tyrants who employ the law of the stronger."[22] Today, global warming continues unabated because of irresponsible human conduct that sends carbon emissions into Earth's atmosphere. Hildegard's insights are complemented by discovery of an ozone hole in the "upper region of the air" and by current discussions that link global warming to impacts of an economic "globalization" controlled by transnational corporations, the oil industry, the international banking system, and powerful governments with overpowering military and economic might at their disposal. Economic globalization controlled by "evil moneychangers" with no sense of ecological responsibility, complemented by wars initiated by powerful nations, are stimuli to climate change and alteration of Earth's life-enhancing rhythms and balance. Drought exists in diverse regions around the globe. Dampness is evident where hurricanes have increased in number and intensity. Earth and people are being harmed as creation's sacramental role is negated and community needs are neglected. The outcome of these events is as yet unforeseeable, but potential consequences for people and planet can be modeled. Prophetic statements about future harm can stimulate people to ensure that such prophecies are not fulfilled in their lifetime, or people can ignore them at their peril.

Spirituality and *sociality* are simultaneously personal and universal terms and "signs" that describe the revelatory and the relational, the individual and the communal, dimensions of life and living. Contemplation of the sacramental universe stimulates relating the spiritual and the social, and consequent commitment to the sacramental commons. The cosmos is seen as revelatory of God; the commons no less so. The commons is the place of projects, the locus of efforts to embody compassion in concrete ways such that the needs of all are met through a just distribution of Earth's earth, air, and water and Earth's goods, organic and inorganic. Among others, St. Francis of Assisi and native peoples of the Americas communed with the immanent Creator Spirit and committed themselves to compassion in community. Their stories follow.

NOTES

1. Biblical texts cited in this book are taken from Michael D. Coogan, ed., *The New Oxford Annotated Bible: New Revised and Standard Version, with the Apocrypha*, 3rd ed. (New York: Oxford University Press, 2001).

2. John Chryssavgis, ed., *Cosmic Grace, Humble Prayer: The Ecological Vision of the Green Patriarch Bartholomew I* (Grand Rapids, Mich.: Eerdmans, 2003), 219.

3. Chryssavgis, *Cosmic Grace*, 126.

4. *Catechism of the Catholic Church* (Washington, D.C.: United States Catholic Conference, 1994), 80.

5. Andrew Louth, *Maximus the Confessor* (London: Routledge, 1996), 110.

6. Louth, *Maximus the Confessor*, 158.

7. Hildegard of Bingen, *Hildegard of Bingen's Book of Divine Works*, ed. Matthew Fox (Santa Fe, N.M.: Bear, 1987), 10.

8. Hildegard of Bingen, *Book of Divine Works*, 227.

9. Hildegard of Bingen, *Book of Divine Works*, 96.

10. Hildegard of Bingen, *Book of Divine Works*, 130–31.

11. Hildegard of Bingen, *Book of Divine Works*, 36.

12. Hildegard of Bingen, *Book of Divine Works*, 26.

13. Hildegard of Bingen, *Book of Divine Works*, 35.

14. Hildegard of Bingen, *Book of Divine Works*, 227.

15. Hildegard of Bingen, *Book of Divine Works*, 134.

16. Hildegard of Bingen, *Book of Divine Works*, 26.

17. Arthur Peacocke, *Theology for a Scientific Age: Being and Becoming—Natural, Divine and Human* (London: SCM, 1993), 341. In his Bampton Lectures, 1978, Peacocke states that "the world is a sacrament or, at least sacramental." See A. R. Peacocke, *Creation and the World of Science* (Oxford: Clarendon, 1979), 290. My own ideas developed independent of, but complementary to, the insights of Temple and Peacocke.

18. Chryssavgis, *Cosmic Grace*, 315.

19. Pope John Paul II, *The Ecological Crisis: A Common Responsibility* (Washington, D.C.: United States Catholic Conference, 1990), §15 (emphasis added).

20. Chryssavgis, *Cosmic Grace*, 18.

21. Chryssavgis, *Cosmic Grace*, 221.

22. Hildegard of Bingen, *Book of Divine Works*, 231–32.

· 2 ·

The Spirit of St. Francis

$\mathcal{F}$rancis of Assisi (1182–1226) is well known as a celebrant of the wonders of creation. His widely circulated and acclaimed song, the *Canticle of Creation* (*Canticle of Brother Sun*), expresses particularly well his love for nature. Narratives about his relationships with the birds of Bevagna and the wolf of Gubbio present practical expressions of that love. During his lifetime, in the turbulent thirteenth century, the pope was a powerful political leader; the Catholic Church owned, in one form or another, half of Europe; the payment of money was replacing a barter system as the primary form of exchange for goods and services; and, in part because of the latter, a middle class of merchants and artisans was emerging and becoming financially independent of the landed aristocracy, a situation that catalyzed clashes between these two social classes. Although his historical era had conflicts, characteristics, and a consciousness markedly different from what exists today, his ideas about Christianity, spirituality in nature, kinship with all creatures, peace among all peoples, simplicity of life, and solicitude for and solidarity with the poor and other outcasts still offer relevant insights to present-day people—for relating to the Spirit immanent in creation, to humans as neighbors, and to the community of all life as co-inhabitants of the Earth commons.

It is important to remember that Francis's consciousness and life were not just about "loving nature," as tempting as it is to summarize them that way. His relationship with nature and human communities—including particularly his compassion and care for the outcasts and the poor—was far more complex and intertwined with his specifically Christian spirituality and with his perception that creation was revelatory of God. Effectively, Francis viewed creation as a sacramental universe and a sacramental commons. He believed that simplicity of life, compassion, and respect for God's creation were fundamental aspects of the Christian message. He *contemplated* creation, *cared* for creation, and *communed* with the Creator through creation. Today, his insights are useful for promoting care for pristine nature and all creatures;

social sustainability; consciousness that people are interrelated to and interdependent with other members of the biotic community; concern for the common good and the good of the commons; peace within a local community, within a national community, and among national communities; and a sense of divine immanence in and transcendence from creation. His understandings of creation and the commons, when understood in this deeper sense, have the potential, if incorporated into human ideology and practice, to have continuing significant impacts on the well-being of Earth and of living communities inhabiting Earth.

IL POVERELLO

Francis was born in Assisi in 1182 to Pica and Pietro Di Bernadone. Pietro was a cloth merchant, and one of the wealthiest men in Assisi. Pica was a loving mother who sometimes shielded her son from his father's wrath; little else is known about her. Since Pietro loved to travel to France to acquire bolts of the finest woven cloth, he insisted that his son be named Francesco. Francis later would accompany his father on such commercial ventures and assist him by selling cloth in his shop. As he grew to adulthood, Francis had a minimal formal education, probably less than his contemporaries in his social class because of his youthful loose living and his brief foray into the life of a soldier. He was very popular among his peers as a fun-loving troubadour and a personable, passionate, and persuasive speaker. Eventually, although born to wealth, he renounced familial and financial security. He returned even the clothes on his back to his father in Assisi's public square, in a dramatic rejection of his former lifestyle. He became known as *Il Poverello*, the "Little Poor Man," and, choosing celibacy, remained devoted to his Lady Poverty throughout his life. His subsequent mendicant lifestyle contrasted with the affluent lifestyle of his family and friends, and also of members of the Catholic Church hierarchy of his era and continent. He taught that he and his followers should live simply and own no property, neither personal (not even religious books) nor communal (no land, not even for farming; no buildings, not even for housing). They were to be dependent on others even for subsistence needs. Through manual labor and begging for alms (they were not allowed to accept money, only food and other subsistence essentials, in either case), they provided for their needs. They were instructed to have a minimal impact on the physical world, but a maximum impact on the material world and on cultural consciousness while promoting spiritual well-being. Francis's friars became a spiritual family, and they sought, by their teaching and preaching and by their own manner of living, to guide people to live simply (the poor already did this, involuntarily living at subsistence level or below), to reject acquisitiveness, and to have a sense of community.

Through his gentleness, humility, sincerity, and persuasive words, Francis was able to convince church and secular leaders, princes and peasants, to support his ideas and accept the commitments of his congregation of friars. According to Franciscan tradition, preliminary approval for the Friars Minor was granted to Francis in 1215 during the Fourth Lateran Council. His dedication to Christianity, and his willingness and even hope to be a Christian martyr (according to St. Bonaventure's assessment of Francis), prompted him to journey through the Egyptian desert at great risk, after the destruction of the fortress of Damietta in 1219 during the Fifth Crusade, to try to convince the Muslim sultan Malik-al-Kāmil to become a Christian. He failed in his quest for martyrdom and in his efforts to convert the sultan, but the latter honored him as a special guest for two months, and, probably as a result of their conversations during that time, proposed reasonable peace terms (which were rejected) to the invading Christian crusaders (who were unsuccessful in their attempt to wrest biblical lands from Muslim control).

Francis suffered from ill health and physical deprivation, and he endured hostility from his opponents. Through all of this, he lived simply and continued to love all peoples, wild creatures, and pristine places, and he had a special compassion for the downtrodden—the poor and the lepers who were a special focus of his ministry.

Just before he died on October 3, 1226, probably as a result of cancer, Francis was nearly blind, had frequent nausea, and had a doctor cauterize his infected eye with Brother Fire. He died in poverty, respected as a great spiritual leader who left a legacy of his life and teachings to guide others to experience the sacredness of creation permeated by divine immanence, to be compassionate toward the poor and outcast, and to build a familial sense of community among people and between people and other living creatures. He was canonized by Pope Gregory IX in July 1228, less than two years after his death. The first biography of Francis, commissioned by Gregory IX, was written over the course of eight months by one of his friars, Thomas of Celano, between 1228 and 1229.

In his social context and with his spiritual orientations, Francis promoted care for creation based on his understanding of God and of God's relationships with humanity and with all of creation. Despite a significant separation in geographic space from most people, and a span of almost eight hundred years in historical time from the present era, and despite linguistic and other cultural differences, Francis offers people today ideas and a vision complementary to and at times congruent with their own. His ideas on and interaction with Earth's creatures within a common cosmic context are remarkably attuned with the best contemporary humanist environmental consciousness and the best religious teaching on caring for creation. Such secular and sacred viewpoints share in common a pronounced respect for creatures and a profound sense of a powerful presence permeating nature, whether or not that presence is acknowledged to be divine.

St. Francis lived heroically—as few others did—the ideals of Christianity as he understood them in his time and place. Christians today who have a more positive view of the body and of an integral human life in historical contexts might explore parallel expressions of what it means to be followers of Christ in their own era and culture.

Francis's appreciation for the intricacies and splendor of the universe, and his relationships with and affection for living creatures did not emerge in a spiritual vacuum; they were present in the Bible and in the biblically based prayers he said daily.

SCRIPTURAL ANTECEDENTS

In the sacred scriptures of Christianity, teachings about God's regard for creation abound. Genesis declares that everything that Yahweh creates is "very good" (chapter 1) and that God reaffirms this in the flood story when Noah, at divine command, saves all living creatures, not just his own family and other humans; and then, by establishing a covenant with the Earth and all creation (chapter 9). Job 38–41 shows Yahweh solicitous of the free creatures of mountain heights and ocean depths. Wisdom states that God loves all of creation (11:24) and that God's spirit is in all things (12:1). In the gospel of Matthew, Jesus describes God caring for birds and flowers (6:26–30). Revelation portrays all the creatures of the air, land, and water, along with humans, praising Jesus (5:13). The Bible teaches that humans should respect creation, and relate to it responsibly. In Genesis humans are instructed to "conserve" and to "serve" Earth (2:15). According to Wisdom, people should see signs of God in creation (13:15). Sirach states, in an early and unconscious reference to Earth's bioregional ecosystemic relationships, that all creatures are diverse and needed (42:23–25). In Acts, Paul notes that God is immanent in creation, for in God "we live and move and have our being" (17:28).

In two poems in the Hebrew Scriptures with which Francis would be very familiar, the Spirit's interaction with all creation is described: Psalms 148 and Daniel 3:59–82.

In Psalm 148, all of creation is called to bless the Lord who brought it into being. In addition to angels and people, a succession of creatures, representing and recalling the totality of creation expressed in the six creation days of Genesis 1, is summoned to worship: sun, moon, and stars; waters above and below; lightning, hail, snow, clouds, and storm winds; mountains and hills; fruit trees and cedars; wild and tame animals, sea monsters, and creatures that fly or crawl. In Francis's breviary, Psalm 148 was prayed each day at dawn as part of Lauds, so its sentiments would have been well ingrained in him as part of his life of prayer. The psalm is unusual in its lack of a distinction between the capability of animate or inanimate, rational or nonrational creatures to praise the Lord. There seems to be an underlying assumption that all creatures offer praise. There is no description of how they might do this, if they are lacking in intelligence or awareness of the Spirit. Some Christian thinkers state that the works of God praise God by their very existence, since they give at least mute testimony to creative divine powers; in Native American Indian spirituality, all of creation is living, from eagles to deer to stones, and so is able to experience its relationship to the Creator. The picture presented in Psalm 148, then, can be envisioned in both traditions, but in different ways: all creatures do indeed praise God, but that praise is conscious for people and unconscious for the rest of creation (Christian perspective) or conscious for all of creation (indigenous peoples' perspective).

Similarly, the song of the three young men in the fiery furnace, as described in Daniel 3:59–82, calls on all creation to praise God. Shadrach, Meshach, and Abednego exhort Yahweh's works to bless, praise, and exalt God. Then they cite individual parts of creation, adding, to rational angels and people, nonrational and inanimate beings: the heavens, including the sun, moon, and stars; waters above and below, including showers and dew, rain, ice, snow, clouds, springs, seas, and rivers; lightning; nights and days, light and darkness; Earth; mountains and hills; dolphins and all water creatures; all birds of the air; and all wild and tame animals. The form this praise might take is not described; there is just the assertion that it might occur. Again, those with a traditional Christian perspective might see a reflected praise; those with a traditional native perspective would view the praise as conscious. The young men's song expressed in the verses in Daniel was also very familiar to Francis. On Sundays and holy days it was added to Psalm 148 at Lauds.

It is evident, when the *Canticle of Creation* is compared with Psalm 148 and Daniel 3, that Francis drew upon these earlier sources, which linked his nature mysticism to his Christian biblical tradition, to express in song and his own language his appreciation for the wonders of the Spirit in creation. While the phrasing in the Bible is active—an exhortation to praise God—and in the *Canticle* it is passive—a hope that God be praised—in all three poems all entities and elements of creation praise God or are exhorted to praise God.

SPIRITUALITY IN CREATION

After his call from the Spirit and his conversion to a new life, Francis came to appreciate ever more evidently the wonders of creation, and began to experience in a profound way the presence of the Creator-Spirit in the works of creation. His *Canticle of Creation* is his most beautiful expression of that experience. It would not have been composed, however, had Francis not been familiar with its scriptural predecessors, and had he not had extraordinary experiences and relationships with creation's living and nonliving members.

Stories of Francis's encounters with living creation abound. Among them are narratives describing how Francis preached a "Sermon to the Birds" near Bevagna in 1213; converted the wolf of Gubbio from his predation; held comfortingly in his hands and then released a waterfowl and a fish while on the Lake of Rieti or Piediluco in separate incidents; and became friends with a falcon during the time in 1224 when he was on Mount LaVerna and received the stigmata, shortly before composing the *Canticle* in 1225. Crickets, crows, lambs, nightingales, and turtle doves are among others of his creature friends; and tradition records that at the moment of his death a flock of skylarks, in fond farewell, soared above, sang near, and settled on the roof of the house where he died.

In the *Canticle of Creation*, Francis expressed most beautifully his relationship with creation and with the Spirit encountered in and through creation. He developed these relationships continually in his daily life, through his encounters and associations with a variety of species and individuals in the biotic community, and his mystical appreciation of abiotic creation.

CANTICLE OF CREATION

Most High, all-powerful, and all-good Lord,
Praise, glory, honor,
and all blessing
are yours.
To you alone, Most High, they belong,
although no one is worthy
to say your name.
Praised be my Lord, with all your creatures,
especially my lord Brother Sun,
through whom you give us day and light.
Beautifully he shines with great splendor:
Most High, he bears your likeness.

Praised be my Lord, by Sister Moon and Stars:
in the heavens you made them bright
and precious and beautiful.
Praised be my Lord, by Brother Wind,
and air and cloud
and calm and all weather
through which you sustain
your creatures.
Praised be my Lord, by Sister Water,
who is so helpful and humble
and precious and pure.
Praised be my Lord, by Brother Fire,
through whom you brighten the night:
who is beautiful and playful
and sinuous and strong.
Praised be my Lord, by our Sister Mother Earth,
who sustains us and guides us,
and provides varied fruits
with colorful flowers and herbs.
Praised and
blessed be you, my Lord,
and gratitude and service be given to you
with great humility.[1]

In the beginning of his *Canticle*, Francis declares that the Lord deserves worship from all creation, although no person is worthy even to say God's name. Then he asks that the Lord be praised *with* all creatures: respect is due to them since they are in community with God. In the next several verses Francis alternates male and female, brother and sister, in his references to inanimate aspects of the created world, beginning with heavenly bodies and then going through the four basic elements—air, water, fire, and earth—acknowledged by the ancients. Brother Sun is praised with God, while the other creatures praise God. Brother Sun is "lord" as well as brother and is in the likeness of God (probably because of solar titles given to God and Jesus in earlier Christian centuries). Then Sister Moon and the stars praise God, as Francis proceeds from the brightest light to the more diminutive lights; these lights are bright and beautiful in the night sky. Elemental creatures then bridge the heavens and the Earth. Brother Wind, the air that embodies him and by which creatures feel his presence, and the clouds and other weather creatures praise God. The mention of clouds and weather leads to Sister Water. She is the liquid form of the clouds, holds a humble position on Earth relative to their presence above, and is useful, precious, and pure. Brother

Fire, the third basic element, is the last of the creatures bridging the heavens and Earth, whose light below complements the heavenly lights above. He leads to Sister and Mother Earth, who complements Brother and lord Sun. Earth is sister and mother: a relative in the family of creation, but also a sovereign, parallel to the lordly sun, who governs her children and nurtures them as a loving mother. The *Canticle* declares, then, that from the mightiest creature above to the mightiest below, all the inanimate yet familial creatures praise God and help humankind.

Francis's appreciation for inanimate or abiotic creation is not apparent in most of the biographies written about him, which focus on his appreciation for the biotic community. Ordinarily, he is on familiar and familial terms with living creatures, but not with their habitat, their Earth home, and the universe beyond. After all, he preached a sermon to the skylarks, not to the sky or stones. Therefore, people familiar with stories about the life and teachings of St. Francis might wonder, when reflecting on his *Canticle*, where are the birds and animals and flowers?

The *Canticle* parallels the first three days of the first creation story in Genesis, in which the bases are established for habitation by the living creatures who will be created to dwell in air, water, and land in the next three days of creation. One might wonder at this point, perhaps, why Francis did not include living creation in his *Canticle*, and if he intended to write a second part in which animate creation, as seen in representative species, would praise God also. An addition to the *Canticle* could directly complement the second three days of the creation story, where life is brought into being; and Psalm 148 and Daniel 3, poems in which both inanimate and animate bodies are called on to praise God. Francis has already offered a subtle transition in his *Canticle* to those biblical readings, by beginning with the heavenly lights and descending to Earth, where living beings dwell. In the Bible, all creatures are called to praise God, whereas in the *Canticle*, only inanimate creatures do so. An addition could show animate creatures also praising their Creator.

People of Francis's own time would not have asked why living creatures were absent from the *Canticle*, nor would they think to suggest a second part to his song. They were already familiar with the melody to which he added his words. As folk singers before and since have done, Francis took a popular song and substituted his words for those of the original songwriter while retaining the existing melody. He sang his poem to the melody of a song that praised the beauty of fields and flowers and other living creatures. He added words about inanimate creation to the melody to make the song complete, its words and melody interacting in a harmony that expressed an awareness that all of nature was interrelated and that all of nature praised God. So Francis did, in fact, include all creatures, nonliving and living. People who heard him sing the *Canticle* would note the old melody linked to the new words, and they could visualize all creatures praising God. The *Canticle* would powerfully evoke a spirituality of creation, an integrated, harmonious relationship of creatures and Creator.

(The originality and beauty of the *Canticle* are recognized and appreciated literarily today. Since Francis wrote at a time when the Italian language was emerging from Latin and French, his poem is considered to be one of the earliest works of Italian literature.)

Francis of Assisi developed his spirituality in creation. Beyond the walls of church buildings and beyond his participation in Catholic worship and in communal prayers with his friars, he encountered the Creator in ways distinct from such experiences of formalized worship in the friars' community settings or in constructed sacred space. He came to realize that while some space might be set aside as sacred and exclude uses other than religious rituals, ultimately all space is sacred space because of divine presence. For Francis, God's presence permeates creation and can be encountered in unique ways in creation; people should respect all creatures, who have an inherent dignity before the Creator; people should live in harmony with creation; and people should respect Mother Earth, who provides for human needs. He believed that the sacred nature of Earth is not intrinsic but derived from its relationship to the Creator.

Although Francis is innovative in his historical place and moment in those respects, he was a product of his time and culture in other ways. He prayed to God and to Jesus, Mary, and Christian saints, and he believed that only Christians would enter heaven. He believed that the supernatural life took precedence over natural life, and urged people to be mindful of life after death. He saw a hierarchy in nature and shared in the anthropocentric tendency common in Christianity (which expresses the belief that creation is ordered to the service of humankind), although he advocated respect for all creation. He did not teach people to have regard for creation because of their self-interest, because they needed Earth and Earth's goods and creatures to provide for human needs; rather, he taught that while creation and creatures were intended to assist humans, they were to be viewed as worthy of familial affection in their own right.

Francis experienced kinship with all creation. In the stories about his engagements with various birds and animals, he seems to sense not only the presence of divine Spirit in other creatures but also their individualized spirits and consciousness. Therefore, what followed for him was that all creation must be respected and all life must be reverenced in their own right or because of the Spirit dwelling in them.

Francis's kind of spiritual encounter outside the walls of church or temple has at times been affirmed and at times attacked by institutional religions. Traditionally, the holy building as sacred place has been favored. However, King Solomon declared during prayer dedicating the First Temple in Jerusalem that Yahweh's presence could not be confined within its four walls (1 Kings 8:27); Jeremiah in his famous sermon in the Temple precincts questioned the relevance of Temple services where worshipers ignored people's needs (Jeremiah 7); and Jesus, in response to the Samaritan woman's question about whether Jews or Samaritans worshiped in the true temple, endorsed neither structure, but declared the time to be coming when true worshipers will worship "in Spirit and in truth" (John 4). One might reason, in the light of all this, that although formal religious practices unite people in a *community* of worship, the faithful as *individuals* more often receive their call from God in an experience of the Spirit in pristine nature. Unfortunately, church authorities usually fear such experiences, especially the mystical ones, because they are outside the guidance or control of institutionally designated religious leaders. But Francis, as a Christian, recognized a transcendent reality immanent within creation. In his spiritual journey, he experienced that reality and called others to share in it.

COMPASSION FOR THE POOR

Francis lived in *voluntary* poverty inspired by his religious understandings; and he identified with and had compassion for those who lived in *involuntary* poverty imposed by their social standing and prevailing political and economic conditions.

Thomas of Celano wrote in his *First Life of St. Francis* that Francis compassionately helped the poor, providing for their basic needs.[2] Among other actions, Francis shared his meager supply of food with people poorer than he was, and, after overcoming his fear of death and disfigurement should he become leprous, he embraced and then went on to minister to lepers separated from their families and from any other human companionship.

Francis called the religious order he established the Friars Minor, or "Lesser Brothers." In an era when the merchant and skilled labor classes were rising in power, and the nobility was trying to retain its power over them, Francis rejected the competition *of* egos and *for* wealth by affirming those who had neither and by establishing his order among them. They were to be a contrast to the social currents of the time. They were to be landless, dress simply, have no money, beg for food when hungry, and aid outcast lepers. They were to live as and among the "least brethren" described by Jesus in the Last Judgment story in Matthew's gospel.

St. Francis wanted the Lesser Brothers to be models of community living, as brothers concerned about each other and as men who shared in common the goods from the commons, while living a simple, subsistence-level life. Their lives stood in stark contrast to the acquisitive efforts of the rising merchant and artisan classes and the avaricious practices of the existing noble class. Their way of life demonstrated that the needs of all might be met if the wants of some were constrained.

Eventually, Francis's model of simple living, love of creation, and compassion for the poorest members of society would help to reform the church and the peoples among whom it ministered.

COMMUNITY IN THE COMMONS

In his life, work, and words St. Francis demonstrated his understanding that creation is revelatory of its Creator—that is, it is *sacramental* in nature; that its goods should be shared—the *common good* was to be sought; and that Earth was a shared home—a *commons* on which all depended for their subsistence and by which all were nurtured.

Today, humans, the reflective consciousness of the cosmos—the universe reflecting upon itself—are particularly aware, if people of faith, of nature's sacramental nature. Creation is *sacramental* because it is the mediation or place of revelation of the immanent presence of the Spirit. Creation should provide for the *common good* because its fruits or "resources" are intended to meet the needs of humans and all other creatures; creation is a *commons* because it is the home of humans and all other creatures, and the locus of their interactive and interdependent and integrated relationships. Creation is not to be viewed solely as sacramental: while people see signs of the Creator in it and can be drawn through its beauty and wonder to contemplate its source of being, they should also be drawn into relationships with its members in themselves, for who they are, and not just for their manifestation of divine presence. Creation should not be reduced to a function, however instrumentally beneficial that might be to meet people's material or spiritual needs. Creation is sacred in itself, not just as the bearer of divine Being. Creation has intrinsic value, not just instrumental value as a provider of goods or mediation of the Spirit.

Francis acknowledged this goodness and value of all creatures. He transcended the anthropocentrism of his time when he called animate and inanimate beings "brother" and "sister." There is no rivalry among these siblings bur rather a mutuality of interests in a familial relationship.

The ideas of Francis regarding Creator and creation would be viewed today as pan*en*theistc, not to be confused with "pantheistic." While *pantheism* sees a unity of Earth and Spirit (God is in and part of Earth as its spiritual essence—however understood—or guiding power), *panentheism* understands Earth to be permeated by the immanent presence of a transcendent Spirit, who is distinct from creation (Earth is in and reveals the transcendent-immanent Spirit). A panentheistic perspective provides insights into the Creator Spirit's loving engagement with creatures.

IN THE WORLD AND NOT *OF* THE WORLD

One of the factors that historically has limited Christian relatedness to and care for Earth has been its focus on a heavenly afterlife. Striving to attain this future life in a separate, spiritual dimension of reality takes precedence over present "earthly" concerns, occupations, and preoccupations. This Christian attitude was affected by understandings and misunderstandings of Jesus' discussion of his relationship to "this world."

The setting of early Christianity was Roman Palestine. Jesus was born in an occupied land among an oppressed people in a remote part of the extensive Roman Empire. He was *in* the world as an ethnic and religious Jew at a particularly trying period in Jewish history. He did not, however, share the economic or political and nationalistic worldviews prevalent among his contemporaries and in that sense was not of the (ideological) world whose perspective he rejected. Jesus taught that his reign or "kingdom" was "not of this world"; that is, it did not conform to his culture's way of thinking and the social, political, and economic consciousness and structures that flowed from it.

In the Gospel of John, Jesus declares that his reign or "kingdom" is "not of this world," while in the Gospel of Luke he states that his reign is "among" his followers. The juxtaposition of these and other biblical texts has led some Christian writers through the centuries to declare that the followers of Jesus must be "*in* the world but not *of* the world." Biblically, *world* can mean a place or a perception, a context, or a consciousness. Thus, in the first text Jesus rejects the ideologies of his time, the ways of thinking contradictory to his message of compassion and love and justice; and he rejects being limited to a particular place when he negates the perspective of those who think his role is to fulfill prevailing Jewish messianic political thought. (The latter expressed the hope that a warrior king, in the spirit of David, would expel the occupying Romans and reestablish the kingdom of Israel as an independent nation in "this world.") Jesus, then, while living in the physical world, is not "of" the world when the latter means an ideology or a particular fixed geographic place.

Francis of Assisi is regarded by many Christians as a faithful disciple of Jesus who, like his teacher, was in the world but not of it. Francis lived *in* the world as a child of the thirteenth century, with its historical people, events, and consciousness. He accepted and adapted to the perceived role—political and temporal, as well as spiritual—of the Catholic Church of the time. Francis, unlike Jesus, was *of* the world in that he shared its operative religious consciousness. While Jesus rejected conservative pharisaic Judaism, and eventually would be in conflict with the priests and other religious leaders of his time, Francis shared the perspective of his time and place that the church and its leaders were to be served as religious guides and as God's representatives despite their personal shortcomings. He asserted that people were called to discipline strictly and even to disparage their body in its present, corporeal, earthly setting, and to develop a spiritual life that would enable the soul to enjoy a future life in heaven. He was, then, "of" the Catholic Christian world in his immersion in the institutional church's authority, religious teachings, and practices.

Francis was not "of" the world, in the sense of world as political or economic ideology. He did not accept his era's money-oriented mentality, social stratification (including in the church), and struggles by individuals and social groups for political and religious dominance over one another (including instances of popes with armies defending their sovereign territory against other temporal lords).

All people are, to some extent, limited by, but not restricted to, the ideas and ideologies dominant or prevalent in their time and place. Francis was no exception. He was very obedient to church authorities, but argued to convince them to permit the founding of his lesser brothers, the Friars Minor. He believed that only the priest brought God among humans, during the Mass, but yet saw signs of God in creation; he did not reconcile his fidelity to Catholic sacramental doctrine with his experience that creation was revelatory of the divine without priestly rituals. He sought to restore the church to God's ways, but he believed that priests should be revered, because of their role at Mass, even when their personal conduct was reprehensible.

Francis lived in two cultural worlds: a *tradition-breaking* medieval social world in a state of political and economic upheaval; and a *tradition-bound* church spiritual world that simultaneously sought, with mixed results, to assert some authority over secular rulers and civil affairs. Like Jesus, Francis transcended his social world, not bound by its ideological, political, or economic limitations. Unlike Jesus, who had conflicts with the pharisees and priests of his time, and even confronted directly the power of religious leaders in the Temple in Jerusalem in his conflict with the moneychangers and animal merchants, Francis let himself be confined, doctrinally and behaviorally, by the Catholic Church, many of whose leaders were similar in outlook to the Jewish religious leaders of Jesus' time as they are described in the gospels.

Francis, then, loved nature and the natural world, to a certain extent, and loved creatures living according to their nature and integrated with nature. But he did not accept humans' place in nature as corporeal beings who are part of the natural world. Humans were to strive to subdue their bodies, even to the extent of doing violence to them to control them, as if people were called to be angels rather than created to be humans. He did not accept people as body-spirit beings in his spiritual teachings, but he did affirm their right to sustenance and charity from their communities.

Ironically, Francis negated creation to some extent. His focus on the next life blinded him against regarding humans as creatures who are inextricably integrated and interdependent with the rest of creation. Francis's relationships were not with humans immersed in historical contexts as living beings who were blessed with all creatures as "very good" in the first biblical creation story, people who naturally live, reproduce, and provide for their subsistence through their work. Francis related to people essentially as embodied spirits who were called to a heavenly afterlife and who on Earth were fallen beings who should reject the physical part of their humanness. Like his contemporaries in the church, Francis regarded life as a time of trial, testing, and sanctification, where the physical was subjected to what was understood to be a "higher" spiritual reality. There was no complementary affirmation of living a fully human life (physical, spiritual, social), no comparable teaching that sanctification might be given to people who live in a holistic way, including by engendering and lovingly raising children, and working responsibly to the best of their ability in their vocation to earn their livelihood to support their family. Francis's perspective, in fact, was an indirect contradiction of the Christian belief in divine incarnation and resurrection in Jesus. If the body is a burden to be subjected to the spiritual, why then did God come among humans, affirming a holistic human, rather than appearing solely as a spirit to draw people away from corporeal existence?

Francis, unlike Jesus, sought to suffer in order to discipline his body's physical needs and wants. Like Jesus, Francis accepted unexpected pain or discomfort as an inevitable consequence of being human or of fulfilling what he understood to be his mission. Jesus spoke both of voluntarily taking up one's cross (choosing to bear hardship or even death by promoting the reign of God) and of enduring involuntarily an oppressive imposition by "going the second mile" when forced to carry the pack of one of the occupying Roman troops who were on patrol (willing to bear an unexpected, and even unjustly imposed, burden). Such hardships might become one's lot as a consequence of doing God's work; one should bear the social consequences of doing what is right and endure the physical exigencies of the human condition. One should not, by contrast, seek deliberately to become ill or to be executed. Francis departed from Jesus' teaching when he sought martyrdom in Egypt (if Bonaventure's data are accurate), when he sought to be humiliated, and when he whipped himself or wore chains and a hair shirt. It should be remembered that when Francis did these things he was doing what people of his time thought were ascetic, self-disciplinary acts. He is, then, "of the world" in that regard, fulfilling the requirements or expectations of the limited and limiting church understandings of his time. In his era, the story of Adam and Eve and their "fall" in a historical Garden of Eden was understood literally. Christians were to acknowledge this "original sin" and their own sins, all of which flowed from their corporeal humanity, and seek salvation by transcending "this world" preoccupations.

Spirituality is the most personal and the most universal experience of the Spirit possible to people. When encountering divine presence, individuals in diverse settings from distinct cultures engage the same divine Being, but express their experience in different languages and with different symbols and stories. *Religion*, through its structures, leaders, doctrines, and rituals, gives spirituality an institutionalized form. While religion is culture based, spirituality is Spirit based. In his life and teachings, Francis expressed his spirituality in terms unique to his era and area, but in his Catholic religion he remained conditioned by his culture.

In the time of St. Francis, Christians holding the theological view that God in Jesus came to save them out of the *physical* world did not realize that they were denigrating the work and world of God-Creator as well as putting the latter in conflict with the work of God-Redeemer. They misread Jesus' saying that his reign is "not of this world," erroneously interpreting "world" to mean their historical, material reality rather than the ideology of their time. Thus, they regarded corporeal existence as something to be endured and overcome. The result of this interpretation ultimately was that they were led away from the wholeness of their existence—that is, away from the material reality that is part of what it means to be human. So while Christians believed on the one hand that Jesus was both divine and human, on the other they rejected this divine affirmation of humanness, and viewed Jesus' role to be to rescue—save—them from that very humanness.

Christians believed that God in Jesus became an individual member of the human species who was born, killed, and raised from the dead. Jesus was not just a spiritual "immortal" who had happily escaped the limitations of bodily existence but rather someone who had become wholly human again, body and spirit. They did not see the contradiction inherent in despising their corporeal existence and the physical Earth ("world") they inhabited, from which they believed Jesus would save them, while simultaneously believing that God created them and the world, came among them as a human being, and was resurrected as a fully human being, not as a bodiless spirit. In contrast to Christians today, they did not recognize that humans are neither imprisoned souls nor angelic spirits; nor that God affirmed the holistic human not by speaking to humanity by means of visions alone, or through a docetic, solely spiritual Jesus, but by being born human, living a human life, dying, and rising to a new type of spirit-body human existence. In the early centuries of Christianity, Marcion and others were declared heretics for teaching that Jesus had no physical body and was not really human. Today, while not teaching that Jesus was not human, Christian churches sometimes act as though that were the case when they focus or seem to focus exclusively on salvation from the world's material reality.

SPIRITUALITY, SOLICITUDE, AND SOLIDARITY

While most people who admire Francis of Assisi today have in mind a friar friend of feathered fauna who also loved all of nature, this spiritual and social troubadour was much more complex than that. It is true that those within the Christian tradition have much to learn from him about relationships with nonhuman creation. But those same Christians should also be at least intrigued, if not inspired, by his ideas on living simply and compassionately, and on seeking to integrate all of this with an engagement with the Spirit immanent in and revealed through creation.

This does not mean, even in an era when increased care for creation and for human community is so lacking and so needed, that an *imitatio Francesco* should be a goal for Christians and other admirers of Francis. As noted earlier, Il Poverello was in many ways a product of the theological, spiritual, and ecclesial consciousness and practices of his time. It does mean that just as Francis sought to be the best he could be insofar as he understood what that was, so, too, should Christians who study his life seek to see how they might be faithful to who they are and what they are called to do. God does not expect Christians to be clones of St. Francis. The Spirit calls people to be human beings striving as best they can in their time and place to be faithful to God as individuals and as communities.

For Francis, all creation has theophanic potential; it can reveal God to the person open to that possibility. A theophany is not limited solely to a spiritual experience of the extraordinary, a direct encounter with the Spirit who is transcendent from creation; it can be a spiritual experience of the ordinary, an encounter with the Spirit who is immanent in creation and revealed through and mediated by creation.

In the spirit of St. Francis, contemporary people might seek ways to live more in harmony with each other and with nature, and to share the common goods of the Earth commons.

ST. FRANCIS FOR THE
TWENTY-FIRST CENTURY

The extremes of Francis's lifestyle need not—should not—be replicated today. But they do counterbalance consumer culture. They are living statements that affluence, class oppression, ethnocentrism, irresponsible sexuality, racism, sexism, discrimination against the weakest members of society, speciesism, and nationalism should neither limit nor define humanity, nor should they thwart human aspirations to live simultaneously within the complementary physical and spiritual dimensions of reality.

Some people might choose the celibate and communal life that Francis chose. This would be their particular calling in the world. It is not a "higher" calling but a complementary calling. God declared all creation to be "very good." Procreation is necessary for creation to continue to unfold, and for life to continue to evolve toward the Creator's vision of what it might become.

In an age of overconsumption of scarce Earth resources, forced extinction of species of wildlife, some Christians' rejection of responsibility for Earth and of Jesus' prayer that God's will be done on Earth as in heaven, disparagement of the poor, dominance of humans over other members of the biotic community, wars and rumors of wars, and pollution of Earth's air, land, and water, Francis of Assisi can inspire Christians to be catalysts for social change who contribute to Earth community well-being.

In the spirit of St. Francis, and while regarding care for creation as an essential part of their faith, people should conserve places of natural beauty, respecting those remnants and reminders of God's creative and creating power. They should ensure that the subsistence needs of all peoples are met, before expending Earth's goods for human wants. They should promote sustainable employment at a living wage, so that all might have dignity and the opportunity to provide for themselves and their families. They should develop or restore and use intermediate technology, which is technology appropriate to people and place. They should make the Earth commons a place in which pure, living water, unpolluted land, and clean air provide the setting for the lives of all creatures. They should promote organic agriculture, energy conservation, and alternative energy development and use. They should recognize the intrinsic value of all creatures, who are not on Earth simply to meet human needs and wants. They should develop an economic system focused on meeting all peoples' *needs*, not some people's *wants*: a simpler lifestyle will be required of all those people who consume Earth's goods well beyond what they need for material and social well-being. They should be mindful of their intergenerational responsibility. People do not love their children and descendants beyond them if they irresponsibly use up in the present the water, soil, energy sources, and minerals that future generations will need. They should promote regional and international peace based on justice, for the common good of humanity and all life, and safeguard the commons shared by all life. They should replicate in their individual and community lives, and in their relationships with other creatures, the harmony between living creatures and their Earth commons that Francis celebrated in the words and melody of his *Canticle of Creation*.

If the spirit of St. Francis were to permeate only people of the Christian faith (let alone his admirers in other traditions), the common good of all peoples would be promoted, the commons would be cared for and would provide for the needs of all creatures, and creation would indeed be sacramental, revelatory of divine presence and of human engagement with that presence.

NOTES

1. Trans. John Hart from the Italian text of manuscript 338 in the Assisi library, cited in Arnaldo Fortini, *Francis of Assisi*, trans. Helen Moak (New York: Crossroad, 1981), 566–67.

2. Regis J. Armstrong, O.F.M., Cap., J. A. Wayne Hellmann, O.F.M. Conv., and William J. Short, O.F.M., *Francis of Assisi: The Saint*, vol. 1 of *Francis of Assisi: Early Documents* (New York: New City Press, 1999), 195.

$\cdot 3 \cdot$

Native Spirits

$\mathcal{T}$he Spirit of St. Francis is complemented across space and time in the lives and teachings of native American Indian peoples in the United States. Francis was well known for his kinship with abiotic nature and the biotic community. The Indian[1] peoples have a strong respect for creation and a heightened sense of kinship with all creatures that complement the perspective of Francis. Non-Indians regard Black Elk as the most renowned traditional spiritual leader. Among traditional Indians of the latter part of the twentieth century, Phillip Deere is among the most revered.

Some native spiritual leaders wove together their traditional cultural perspective and the insights of Christianity. Such representative native elders include the Lakota Black Elk (1863–1950), a warrior who became a cultural leader, a healer, and a spiritual icon for his own and other peoples and who served as a catechist for the Jesuits; and the Muskogee Phillip Deere (1926–1985), an elder noted for his human rights work, his spiritual insights, and his healing abilities and who had served for nearly two decades as a Methodist preacher. Unlike Francis during his lifetime, Black Elk and Phillip were healers ("medicine men"). Like Francis, both engaged the Creator in creation and expressed their kinship not just with humans but with all creatures.

In various aspects of his life, Francis shared ideas and practices in common with traditional Indians, peoples not yet contacted and not yet erroneously called "Indians" or "Americans," or "Creek" or "Sioux" but known by their native names in their native territories. Francis and the first spiritual leaders of what would be called later the "Americas" respected other peoples, wild creatures, and pristine places, and they believed in sharing natural goods. All expressed compassion and promoted harmony; all believed in living simply, seeking only a sufficiency of goods to meet life's necessities. From three distinct cultures and diverse historical contexts, Francis, Black Elk, and Phillip offer complementary reflections on caring for creation as a whole and as specific creatures, and for relating to the Spirit through creation. They experienced the

41

fullness of the sacramental commons and shared that experience with their respective peoples.

Francis of Assisi from the Christian tradition, a native of Italy; Black Elk from native and Catholic Christian traditions of the Lakota (Sioux) nation in the midwestern United States, from South Dakota; and Phillip Deere from native and Methodist Christian traditions of the Muskogee (Creek) tradition in the southwestern United States, from Oklahoma, are proponents of panentheistic perspectives. From their respective social contexts and spiritual orientations, Francis, Black Elk, and Phillip promoted care for creation based on their understandings of the Spirit and of the Spirit's relationships with humanity and with all creation. They offered complementary and at times congruent ideas and visions of human relationships with the Spirit and the Spirit's creation, each incorporating a pronounced respect for creatures and a profound perception of the presence of Spirit in the cosmos. All experienced spirituality in creation. Whether they roamed forests or mountains, walked along rivers, or paused to pray with animals, they encountered in these sacred places and moments the Spirit who brought all into being. Such encounters were significant spiritual experiences that stimulated them to share with others the peace, insights, and gifts they had received in places within pristine creation. Francis, Black Elk, and Phillip had parallel personal lives and complementary calls by the Spirit that led them away from familial and financial security.

In Christian missionary activities over the centuries, the complementarity of religious traditions was rejected, not respected. Often, diverse religious traditions were feared, negated as being devil worship, regarded as competitors, seen as inferior, or deemed condemned by the divine being whom a particular culture worshiped, and so they were to be eradicated and replaced. Consequently, native peoples in the Americas have been victims of physical and cultural genocide; their spiritual leaders often were especially persecuted.

BLACK ELK, LAKOTA ELDER

Black Elk was born poor, and his dedication to his people and their well-being ensured his continuing poverty because of the sacrifices he made. The oral autobiography of this Oglala Lakota spiritual leader and healer was recorded by John Neihardt, Nebraska's poet laureate, and published in 1932 as *Black Elk Speaks*. Readers of the book usually do not realize that Black Elk became a Catholic in 1904,[2] after the time described in the book, and was sent by the Jesuits as a missionary and catechist to the Lakota and other Indians. Since during his lifetime native traditions were disparaged and he saw

Christianity as a more powerful religion, Black Elk publicly (but not entirely in private) set aside the old ways when he became a Catholic, with a consequent loss of significant ancient wisdom, spiritual practices, and healing knowledge for both native peoples and Christianity.

The spiritual richness in Black Elk's narration of a vision he had while leading a Ghost Dance, when he was still a traditional spiritual leader and healer, reveals his depth of perception of and his engagement with divine presence. In the vision, Black Elk soared in the form of a spotted eagle and then landed near a village:

> As I landed there, I saw twelve men coming toward me and they stood before me and said, "Our Father, the two-legged chief, you shall see." Then I went to the center of the circle with these men and there again I saw the tree in full bloom. Against the tree I saw a man standing with outstretched arms. As we stood close to him these twelve men said: "Behold him!" The man with outstretched arms looked at me and I didn't know whether he was a white or an Indian. He did not resemble Christ. He looked like an Indian, but I was not sure of it. He had long hair which was hanging down loose. On the left side of his head was an eagle feather. His body was painted red. (At that time I had never had anything to do with white men's religion and I had never seen any picture of Christ.) This man said to me: "My life is such that all earthly beings that grow belong to me. My Father has said this. You must say this." I stood there gazing at him and tried to recognize him. I could not make him out. He was a nice-looking man. As I looked at him, his body began to transform. His body changed into all colors and it was very beautiful. All around him there was light. Then he disappeared all at once. It seemed as though there were wounds in the palms of his hands. . . . It seems to me on thinking it over that I have seen the son of the Great Spirit himself.[3]

In this narrative, Black Elk appears to have encountered Christ before engaging Christianity to any extent. He sees a universal Christ, for "he did not resemble Christ"—that is, he was not like the anglicized Christ of pictures—but "I have seen the son of the Great Spirit himself," who "looked like an Indian." (Similarly, in the narratives of the appearances of the Virgin of Guadalupe in Mexico, Mary looked like an *india* to Juan Diego on the hill of Tepeyac in the sixteenth century.) The Indian Christ seen by Black Elk has his arms outstretched on the Tree of Life, and becomes transfigured, in imagery congruent with scenes in the Gospels.

Prior to this vision, at the age of nine, Black Elk had fallen into a twelve-day coma and experienced the most significant event of his life, a Great Vision that would guide him for decades until his death. In his Great Vision, he was transported to the clouds and to Harney Peak in South Dakota. There he was instructed, by way of symbolic gifts presented to him, that he would be a warrior, healer, and spiritual guide. He saw coming very destructive wars and the suffering of his people, but the vision ended with a scene of hope. He stood on the top of Harney Peak and saw all the peoples of the world in a community of circles set within a great circle of harmony; and in the center of the great circle stood a Tree of Life. Black Elk became a healer in 1882 and was renowned among his people and beyond. He was associated in one way or another with major and traumatic events in his people's history: Custer's defeat and death; the killing of his cousin, Crazy Horse; and the U.S. cavalry's massacre of hundreds of Lakota men, women, and children at Wounded Knee in South Dakota.

Black Elk's experience of the revelatory commons is expressed in his statements to his interviewers. He speaks of his relatedness to other creatures and to Mother Earth, and of how the native peoples generally lived in harmony with all life such that all had an abundance of Earth goods to provide for their needs. The people killed other animals only as needed for survival. All people recognized the presence and power of the Creator Spirit present in creation.

When he described the wind whispering in the leaves of the cottonwood tree in the center of the Sun Dance circle, Black Elk's words complemented Psalm 148 and the images presented by Francis in the *Canticle of Creation*: "you can hear the voice of the cottonwood tree; this we understand is its prayer to the Great Spirit, for not only men, but all things and all beings pray to Him continually in differing ways."[4] The cottonwood trees are prayerful and sacramental. Their prayer reminds humans that all creation prays to the Creator.

The unity of all creation, and its communal offering of prayers to the Creator Spirit, the Father Wakan-Tanka, is present when the sacred pipe is smoked. According to Black Elk, when White Buffalo Calf Woman appeared to the Lakota people and gave them the ceremony of the sacred pipe, she instructed them that the bowl of the pipe represents Earth; the buffalo calf carved in the stone signifies all of the four-legged creatures who live on Mother Earth; the wooden stem represents plant life, the rooted ones; the eagle feathers that hang from where the stem is joined to the bowl represent the eagle messengers (which are viewed also as extensions of Wakan-Tanka and whose feathers are viewed as rays from Wakan-Tanka) and all winged creatures. When a person prays with the pipe, they are joined with "all the things of the universe . . . when you pray with this pipe, you pray for and with everything."[5] People who pray with the pipe "must always remember that the two-leggeds and all the other peoples who stand upon this earth are sacred and should be treated as such."[6] In the sacred pipe, then, the revelatory or sacramental commons is represented: all creatures converse with the Great Spirit; all creatures are sacred and should be respected. (The commons implication of this is that all are entitled to the Earth goods they need.) Earth, from whom all living creatures have come, is sacred, humble, and nourishing, and with her as their home and Mother all people live as relatives.

This understanding that all living beings are related (all are "members of the biotic community," in today's scientific terminology) is sometimes expressed in an elder's opening prayer for a ceremony or a meeting. The elder will begin, "Greetings all my relatives. Greetings to all the two-legged people. Greetings to all the four-legged people. Greetings to all the winged people. Greetings to all the finned people. Greetings to all the rooted people." The prayer, in the Lakota tradition, might end with *"Mitakuye oyasin"* (We are all related). In a similar vein, Black Elk taught that the most important reason why people went through *Hanblecheyapi*, or "Crying for a Vision," was because "it helps us to realize our oneness with all things, to know that all things are our relatives."[7]

Black Elk refers to the revelatory or sacramental nature of nature when he instructs people, as they walk "the sacred path of life," to "be attentive as you walk," that is, to remember that they are always in the presence of the Great Spirit, and should "be attentive to all the signs that You have given us" for instruction and to experience divine presence.[8] Later, he observes that people will experience a great peace of spirit "when they realize their relationship, their oneness, with the universe and all its Powers, and when they realize that at the center of the universe dwells *Wakan-Tanka*, and that this center is really everywhere, it is within each of us."[9]

The experience of relatedness to, and oneness with, all creation as described by Black Elk resonates with Francis's sense of kinship with all the "brothers and sisters" in the biotic family and the greater cosmos. It is present also in the teachings of Phillip Deere.

PHILLIP DEERE, MUSKOGEE ELDER

Phillip was born into poverty, and his spiritual vocation kept him poor. A carpenter by trade, he was also an international spiritual leader, a human rights activist, and a healer. His activities in these areas prevented him from holding long-term employment to support his wife and six children. Phillip's poverty in a sense was *in*voluntary, in that had he been solely a carpenter he would not have had to live a life of deprivation for himself and his family, nor would he have had to set aside family responsibilities in order to travel to help others. In another sense, his poverty was voluntary, insofar as it was occasioned by his spiritual calling: one's response to the call of the Spirit—the Great Mystery, in his people's tradition—is a personal choice. In the Muskogee spiritual tradition, a man or woman who was gifted with healing powers by the Great Mystery was required to give themselves to meet people's needs, no matter what the personal cost might be. They might have an ordinary occupation—a carpenter, for example—but when someone requested their help, they had to put aside their "gainful employment" to exercise their extraordinary vocation. They were expected to provide the needed assistance without expectation of remuneration and without consideration of the petitioner's ethnic or economic background. As a consequence, Phillip lived on allotted land in an unfinished home he was gradually building that had no indoor plumbing and a wood stove for cooking and heating. Near his dwelling was an open-walled roundhouse, with its central fire, that he built for sacred ceremonies.

Phillip Deere, like Francis of Assisi, was well known among his people and also to other peoples as a spiritual leader. Unlike Francis, he was married with a family, as is usually the case with indigenous spiritual leaders. Like Francis, he traveled the world offering guidance; people sought him out at home and abroad; and he lived in poverty. Unlike Francis, he was a healer ("medicine man" or "shaman" in nonnative terminology) renowned across continents and a human rights activist. In his teachings, Phillip was a bearer of the traditions of his people, but he was also reflective and adaptable to new situations and ways of thinking.

Phillip Deere had little formal education, though he was literate and of profound intellect. He had a prodigious memory in which he retained prayers and healing chants in Old Muskogee, creation stories and the ancient migration legend of his people's history in Muskogee and English, and federal and state governments' treaty provisions in English. His people still retained oral history as the primary means of passing on their heritage, and Phillip was a Muskogee historian and storyteller in that tradition. In his words: "I never finished with my grade school. . . . At home the elders taught me something that will never be found in libraries. They told me of prophecies; they told me of the use of herbal medicines. I was told about the sacredness of the earth. I was told of my own religion. And this I preserved for many years."[10] In the Muskogee tradition, parallel to biblical understandings, a Creator fashioned the universe. The Muskogee story of creation, of course, springs from local cultural understandings and surroundings, as did the ancient Hebrews' story. In Phillip's oral tradition, at one time the Earth was flat. There were no mountains or hills, today's trees were then only low bushes that bore fruit, and people were short with axe-shaped heads. The Creator—the Great Mystery—told four birds to fly around the Earth without flapping their wings.

The eagle, horned owl, buzzard, and falcon hawk circled the earth. On their third time around the buzzard flapped his wings, and dramatic changes occurred: rocks grew to mountains, bushes became trees (some now without fruit), and people changed. Thus, the buzzard is credited with bringing positive changes to the world and is especially honored. Only the spiritual leaders are allowed to use buzzard feathers, which they employ in healing wounds. It is worthy of note that here, as elsewhere in native traditions, creatures that people in other cultures sometimes fear or look down on are shown to do something positive. In this case, the buzzard, which some would find repulsive as a carrion bird, is shown in a positive light at the primordial time of creation (as the stimulus for positive changes to the Earth) and in the present time (as an aid to healing).

In contrast to the biblical story (and more accurate, historically and scientifically), the Muskogee creation story does not present the first people living in a paradisal state. Then, as now, they had to worry about illness and conflicts with other animals. Phillip describes conditions this way:

> At one time, in the early days of the creation, we were told, at one time the human beings had no friends, and could have been destroyed by huge animals, large animals that were giants that walked upon this earth at one time. There was sickness coming upon the people, with no cure whatsoever. In the old times, people had no protection against illness or other animals. Then the plant people said, "We, too, are trampled down, we, too, are beaten down, we, too, are wounded at times by these animals and by these bugs and insects. We will be your friends. We will help you." And so this is how every herb became useful to us. So, there's an herb for every illness, and they'll work if the right medicine person can be found. . . . Some cures are learned in dreams.

In this teaching, plants serve as healers of the people, a function parallel to that of the tree of life in the Garden of Eden (Genesis 2:8; 22–24) and in the new Jerusalem (Revelation 22:1–2). In the latter biblical passage in particular, there is a congruence with Muskogee thought about the healing qualities of plants, for the tree of life in the new Earth of Revelation has leaves with healing power. There is an interesting contrast here as well: In the biblical story people lose access to the tree of life when they are expelled from Eden and shift their mode of existence; in the Muskogee story people find assistance from life-sustaining plant people when they shift their mode of existence. The Muskogee story also recognizes a community of life in which all creatures, not just humans, are *people*. Other living beings can communicate with humans, and have reciprocal relationships with them. The Muskogee received medicinal help from plant people, but they cultivated plants, too, such as corn. They provided life for, and received life from, the plant community.

The Great Mystery, when bringing about the creation, instilled certain "natural laws" within it that govern creation as a whole and guide each creature to live its specific way of life:

> In the beginning when the Earth was created, when everything came about, everything was given original instructions of life and everything followed those instructions of life. The Earth has its duties to perform, the sun, the moon, the stars. Everything was given instructions of life. And the trees have never failed to follow those instructions. They have never made a mistake. The rivers have never made a mistake. Every plant, every animal, every bird, every fish have never made a mistake. They still follow those original instructions of life.

The circle symbolizes creation living in accord with the Creator's natural laws, and it also represents the life cycle of all creatures as one family:

> And at that time, in our understanding, that creation was in a form of a circle. . . . We know that the sun is round, the moon is round. That's where the sacred circle, the sacred hoop comes from. When it was learned that the Earth was round it was not a surprise to the Indian people because they already knew that the Earth was round because all creation followed that circle. That circle represented the circle of life. The trees, they grow old and the little ones take their place, and it's been that way for thousands of years. The people, they grow old and the young ones, they take their place. This is all part of that circle and it is the cycle of life that has been going on for thousands of years. We call it a circle because it is a measurement of no beginning and no ending. This is where we found a way of life. This is where what is called Indian civilization came from. In our study of nature we found the circle. Therefore the tepees, sweat lodges, and many ceremonies that we have are still in the form of a circle. In this circle we found life, we found a way to survive. It became sacred to our people. In a traditional council you will find the elders sitting in a circle and not in rows.

The sacred circle, representing harmony, wholeness, and the cycle of life, is a symbol shared in common by native peoples.

Humankind existed in creation as a part of it, with no special privileges and with no superior position. All creatures were loved by the Great Mystery, and all were to be respected in their own right. They were not created to serve people but to share in Mother Earth's bounty as a community of life:

> We were told to respect everything within the creation because we were the most dependent in this creation. The human being is the most dependent

being in creation. We find that among our Indian stories, that of everything that was placed here, human beings came last. And if you will study your Bible, the Book of Genesis, you will find that human beings came last. They came last because they had to depend on everything that was created on the days before. We are the most dependent within this creation. The bear is born prepared, the elk and the moose and all the animals are prepared when they are born. Many of the animals that were born last night are walking this evening. Even a tiny chicken that was born this morning is already walking, but how long does it take for a human being to start walking? How long do you have to carry that baby before it learns to walk? We came unprepared so we have to depend on these animals. We have to depend on the plants for our clothes because we are not prepared for our winter. We are not prepared for the snow. So we are the most dependent and most pitiful among this creation, but somewhere down through history we made ourselves believe that we are better than everything within the creation and that we could make things better. But in the traditional ways of thinking we're only part of the creation. We were placed here to sustain life. . . . We looked at the sun with respect, we looked at the Earth with respect, we looked at the mountains and the rivers with respect. We learned to respect the creation at an early age. . . . Somewhere down the history of the human race we began to wander away, and we drifted away from those natural ways of thinking to where we no longer think like our ancestors did, and we forget about nature. We no longer believe in life as our ancestors did.

The old ways have been changing, in particular because of the attractions of the consumer society, the loss of employment opportunities, and economic stagnation resulting from the capitalism that displaced communalism; and psychological depression, spiritual ennui, and loss of dignity caused by broken treaties and physical and cultural genocide. Phillip has remained hopeful, however, because in recent decades native youths have begun to seek out surviving elders to explore an integration of the old ways into their lives. His annual "Youth and Elders Conference" brought together, from across the United States and Canada, young people and spiritual leaders from numerous native nations. They explored together traditional spiritual ways:

If we want our children to grow up, healthy people, healthy human beings, we feed them proper food so they will grow up physically strong. But what provisions have we made as a spiritual food for them? If there is no spirituality in this person he is not balanced. . . . We have to look at a human being as two in one. This is the teaching of my ancestors and also this is the teaching of the Bible. It teaches us that the dust alone could not live, and so the spirit had to enter this dust in order for it to become a living being.

The traditional spirituality advocated by Phillip has links, then, to Christian spirituality. It takes a different path, however, in its emphasis on the relationship of spirituality to creation:

> In the early days our people studied nature. They studied everything in nature and they learned to survive off what was in this creation. In learning and understanding the medicine ways, many times they fasted to learn. They searched out food that they could survive on, plants that could heal their sick. They learned to survive off the creation, and the strong belief was that there was enough placed here within the creation to sustain life, that we did not need to take anything away, we did not need to add any more, everything was placed here. And so thanks was given to everything.

This expression of gratitude, of course, is also the attitude of Francis of Assisi toward creation. So, too, is the notion of living in harmony with the natural environment, not taking more than is necessary, not needing to add anything to the goods provided by Mother Earth.

For Phillip and Francis, people should be conscious and appreciative of what Earth provides, recognizing that although they have a spiritual dimension to their lives, they must also care for the natural home that is their earthly dwelling:

> So we have to turn around and respect Mother Earth. We cannot say that "I am just a pilgrim passing through," so I have no use for the Missouri River. We cannot say that "I a Baptist," "I a Methodist," or 'I am a Catholic," so I have no use for this tree. We have to understand who we are, what we are, where did we come from. We are the caretakers of this land and we are part of this creation. So we must respect Mother Earth.

In Phillip's experience with Christians, he observed that some would say that it did not matter what they did to their earthly home since they had another home waiting in the next world. This, he believed, made them careless with or exploitive toward Mother Earth. There could be harmful consequences from such an attitude and the practices it engendered, particularly if people claimed to be above other creatures and regarded them as having worth only to the extent that they served humankind. The Muskogee tradition, by contrast, offers an alternative understanding:

> We believe in natural laws of love, peace and respect. We learned this thousands of years ago and this was the life of our people. When we destroy anything within the creation, we feel that we destroy ourselves. . . . So we must preserve what we have. . . . We have felt ourselves to be a part of the creation:

not superiors, not the rulers of the creation, but only part of the creation. If we understand those natural ways, natural laws of love, peace and respect, we will be able to get along with everyone. We will learn to love and share with everyone.

What follows is that spiritual people must be conscious of their responsibilities to the Creator and grateful that this Great Mystery is solicitous of them as a loving parent, called *Father* in the Christian tradition; and they must be conscious of their responsibilities to, and grateful for the nurturing of, *Mother* Earth:

> When we learned about Christianity we heard about the Father. We learned to pray to the Father, and in the churches every Sunday we heard about Father. To this day we still hear about Father. But we never hear anything about Mother. . . . But every Indian knows what you mean when you say, "Mother Earth." Traditional people know what you're talking about. . . . We must all learn to say "Mother" as well as we say "our Father." And in this way of life we will have balance.

The balance that Phillip Deere calls for includes the understanding that spirituality is not something reserved only for a part of one's week; it must permeate every moment: "Native religion to us is a way of life. That religion is based on this creation and its sacredness. In this religion every day was a sacred day to us. Religion did not take place just Saturdays or Sundays. Every day of our life was a holy day." The Muskogee elder Phillip Deere walked gently on Earth and respected all of Earth's living beings. He lived as a relative of all creation and traveled with the Great Mystery. In his presence, youths and elders alike engaged a spiritual leader who walked with the Spirit, a holy man who not only taught about spirituality but lived connected to the Spirit who is its source and to all creatures.

FRANCIS AND BLACK ELK

Francis of Assisi and Black Elk from South Dakota shared in common a Catholic faith whose traditional doctrines had changed little during the almost seven hundred years that separated their historical times, and across the thousands of miles that separated their geographic places. However, for Francis that faith was firmly within the dogmatic constraints of Catholicism, while for Black Elk it was interwoven with Lakota spirituality, a weaving that was to a certain extent "sacramentalized" or symbolized in Black Elk's Ghost Dance vision of Jesus as an Indian. Francis was not noted as a healer during his lifetime, although healing miracles were attributed to him posthumously; Black Elk, before he became a Catholic, was widely respected as a traditional healer who used herbs and prayers to cure people. Both Francis and Black Elk lived and died in poverty due to the diverse exigencies of their respective callings. Francis was single and celibate, lived in poverty, had spiritual rather than biological children in his brothers, and disciplined his body to repress his sexuality. Black Elk was married and had children, and he lived in poverty. Both spiritual leaders were Catholic missionaries and Black Elk, baptized as Nicholas, additionally was a baptismal godfather to scores of Lakota children.

FRANCIS AND PHILLIP DEERE

In their formal education, Francis and Phillip had similar backgrounds. Francis had more education, as a member of the rising merchant class, but less than youths who were offspring of the nobility. Phillip had little formal education because of the poor quality of public schools in his area, racism against native peoples, and his family's need, even when he was a child, for him to work to help support them. In addition, Phillip's command of English was restricted because it was his second language, Muskogee being his first. When he became a traditional healer, he learned healing chants and the names of medicinal herbs in his third language, Old Muskogee, which was not understood even by the traditional people who spoke Muskogee as a first language. Phillip knew 424 healing chants in Old Muskogee. Each chant contained a symptom of illness, the name of the healing herb for that symptom, and a prayer to the Great Mystery to make the healing process efficacious.

Francis and Phillip both were Christian preachers, in their own way. Francis believed and taught Catholic doctrine. Phillip was a Methodist pastor for a time, before returning to traditional Muskogee beliefs and practices. Shortly before his death, the Methodist Church reinstated him with his clergy credentials, honoring him as a holy man whose life and teachings were universal, not limited by beliefs and rituals specific to a single faith tradition.

Francis and Phillip were both noted for their skills in public speaking. Francis convinced the pope to support his religious congregation, and while he failed to convince the Muslim sultan Malik-al-Kāmil to become a Christian, the latter welcomed him and provided for him for months as an honored guest. Phillip was a traditional orator who held people spellbound for hours as he spoke of the teachings of the Great Mystery, human rights issues, and care for Mother Earth; as he journeyed throughout the Americas to teach and to heal; as he went to state and government offices in Oklahoma and Washington to plead for justice for his people, while being attacked in the press as a "renegade"[11] for these efforts; and as he journeyed to Geneva, Switzerland, each spring to testify before the United Nations International Human Rights Commission about injustices suffered by indigenous peoples of the Americas. He was the spiritual guide for the American Indian Movement and for the International Indian Treaty Council.

In other aspects of their lives, too, Francis and Phillip had similar ideas and practices. Each loved all peoples, wild creatures, and pristine places. Each took risks to provide compassion and to promote harmony. Each lived simply.

Francis and Phillip died in parallel circumstances. Francis was nearly blind, had his eye cauterized in a failed attempt to heal it, had cancer, and suffered from nausea. Phillip had cancer in his left eye, sinuses, and cheek, and he was partially blind and nauseous; medical treatments were unavailing (by tradition, he was not allowed to attempt to heal himself and was the recipient of donated medical treatment, herbs from other healers, and healing prayers from traditional spiritual leaders and Christian ministers, but declined surgery). Both died in poverty. Both were respected as great spiritual leaders in their respective traditions and beyond. Both left a legacy of example and teachings to guide others to walk the way of the Spirit.

FRANCIS, BLACK ELK, AND PHILLIP DEERE

Francis of Assisi, Black Elk, and Phillip Deere developed their spirituality in creation. Beyond the walls of church, sweat lodge, and roundhouse they encountered the Creator in ways distinct from their experiences as leaders of formalized worship in constructed sacred space. They came to realize that while some space might be set aside as sacred and be exclusive of other than ritual use, ultimately all space is sacred space because of the presence of the Creator.

In the area of spiritual relationships to creation, Francis the Catholic, Black Elk the Lakota elder and Catholic, and Phillip the Muskogee elder and occasional Methodist, have their closest parallels as well as significant differences.

In the shared thought of these spiritual leaders, the Spirit permeates creation and can be encountered in unique ways in creation; people should respect all creatures, who have an inherent dignity before the Creator; people should live in harmony with creation; and Mother Earth provides for human needs.

Their thought is differentiated in that Francis believed that the sacred nature of Earth is derived from its relationship to the Creator, while Phillip believed Mother Earth to be sacred in herself. Francis prayed to God and to Jesus, Mary, and Christian saints, and he believed that only Christians would enter heaven; whereas Phillip prayed to the Great Mystery and to lesser spirits to aid him in his healing ministry, and he believed that all who walked with the Great Mystery, however they understood that divine being, would be welcomed into a blessed next life. Francis believed that the supernatural life took precedence over natural life, and he urged people to be concerned about life after death. Phillip saw the present life and future life as different but not discontinuous aspects of reality, and he prioritized the natural life, teaching people to be conscious of living according to the laws of the Creator and the needs of Mother Earth. Francis saw hierarchy in nature and shared in the anthropocentrism, common in Christianity, that understood creation to be ordered to the service of humankind, although, despite that view, he did advocate respect for all creation. Phillip regarded all creatures as equals; none had a special place in creation or was worthy to make a special demand on the Creator. People, in fact, were dependent on other creatures for their very survival, and they should be grateful to and respectful toward those creatures and to the nurturing Mother Earth, rather than seek to dominate them.

Francis, Black Elk, and Phillip were mystics. For Black Elk and Phillip, it was part of their religious tradition that their lives should interrelate with Creator and creation. By contrast, Francis's spirituality was distinctive in Christianity. He was drawn by the Spirit into a kinship with creation that enabled him to share in part the type of relationship experienced later by Black Elk and Phillip.

Francis, Black Elk, and Phillip saw themselves as part of and in kinship with the natural world. One might speculate whether or not the Christian mystic and the native elders sensed the presence of Spirit in those parts of creation that are seen by others as inanimate creations or nonrational creatures, or whether or not they sensed an individualized spirit life in them. In either case, the implication should be for others, as it was for them, that all creation must be respected and all life must be reverenced, in their own right as well as because of the Spirit dwelling in them. This respect and reverence, and belief in and openness to the Spirit, have led them and others to sacramental moments in the Earth commons.

SPIRITUALITY IN CREATION

Francis and Phillip expressed their spirituality in terms appropriate to and conditioned by their respective cultures. Their teachings recount their parallel experiences with the Spirit in creation.

Phillip Deere described how in past centuries Christian missionaries preached against Muskogee ceremonial grounds, comparing their burning sacred fire to hell fire, and condemning them for worshiping fire. But since he was well versed in the Bible, Phillip reflected on the Exodus story of Moses hearing God's voice come from a burning bush. God did not speak to Moses in human form but from fire. Thus, although Moses received his call at a burning bush, and although Francis referred to fire as "Brother Fire," the missionaries (in this case, Protestant Christians) had equated the Muskogee sacred fire only with hell fire, not a sacred fire (as for Moses) or a kindred part of creation (as with Francis). Phillip continued to use the sacred fire in his ceremonies.

In a Catholic church constructed in the U.S. Northwest in the nineteenth century, a similar denigration of native spirituality is depicted in a large mural. A missionary priest holds aloft a crucifix as he addresses a native family. In the sky above him, an angel holds a flaming sword extended toward demons who are being chased into the fires of hell, away from the family above whom they hover. The simple but graphic message is, of course, that native peoples worshiped Satan and walked with devils prior to the arrival of Catholic missionaries. In stark contrast to the scene in the mural are the twentieth-century words of the United States Catholic Bishops in their 1992 pastoral letter, *1992: A Time for Reconciling and Recommitting Ourselves as a People*. The bishops state that "the coming of religious faith in this land began not 500 years ago, but centuries before in the prayers, chants, dance and other sacred celebrations of Native people."

The national bishops' letter was issued five years after a regional document, *A Public Declaration: To the Tribal Councils and Traditional Spiritual Leaders of the Indian and Eskimo Peoples of the Pacific Northwest*, signed and issued by Catholic, Episcopalian, Methodist, and Lutheran bishops, and the ranking officials of the American Baptist Church, Presbyterian Church, Christian Church, and United Church of Christ. It was an ecumenical statement of apology and commitment. It apologized for past wrongs committed by missionaries and church leaders and laity, and it called on members of Christian denominations to "a commitment of mutual support in your efforts to reclaim and protect the legacy of your own traditional spiritual teachings. . . . The spiritual power of the land and the ancient wisdom of your indigenous religions can be, we believe, great gifts to the Christian churches."

In the light of such statements, people of all faiths might hope for a reappraisal and respectful appreciation of the life and teachings of spiritual leaders such as Black Elk and Phillip Deere (and David Sohappy, discussed in chapter 8).

Francis, Black Elk, and Phillip Deere were kindred spirits. Each had a sense of creature kinship, a relational consciousness that recognized the unity of being. For Francis, it was a familial creature kinship: others were "sister" and "brother." For Black Elk and Phillip Deere, creature kinship was both familial ("all my relatives") and communal ("winged people," "finned people," and "rooted people," among other living peoples). Francis extended sibling relationships to abiotic nature, such as "Brother Sky," although he viewed Earth as both "mother" and "sister"; Black Elk and Phillip believed that abiotic nature, including stones, was alive, but they reserved familial terms to parental designations, such as "Mother Earth" or "Grandfather Sky." All three holy men engaged the Creator and all creatures as related beings.

People with a relational consciousness and community commitment respond to the Spirit's call to renew Earth and to explore the wonders of the wider cosmos. They have a spirit of appreciation for the laws of the Creator and are conscious of their responsibility to conserve the integrity of creation. All people are invited to learn anew, in the spirit of Francis, Black Elk, and Phillip, respect for Earth and all life, and gratitude for Earth's goods. This human consciousness and commitment will be facilitated when people seek the Spirit and spirituality in creation and work to conserve the sacramental commons.

NOTES

1. Traditional native peoples of the United States use the word *Indian* as a generic designation but use their particular nation (e.g., Navajo, Muskogee, etc.) as their specific community.

2. Black Elk's life as a Catholic is described in Raymond J. DeMallie, ed., *The Sixth Grandfather: Black Elk's Teachings Given to John G. Neihardt* (Lincoln: University of Nebraska Press, 1985); Clyde Holler, *Black Elk's Religion: The Sun Dance and Lakota Catholicism* (Syracuse, N.Y.: Syracuse University Press, 1995); Michael F. Steltenkamp, *Black Elk: Holy Man of the Oglala* (Norman: University of Oklahoma Press, 1993); and Damian Costello, *Black Elk: Colonialism and Lakota Catholicism* (Maryknoll, N.Y.: Orbis, 2005). Steltenkamp's book includes interviews with Black Elk's daughter, Lucy Looks Twice, and photographs of Black Elk as a catechist.

3. DeMallie, *The Sixth Grandfather*, 263, 266.

4. Black Elk, *The Sacred Pipe: Black Elk's Account of the Seven Rites of the Oglala Sioux*, ed. Joseph Epes Brown (New York: Penguin, 1976), 75.

5. Black Elk, *Sacred Pipe*, 6–7.

6. Black Elk, *Sacred Pipe*, 7.

7. Black Elk, *Sacred Pipe*, 46.

8. Black Elk, *Sacred Pipe*, 64.

9. Black Elk, *Sacred Pipe*, 115.

10. This and subsequent quotations from Phillip Deere were recorded by this writer in

interviews in Great Falls, Montana, in 1984, and at his home in Okemah, Oklahoma, in 1985.

11. Phillip Deere told me while I was visiting him at his home that when non-Indians used the term *renegade* to attack him personally and in the press, he regarded it as an honor. It meant that he was doing something good for his people.

II

COMMONS

$\mathcal{T}$he commons is the local cosmos and is revelatory of the creating Spirit-immanent. In creation, people who are open to engagement with the Spirit experience sacramental moments in sacramental places in the sacramental commons in the sacramental universe. In the commons, human history emerges within geologic history and biotic history, but with its own cultural history. Commons consciousness motivates people to promote commons integrity. Creation consciousness in the commons prompts people to promote commons integrity by conserving abiotic forms of nature such as water, and biotic forms of nature such as salmon. The potability and accessibility of water and the survival of aquatic species are inextricably intertwined. Humankind is responsible for ensuring the intergenerational sustainability of the commons, commons goods, and commons creatures.

· 4 ·

Sacramental Commons

$\mathscr{T}$he sacramental universe is localized in the *sacramental commons*. People most often experience the revelatory nature of creation when their engagement and focus shift from the macro to the micro, from cosmos to commons. The sacramental commons is a revelatory *locus*, the place of Spirit-spirit engagement and relation. Sacramentality is evident in specific settings, such as local bioregions, conserved pristine places, urban centers, or rural communities. The sacramental nature of commons places is seen in their revelation of divine aesthetics and divine creativity in the beauty of creation, or of human imagination and artistry where human structures are integrated well within abiotic nature and with respect for the habitat of the biotic community, and evidence responsible human use of Earth goods. The immanent presence of the Spirit is sufficient to make both types of space—dynamic creation and designated construct—sacred space. Sacramental places have the potential to inspire people to view environmental issues as creation issues and spiritual issues, and to consider how the Spirit intends the intricate diversity of creation to provide a commons and commons goods for the common good of the ecosystemic biotic community and its human community.

A sacramental commons is a place within a planet's, an area's, or a community's space which at special moments is revelatory of God-immanent, and in every moment is the sign of a divine intention that natural goods be shared among members of the biotic community for their sustenance. A sacramental universe is the totality of creation infused with the vision, love, creative presence, and active power of the transcendent-immanent Spirit. A sacramental commons is enSpirited and enspirited creation, which becomes the locus of moments of human participation in the interactive presence and caring compassion of the Spirit immanent, who permeates and participates in the complex cosmic dance of energies, events, elements, and entities. A sacramental commons is transparent to the eyes of faith. It mediates and reveals the immanent presence of the engaged Spirit.

61

People who appreciate the sacramentality of the commons draw spiritual energy from the visible and invisible dimensions of the world around them, and derive strength to make social commitments to conserve the commons and care for community. A *sacramental consciousness* integrates spiritual consciousness (which is Spirit consciousness) with self-consciousness (an individual's reflective and reflexive awareness); social consciousness (an understanding of social relations, social structures, and social injustices in human communities); species consciousness (understanding the needs of humankind, and means for humanity's balanced and collaborative, as well as competitive, relationships with other species); and spatial consciousness (a sense of place, of the natural and social environments that are the contexts of individual and community existence). Spiritual consciousness leads to social engagement and to sociospatial commitment to the well-being of Earth, the community of life generally, and people and peoples. To the extent that such material and social relationships are missing or minimized, the relationship to Spirit is absent or diminished.

COMMONS AND SACRAMENTAL COMMONS

Sacramental moments are experiences of the loving and creative presence of the Spirit. Creation is born from divine imagination and flows toward divine vision. It is the locus of the human experience of divine presence. People perceive signs of the Spirit in creation, signs that might or might not be acknowledged but that in either instance link innermost human being with divine Being. People have moments of engagement with the Spirit when they are open to the loving and creative presence of the spirit in evolutionary creation. The sacramental commons is not only the locus of engagement of Creator and creatures. It is also a shared space whose common goods should equitably provide for the needs of those creatures.

The *commons* is the place in which dynamic natural history evolves, diversifies, and complexifies, and the base from which cultural history develops in all its intricacy. Human natural history and human cultural history develop together. Human property in land and goods is part of a human commons that is to provide for human needs. In a complementary way, Earth is a commons: a shared space that is the source of life-providing common goods for all creatures. The Earth commons is not intended solely for humans' use and enjoyment, although as part of the biotic community they are to share in its goods. Earth provides for all creatures as they live related to and dependent on each other in integrated bioregions.

A sacramental place is naturally a commons: a home shared by all the members of the community of life in which their food and habitat needs are integrated, their competitive needs are balanced, their relationships are interdependent, and their associations are consciously or unconsciously collaborative. It is "naturally" a commons because the eternal numinous presence immanent in the universe creates freely from love, sharing that most essential aspect of intrinsic divine communion with extrinsic creation. The divine spiritual commons of love is imaged in the cosmic natural commons, which concretizes divine creativity and sustains commons residents with commons goods.

JUSTICE IN THE COMMONS

In the commons, human communities are called to pursue the common good. Pristine creation is the mediation of the Spirit immanent and transcendent. The Creator Spirit has provided, through the evolutionary dynamics of the biotic community and the complementary availability of air, land, and water, a sufficiency of goods—when they are justly distributed—to meet everyone's needs. The poor are the revelation and mediation of Christ Jesus, the Logos Incarnate in the Christian tradition. Ecojustice is the act of linking responsibility for the natural world with responsibility for the neighbor. The good of the revelatory commons and the common good of the revelatory poor are inseparable. The commons good and the common good are woven together. In past eras, biblical peoples communed with the Spirit in creation and communally shared Earth's goods and the fruits of their fields and vineyards. In past ages and into the present one, native peoples around the world have linked spirituality and the commons, and experienced the sacred through an integration, in community, of Creator Spirit, Mother Earth, and kinship with the biotic community. They had no land ownership, regarded property as communal, and worked together to provide for their people. Today, peoples of diverse religious traditions should recall and reenact this linkage of spirituality, compassion, and community that is part of the biblical heritage of Christians and Jews, and affirmed in the sacred texts, oral teachings, and community practices of other peoples.

People should understand that the commons they share is sacramental, reflect on the implications of that understanding, imagine what it would look like in its best possible state, and act to begin to make that a reality for themselves and for the generations to come. Earth as *sacramental* is a revelation of Spirit's loving creativity: in its diversity of life and topography, and in its ability to provide food and shelter for its inhabitants. Earth as *commons* is an area shared by all of the members of the community of life. It provides for their needs while humans sustain or renew its integrity, as needed (to remediate or repel human practices of despoliation of context and diminution of creatures).

People should not suffer from poverty or hunger in a sacramental commons. Just as when in the dedicated sacred space of a church building Christians share in the presence of Jesus when they partake of sacramental communion, so, too, in the created sacred space of a bioregional commons permeated by the presence of the Spirit Immanent, all should be able to partake of bread that gives life. People conscious of the sacramental commons do not limit sacred space to buildings they construct, nor their communion with Spirit and with each other to ritual moments in such buildings. In a sacramental commons the community of faith is a sharing community that expresses in a concrete and visible form the meaning of "Holy Communion" shared in church. The invisible and visible aspects of reality blend into a moment and way of life of sacramental unity and sacramental totality, with bread for the spirit complemented by bread for the body.

In religious rituals people's spiritual being is nourished individually and communally. Similarly, in nonreligious settings the human community in its corporeal, material being shares in and is nurtured by the commons; and the biotic community as a whole shares in and is nurtured by the commons. People are corporeal and spiritual beings; the complementary sacraments of church and commons holistically uplift the integral human being. In both instances the human is being and becoming, a dynamic entity growing physically, socially, and spiritually. The sacramental universe, the sacramental rituals, the sacramental community, and the sacramental commons are the context for that growth and in sacramental moments influence it.

In the sacramental commons, spiritual hunger and physical hunger are satisfied. Human encounters with the works of the transcendent Creator Spirit who continues and immanents evolutionary creation, becomes incarnate, and is present with and seeks to guide people, become one communion and engagement with Spirit's work of spiritual and material liberation. Sacramental communion in a church building is complemented and enhanced by sacramental communion in nature's outdoor cathedral of creation: among human communities and between human communities and the Spirit who gives life and integral liberation.

Conscious of the sacramental commons and sacramental community, Christians encounter a new way to understand the teaching of Jesus presented in the Last Judgment story in Matthew 25:31–46. In the narrative, the Son of Man invites into the kingdom people who have fed the hungry, given drink to the thirsty, welcomed the stranger, clothed the naked, cared for the sick, and visited those in prison. The Son of Man declares that whatever people did for these oppressed ones, they did for him. Their practical works for the poor are primarily justice-based distributions of the Earth's goods: food from the soil's nutrients, the sun's rays, and the sky's rain; drink from water; clothing from plant fibers and sheep wool; medicine from herbal plants. The Son of Man is an invisible and immanent presence among the people awaiting the distribution of goods from the Earth in which the Spirit is invisible and immanent.

The Earth commons and the bioregional commons, in order to be sacramental, must be revelatory of the creating and liberating Spirit in pristine nature, the biotic community as a whole, and the human community's acts of compassion and justice that image the Spirit's mercy and justice. The commons must provide justly for the needs of all humans, a distribution that requires that the basic needs of all take priority over the wants of a few.

The land of the Earth commons that is required as human space, to sustain life and enable livelihood, must be shared equitably among humans. The goods of the commons—also called "resources," which can imply anthropocentrically that these goods are intended solely for humans—must be equitably shared among human communities and individuals. Biblically, the Jubilee Year provisions were promulgated to ensure that commons goods were used for the human common good and the common good of all biokind.

Jesus proclaimed the Jubilee Year during his Nazareth synagogue sermon (Luke 4:16–21). In the synoptic gospels, Jesus teaches the "Lord's Prayer": Christians are to pray for bread and for the coming of the Spirit, so that the Spirit's will might be done on Earth as in heaven. In the visions of Revelation the seer describes a time and place when people's needs for food and medicine are satisfied from the fruits and leaves of the Tree of Life, and their sorrows are dissipated by the brilliant presence of the Spirit. In the exhortation to love the oppressed, in a proclamation of jubilee justice, in a prayer for bread and justice, and in a vision of the time when there shall be no oppressed, the Christian Scriptures express a sacramental vision and a sacramental hope for the sacramental commons.

The sacramental universe is continually localized in the sacramental commons. That sacramentality of creation is locally experienced when Spirit and spirit consciously engage in sacred space, which is every space in creation because of the universal presence of the Spirit-immanent. People can experience the presence of Spirit unexpectedly in sacred moments in sacred space (a potentiality which ultimately is present in all pristine creation) when they are open to seeing signs of the Spirit in the world of nature, and open to the loving and creative presence of the Spirit in evolutionary creation; or, when they work to effect justice and transform society, and experience the divine presence among the oppressed. Sometimes a spontaneous sacramental moment reveals divine presence and activity in dynamic creation in a vision or new insight; at other times, it is through an overwhelming consciousness of the Spirit's presence in nature or in a community of the poor. In sacramental communities, people work to ensure that at least the subsistence needs of humankind are met and that the evolutionary well-being of all biokind is promoted.

Pristine creation is the mediation of the Spirit immanent and transcendent. The Creator Spirit has provided, through the evolutionary dynamics of the biotic community and the complementary availability of air, land, and water, a sufficiency of goods to meet everyone's needs when they are justly distributed. The poor are the mediation of Christ Jesus, the Logos Incarnate (the creation-creating Word becomes the community-creating Word) in the Christian tradition. Ecojustice is the act of linking responsibility for the natural world, engendered by engagement with the Spirit, with responsibility for the neighbor, as required by Jesus as the Son of Man present among the "least brethren." The good of the revelatory commons and the common good of the revelatory poor are inseparable. Commons good, common good, and common goods are integrated. In acknowledging a "sacramental commons," people express an appreciation of the sacredness, integrity, and life-sustaining qualities of creation.

SACRAMENTAL COMMUNITY

People participate in interactive and revelatory creation as members of a *sacramental community* in which every part of creation—each aspect of abiotic nature and each member of the biotic community—is a sign of the immanence of the Spirit to every other part, to the extent that they can be aware of it. People who are conscious of this sacramental community are inspired to care for creation and are concerned about fulfilling their responsibilities toward Earth as their home and toward humans and other members of the community of life who are cocreatures loved by the Spirit.

A sacramental community happens in a time and place in which people integrate the spiritual meaning of "sacramental" and the social meaning of "commons," and engage in concrete efforts to relate to and promote the well-being of all life, particularly the common good of the most vulnerable. In the Earth commons people are called to care for creation, celebrate the diversity of life, and communally share in Earth's goods.

Exploitation of Earth emerges not only when humans act from greed, but also when people claiming to be Christians use their "personal relationship to Jesus" and their concern about "getting to heaven" as excuses to neglect their responsibilities to God's creation and to the poor of the Earth.

They state that since Earth is only a passing home, a preparation for their enduring heavenly home, they need not care for it.

An appreciation of the sacramental commons in a sacramental universe will prove invaluable for Christians who confront present environmental crises. Care for creation—in the double sense of "care about" and "take care of"—would be heightened if people would acknowledge and engage with the Spirit immanent in the created world. Where this occurs, people are able to confront the exploitation of creation and offer alternative values to those prompted by greed and religious escapism and by religiously, politically, or economically self-serving doctrines of salvation.

People, then, are called to caretaking within creation. They are part of nature, not transcendent from nor over nature. As creatures in and of the natural world, they are called to serve nature. In the second biblical creation story, people, through Adam, are instructed to "conserve" and to "serve" garden Earth and its integrated biotic community. Today, people's consciousness of integrated practices of caretaking guides their efforts to:

- Care *about* creation: people are lovingly concerned about the integral universe emerging from the vision and through the creativity of the Spirit.
- Care *for* creation: people responsibly use their intellect and skills to integrate the needs of ecosystems and of Earth in those areas of the planet under their care, and to responsibly draw from creation those goods needed for human life and health.
- Care *in* creation: people respect and serve creation as their community, home, and habitat, and live as biotic kin in the biotic community, concerned about individual and species well-being.

Reality is indivisible. The invisible is woven with the visible in an abiotic-biotic/human-divine communion. Recognition of the totality of reality promotes experience of community in the cosmos and commons permeated by the Spirit-immanent. The sense of community has the potential to effect a substantial transformation in environmental policies and practices.

COMMONS PERSPECTIVES AND PRACTICES

A substantive shift is needed in attitudes toward ecological issues and humanity's place in the biotic community and its relation to Earth as a whole. Anthropocentrism must be set aside and replaced by an awareness that all members of the biotic community have an inherent goodness and value that should be respected; that people should relate well to other creatures and share with them a common Earth home viewed as a commons; and that "common good" understandings should be extended to nonhuman creation. The sacramental commons embodies a sense of the sacred in creation and a sense of shared places in distinct but connected biosystems.

It is essential that the commons nurture the members of the biotic community. In order that it might fulfill this function, the commons should be able, without human intervention (except where prior human interference has disrupted these roles), to promote the *common good* of Earth inhabitants:

- Enable living creatures' access to food and shelter, and to space to meet reproductive needs (and, for humans, access to Earth goods needed to provide clothing, energy, and health care);
- Provide breathable air, potable water, and uncontaminated soil;
- Integrate competitive needs;
- Stimulate adjustment to interdependence; and
- Provide a context for collaborative relations.

SACRAMENTALITY IN RURAL
AND URBAN SETTINGS

In some rural areas of the United States, fifth-generation farmers and ranchers work with the land to provide for their families, the nation at large, and the world beyond. In other rural areas, which often are more desolate or at least not as productive agriculturally, native peoples with ten thousand more years of history than Euro-American farmers live on the remnants of their ancestral territories. These are places where the bones of their distant ancestors are buried, places where they interact for life and livelihood with the creatures of land, air, and water and with the common habitat they share.

Traditional Indians and responsible agriculturalists share common values. They have a similar sense of family and of intergenerational responsibility. They worry about the impacts of changing weather or climate on their food sources. In their respective ways of life, they work well with the land. A farm or ranch integrated well within the landscape, and worked in harmony with Earth's rhythms by people who care for it with love and pride, are sensitive to the land's carrying capacity, are respectful of other members of the biotic community, and consider the needs of their neighbors and the limits of soil, air, and water, parallels the precontact existence of most Indians, and postcontact experience of Indians who have the greatest degree of territorial sovereignty and, when they have some control over their own economic development, respect still Mother Earth, themselves, and other living creatures. The land they care for is sacramental through their work and their prayers, whether the latter are based on the Holy Bible, the Sacred Pipe, or both. The respective acts of agriculturalists and Indians to balance human needs with the requirements of all life in the bioregional ecosystem show at least an unconscious sense of the commons which, unfortunately, is contradicted by some Euro-Americans' assertions of their presumed absolute property rights, or their overenthusiastic endorsements of capitalism as an economic system, even though its unabashed individualism and competitiveness ultimately contravene community.

In *The Unsettling of America*, Wendell Berry reflects on two types of farmers: the exploiter and the nurturer. The *exploiter* seeks money, evaluates land solely in terms of its short-term profitability, wants to earn as much as possible with the least expenditure of labor, and often works for an institution or organization. The *nurturer* seeks health for themselves, their family, their community, their nation; wonders what might be the land's carrying capacity (its dependable productivity into the future); wants to work as best they can; and serves Earth, their place on it and their family. The nurturer helps agricultural land to be a sacramental commons.[1]

Rural communities, too, can provide experiences of sacramentality. Homes, businesses, schools, and churches are signs of common interaction for the good of the whole. People in these community and familial places are able to share or otherwise distribute the goods of the commons, to be good neighbors, and to do all of this conscious of their responsibilities to the Creator and creation. As rural people form a vision of a better future, they might at the same time recall the best of their past while not idealizing it—or, for that matter, overlooking what is good in the present or losing hope for the future.

The urban commons, too, can be sacramental. It is not only in dedicated city parks that this is possible, but in the dedicated lives of ordinary people. Human community in its lived reality as well as in its social structures and skyscrapers can be revelatory of the Spirit.

In urban settings, people's affinity for nature, their sense of kinship with the not-human, sometimes is revealed in their choices of home decor and daily companions. Potted house plants and flowers in vases or simply in a water glass abound in urban settings; flower shops and flower vendors sell them to eager urbanites. Pets of diverse species (dogs, cats, fish, and birds being the most common) dwell in houses and apartments, inviting conversation with their human companions. These domesticated plants and animals represent not only themselves as related members of the biotic community, but also the free biota who dwell in pristine nature's air, land, and water.

PLACE, PROPERTY, AND PREEMINENCE

People's basic perspective on the human position in creation generally represents an attitude of *domination, dominion, stewardship*, or *relation*. In the *domination* attitude, seen not only in religion but also in politics, economics, and science, people are believed to have a sovereign right over Earth and Earth goods. In the *dominion* worldview, people essentially see the world as created for humans. People are to own and use a world that has been created for and is oriented toward them. In the *stewardship* perspective, people are viewed as managers of creation on behalf of the creating Spirit, who entrusts this role to them. In the *relational* perspective, people see themselves as one part of a dynamic biotic community living in egalitarian relationships in ecological systems where competition as well as collaboration characterize the interaction of species. The relational perspective is best able to see creation as a sacramental commons.

Humans grouped as a species or as a community sometimes have ambiguous relationships with nature. Many appreciate the marvelous beauty surrounding them, and see themselves as having dominion over what they see, in the sense of responsibility for it as a medieval lord did for his estate; or, they might see themselves as stewards caring for God's creation; or, they might see themselves as an integrated and related part of a whole. Other people might advocate primarily some economic gain to be made by destroying Earth's beauty, perhaps viewing themselves as the absolute lord who has the power to dominate, who is charged by God with "improving" nature to provide for human well-being and is entitled to maximize personal profit in the process. Destructive practices more often will result from the latter, economically focused perspective that, if unchecked, will leave Earth eventually with despoiled land, poisoned water, and polluted air. Constructive practices will result more commonly from those who appreciate the land, and alter it carefully and to some extent reluctantly, only as needed; their respect for the commons, if it is more extensively and universally practiced, will lead eventually to a transformed Earth and transformed communities.

There is an ambiguity, too, in the way Christian churches regard the human role in creation. Anthropocentric teachings coexist and conflict with relational teachings: people are taught variously that they are above all creation, or that they are stewards of the rest of creation, or that they are integral members of an interrelated and interdependent creation.

Traditionally, most churches have taught that humanity is at the top of creation. The ordinary citizen in the pew might transform that perceived species superiority into an excessive individualism—essentially anti-biblical—expressed in such statements as "I have a God-given right to do what I want with my land." But there is no such "God-given right" to private property in land. Individual ownership is a human construct; shared space is the Creator's intention. Biblically, there are three levels of land ownership, in descending order: Spirit-community-individual. Each is subordinate to the one before it. The Creator Spirit alone has absolute jurisdiction over Earth, and then community needs take precedence over individual wants (and even needs, in some cultures). In civil law, the concept and practice of "eminent domain," when used properly and justly, recognizes the preeminence of this community right to meet community needs. Church teaching and civil law coincide here in refuting the notion of absolute private property rights.

In the Catholic tradition, Popes Paul VI and John Paul II incorporate this biblically based understanding when they declare that all property has a "social mortgage." Private owners essentially "mortgage" their land from the community and are to use it to benefit themselves and the community. (While stating this teaching in Cuilapán, Mexico, in 1979, John Paul II advocated land expropriation—with just compensation—and land redistribution to the poor, who would then be able to work it to provide for basic human needs.)

Perspectives on the revelatory nature of nature are found not solely in religion-related writings. The life and work of naturalist John Muir, for example, reveal his keen appreciation for creation and Creator.

JOHN MUIR IN THE SACRAMENTAL COMMONS

On several occasions, the naturalist John Muir (1838–1914) had moments of divine engagement in pristine places. Once, as he traveled through a Canadian swamp in 1864, he unexpectedly came on a rare treat: a group of white orchids. Marveling at their beauty, Muir realized that had he not traversed the swamp in this particular place, no human would have seen the orchids. Reflecting further, he realized that other wonders of creation are not seen by people. He concluded that nature does not exist solely for human benefit and use. In fact, he realized, most of Earth's creatures exist for themselves and for their Creator.

John Muir was born in Scotland in 1838 and migrated with his family to the United States in 1849. He grew up on the family farm in Wisconsin and became a skilled farmer, inventor of practical tools and machines, and explorer of local landscapes. He left home at age twenty-one intending to work in a machine tool company but then studied science at the University of Wisconsin in Madison, taking only courses that interested him. After several jobs and additional inventions, he went on a "thousand-mile walk" from Indianapolis to Florida. Further travels took him to the mountains of California, where he worked as a sheepherder while continuing his scientific studies, which were focused on botany and geology, in open nature rather than in a classroom or laboratory. His particular place of exploration was the Yosemite region. He traveled light and camped frequently in the forests and on the mountains in the area, and he became noted as an excellent guide and a passionate defender of nature. He married, had children, and became a farmer, but continued his scientific explorations around the world. His efforts to protect wilderness areas stimulated development of national parks and forests. He cofounded the Sierra Club in 1892 to continue conservation efforts when politics and greed interfered with the government's role to protect U.S. lands for responsible public use and enjoyment. He served as its president until his death in 1914.

Muir had numerous biographical similarities with Francis of Assisi. He might, in fact, be regarded as a modern-day St. Francis, despite differences of culture, time, and place. He had grown up in a Protestant home, but was not intellectually or spiritually confined by any particular creed. He was married with children, and affirmed fullness of life on Earth. He founded not a mendicant community, but an environmental organization; his extended community was a group of friends and acquaintances who shared his passion for "wild" or free nature. Muir did share with Francis a strong regard for and sense of kinship with the biotic community. Like Francis, he lived simply for much of his life, and he had a profound spiritual sense, which is communicated through his journals. Like Francis, he loved birds, appreciated free nature, saw a relationship between Creator and creation, and recognized the presence and voices of God in creation.

In his journals, Muir writes about his affection and appreciation for birds. Once, while he sat dejectedly by a stream, a small bird emerged from the rocks and "preached me the most effectual sermon on heavenly trust that I had ever heard through all the measured hours of Sabbath, and I went on not half so heart-sick, nor half so weary."[2] On another occasion, when Ralph Waldo Emerson departed Yosemite after visiting him, Muir's sadness was alleviated when "the birds, robins, thrushes, warblers, etc., that had kept out of sight, came about me, now that all was quiet, and made cheer."[3]

Muir shared with Francis a panentheistic perspective. He was aware of the revelatory or sacramental character of nature. When he studied flowers at the University of Wisconsin, initially he was attracted by their exterior beauty, but then he discerned "their inner beauty, all alike revealing traces of the thoughts of God, and leading on and on into the infinite cosmos."[4] Like Thomas Berry and others a century later, Muir could appreciate flowers and other parts of nature not only in themselves, but also as creatures that mediated the Creator and creation. On a hike into Yosemite, he observed "the spiritual glow that covered it."[5] His sense of a spiritual reality was expressed, too, when he declared: "But we know that much that is most real will not counterpoise cast-iron, or dent our human flesh."[6] In a similar vein, he wrote that "the clearest way into the Universe is through a forest wilderness,"[7] and "In God's wildness lies the hope of the world—the great fresh, unblighted, unredeemed wilderness."[8]

Muir had a particular affinity for trees. He called himself "a tree lover sauntering along the mountains to study Sequoia."[9] Wandering among the sequoias, watching the sun splash them with light and seeing the shadows and colors on and around them, Muir observed that "every tree seemed religious and conscious of the presence of God,"[10] a thought mirrored decades later by the Jewish philosopher Martin Buber, who reflected on the possibility of arboreal consciousness in his masterpiece *I and Thou*.[11] Muir declared that in Alaska "I had nothing to do but look and listen and join the trees in their hymns and prayers."[12] He described the solace he received from trees, and urged others to experience it, when he wrote, "Come to the woods, for here is rest. There is no repose like that of the green deep woods."[13] Once, in 1874, he decided to absorb fully the experience of a storm from the perspective of a tree. He climbed a hundred-foot-tall Douglas fir during a December windstorm in northern California. For several hours he clung to the tree as it swayed in the wind, and watched other conifers below him swaying like grass. The music of the wind through the trees, and the forest scents that it freed and dispersed, accompanied his visual and tactile experiences. Muir lamented the wanton destruction of trees, and advocated federal protections for them, observing that "Any fool can destroy trees," and that although "God has cared for these trees," including by saving them from natural disasters, God "cannot save them from fools—only Uncle Sam can do that."[14]

Muir advocated rights for nature, and recognized what would later be called the intrinsic value of individuals and species in the biotic community. When discussing hunting, he noted that laws were finally being passed that provided protection for animals, "partly, let us hope, from a dim glimmering recognition of the rights of animals and their kinship to ourselves."[15] Muir presents here two key ideas: first, members of the biotic community are kin to each other, a thought reminiscent of Francis addressing creatures as "brother" and "sister"; second, animals have rights.

Muir expressed a sense of the Earth commons, and of a common kinship bonding the biotic community, when he wrote that "we all dwell in a house of one room—the world with the firmament for its roof."[16] Although he affirmed this bond, he lamented that "most people are *on* the world, not in it—have no conscious sympathy or relationship to anything about them."[17] He rejected the anthropocentrism at the heart of this attitude, declaring that the idea that the world "was made especially for man" is "a presumption not supported by all the facts."[18] It does not occur to the anthropocentric mind that

> Nature's object in making animals and plants might possibly be first of all the happiness of each one of them, not the creation of all for the happiness of one. Why should man value himself as more than a small part of the one great unit of creation? And what creature of all that the Lord has taken the pains to make is not essential to the completeness of that unit—the cosmos?[19]

Muir noted further that all creatures came from the same "dust of the earth," that stars and Earth have been on their journeys since time immemorial, and species have come and gone over the ages since long before humans emerged to "claim them."[20]

In an interesting insight, Muir notes that people credit plants with limited sensation, and minerals with none, but wonders whether even minerals might have some kind of undetected sensation which humans in their "blind exclusive perfection can have no manner of communication with."[21] His thoughts here complement teachings from Indian traditions.

Muir saw the unity underlying Earth interactions of both the biotic community and abiotic nature. He observed that when people try to view anything in isolation they find it tied to everything in the universe: "The whole wilderness in unity and interrelation is alive and familiar . . . the very stones seem talkative, sympathetic, brotherly. . . . No particle is ever wasted or worn out but eternally flowing from use to use."[22] In fact, "Everything is so inseparably united. As soon as one begins to describe a flower or a tree or a storm or an Indian or a chipmunk, up jumps the whole heavens and earth and God Himself in one inseparable glory!"[23] This statement has traces of the spirit of Francis of Assisi, affirms the poetic insight of William Blake (1757–1827) that one can "see heaven in a grain of sand," and anticipates scientific discoveries of the relationships of species in ecosystems, and of the interactions of particles in quantum physics.

Muir regarded God, according to his daughters, as a "loving, intelligent spirit creating, permeating, and controlling the universe."[24]

John Muir was a spiritual brother to Francis of Assisi, and the spiritual father of many environmentalists in the twentieth century and beyond. His influence in humanist circles complements that of Francis in Christian circles; and both men inspire people across ideological boundaries.

Millennia before Muir, the author of Job (38–41) wrote of the Creator's concern for living creatures, from eagles soaring above high mountains to fish swimming in deep oceans—creatures who did not serve humans, whose ways were unknown to humans, who were loved by the Spirit for what they were themselves, not for what they provided for humanity.

The insights from Job and John Muir conflict with anthropocentric ideas and practices that are destroying the Earth and harming living creatures. The insights suggest the need for a creation-centered consciousness which acknowledges a Creator's work and expresses appreciation for the complexity of creation. In this perspective, human needs and ecosystem integrity are related to each other in the sacramental commons that is home and habitat for the biotic community.

COMMONS RESPONSIBILITIES

Humans have abilities and responsibilities according to their species, and their participation in the community of life is enhanced by their affirmation that they are indeed a part of nature, not separate from nor above it. John Muir, among others, noted this interrelationship.

In the first creation story in Genesis, the Bible states that humans are "images of God." The Bible teaches in the same story that God calls all creation "very good." This was not just a description of an artist taking justifiable pride in a job well done; it was a pronouncement about the inherent nature of nature. People who claim to be God's "images" must restore and conserve that goodness where it has been diminished by human conduct. In subsequent biblical passages—such as the Flood Story, where *all* creatures are to be saved, and where God makes a covenant with Earth and *all* creatures; and in Job 38–41 and Matthew 6:24–34, where God is solicitous of all creatures—God's loving concern for these very good creatures is expressed. As people consider the implications of this, they might use their time- and culture-limited understandings of the mystery of the Spirit, and of the Spirit's parental solicitude for all creatures, to understand their complementary role in creation, and to fulfill their commons responsibilities. As "images of God" humans are called to be the caring and creative consciousness of creation. Human care for creation should extend to all companion creatures: the organic and inorganic, golden eagles, king salmon, and grizzly bears as well as the air, water, and land. All are essential; each part is needed for the integrated working of the whole. Individuals, species, and ecosystems require this interaction. John Muir declared, "The universe would be incomplete without man; but it would also be incomplete without the smallest transmicroscopic creature that dwells beyond our conceited eyes and knowledge."[25] All creation has intrinsic value that is independent of a human-assigned instrumental value based upon a human-centered assessment of a being's potential benefits for human life and livelihood. In the sacramental commons, humans are responsible for safeguarding creation and community by conserving the common good of biokind and of Earth.

The Earth commons is an evolutionary commons. It hosts human communities' evolution (biological; historical: changing political, economic, and religious perspectives), within the context of biotic communities' evolution (development, diversification, and complexification of life; emergence and extinction of species) and changing natural environments (caused by storms, fires, floods, droughts, earthquakes, tornadoes, tsunamis, and tectonic plate shifts). When people realize that this dynamic and evolutionary commons is sacramental, they realize also that they are called to safeguard creation and community through responsible engagement with Earth's biokind.

In the song "America the Beautiful," U.S. residents celebrate the wonders of the Spirit's creation in their part of the Americas, and ask God's blessing upon the nation's people. The song rejoices in spacious skies, productive agricultural lands, majestic mountains, and boundary ocean waters; and offers a prayer that God's grace will be shed on this bounteous and wondrous beauty, whose natural goodness, people hope, will be crowned by "brotherhood" (today: "community") from coast to coast. These themes of celebration and petition complement well the concern for creation expressed in John Muir's observation that "in God's wildness lies the hope of the world."

When humans recognize the presence of the Creator in creation, and relate to other people and other creatures as an integrated life community, and when they leave selected pristine places as they were created and use carefully other places and goods essential for meeting their needs, then they will inhabit a good place. Earth will become their shared sacred space and will be able to take care of them. The sacramental commons will nurture humankind and all life, as the Creator intended, while they walk with all life in the presence of the Spirit and live as creation's caring and creative consciousness.

People need a sacramental commons to be fully human, to be holistic beings in their Earth setting. Humans are body *and* spirit: neither solely corporeal beings lacking an immortal soul, nor solely angelic beings who are not dependent on nor responsible for Earth. People are called to be a *community*: to care for each other and for Earth, their common home. People are related to the entire *community of life*: they interact, at times reciprocally, to meet their respective needs. People are called to see the Earth as a *global commons*, a shared home providing for all creatures; and to see private property as part of a *community commons*, whose benefits are to be distributed justly to meet human needs.

In all of creation people can see signs of the creating Spirit. When they are open to the Spirit, people discern and experience in diverse ways in their spiritual and social being the loving presence of Spirit within themselves, and discover and embrace it in others. They can be sacramental people who live sacramental moments in sacramental places of the sacramental commons in the sacramental universe.

Humans share with other species a common origin in the creative acts of God that began billions of years ago and continue to unfold around them, and a common bond as participants in the dynamics of their planet. People should be grateful for what other lives provide for their lives, and be respectful toward them and toward the Earth that is their common home.

People are creatures and caretakers in creation. They share with other creatures common origins both from God's creativity and in the expanding singularity—the dynamic development of the primordial universe—whose elements and energy are embodied in all creation and creatures. They are distinct from other creatures in their extended, self-reflective and relational consciousness: extended in its ability to comprehend the diversity and vastness of all creation and its component parts, systems, and communities; self-reflective in its understanding of its limitations and possibilities, and its creative projections and hopes; and relational in its engagement with the transcendent-immanent Spirit and the conscious biotic community.

If people view the commons as sacramental, presenced by the Spirit and intended by the Spirit to be the place from which the biotic community derives its sustenance and from which human communities provide for their common good, they should be inspired to treat their bioregion with respect, to care for it responsibly, to seek signs of the Spirit in it, and to distribute its goods justly. The integration of community property, community values, and community sharing leads to communion not only among humans but between humans and other creatures and between all life, Earth, and the creating immanent and transcendent Spirit.

NOTES

1. Wendell Berry, *The Unsettling of America: Culture and Agriculture* (New York: Avon Books, 1978), 7–8.

2. Edwin Way Teale, *The Wilderness World of John Muir* (Boston: Houghton Mifflin, 1954), 86.

3. Teale, *The Wilderness World*, 165.

4. Teale, *The Wilderness World*, 70.

5. Teale, *The Wilderness World*, 125.

6. Teale, *The Wilderness World*, 320.

7. Teale, *The Wilderness World*, 312.

8. Teale, *The Wilderness World*, 315.

9. Teale, *The Wilderness World*, 210.

10. Teale, *The Wilderness World*, 219.

11. In each *Thou* we address the eternal *Thou*. I consider a tree. . . . It can . . . come about, if I have both will and grace, that in considering the tree I become bound up in relation to it. The tree is now no longer *It*. . . . The tree is no impression, no play of my imagination, no value depending on my mood; but it is bodied over against me and has to do with me, as I with it—only in a different way.

Let no attempt be made to sap the strength from the meaning of the relation: relation is mutual. The tree will have a consciousness, then, similar to our own? Of that I have no experience . . . I encounter no soul or dryad of the tree but the tree itself.

Martin Buber, *I and Thou*, 2nd ed. (New York: Charles Scribner's Sons, 1958), 6–8.

12. Teale, *The Wilderness World*, 275.

13. Teale, *The Wilderness World*, 314.

14. Teale, *The Wilderness World*, 230.

15. Teale, *The Wilderness World*, 314.

16. Teale, *The Wilderness World*, 312.

17. Teale, *The Wilderness World*, 313.

18. Teale, *The Wilderness World*, 316.

19. Teale, *The Wilderness World*, 317.

20. Teale, *The Wilderness World*, 317.

21. Teale, *The Wilderness World*, 317.

22. Linnie Marsh Wolfe, *Son of the Wilderness: The Life of John Muir* (Madison: University of Wisconsin Press, 1980), 123–24.

23. Wolfe, *Son of the Wilderness*, 171.

24. Wolfe, *Son of the Wilderness*, 232.

25. Teale, *The Wilderness World*, 317.

· 5 ·

Living Water

$\mathcal{W}$ater is Earth's lifeblood. Water gives nourishment and life to the Earth commons. Without water, no life could exist on Earth. With water, the biotic community exists, thrives, diversifies, and complexifies: in the air, on the land, and in water itself. Water provides life: it has minerals for all, insects for salmon, and salmon for eagles and bears. Water provides for life: it is a sustaining medium for fish and a sustaining liquid for all creatures to drink. Water enables beautiful seascapes and enriches beautiful landscapes; it refreshes the eyes, the mind, and the spirit. Water is simultaneously a material good and a spiritual good when people encounter the providential presence of the creating Spirit as they drink the water that sustains their life. Living water should be water for life: literally, as it nourishes and cleanses physically; figuratively, as it flows over the body in rituals signifying spiritual cleansing and life in the Spirit.

WATER POLLUTION AND PRIVATIZATION

When water is *pure*, its life-giving role can be fulfilled. When water is polluted, it endangers health and life not only for humankind, but for all the biotic community. When water, one of the commons goods that Earth provides, is freely available to the human and biotic communities for their nourishment, health, and life, it is used as a common good, a benefit for all to share; and it is distributed for the common good, for the well-being of all life. When this happens, the good of the local commons and of the Earth commons are enhanced. When water is privatized and allocated only to those people(s), industries, or commercial purposes determined by its owners, the role of water as a common good and the function of water to provide for the common good are eliminated. The common goods (Earth benefits), common good (community well-being), and the commons good (well-being of Earth habitat) are jeopardized by the pollution and privatization of water.

79

When water is *polluted* by residential, industrial, or agricultural effluents, it loses its life-giving properties and the role it plays in the cycle of life. It no longer provides for the needs of the commons or for the common good. It no longer has a sacramental character as a sign in nature of the Creator Spirit. Polluted water's impurities, which drive organisms away from living in or consuming water, or poison them when they do use water as their habitat or to slake their thirst, hide and dilute the essence of the pristine water that once flowed as a sign of the Creator's artistry, solicitude for life, and immanence in creation.

When water is *privatized*, it is prevented from providing freely to living beings its life-giving nourishment. Only the affluent or those with sufficient disposable funds are allowed to partake of privatized water; the economically deprived and politically dispossessed are excluded from this subsistence need. When water is privatized, its sacramental role in the commons is denied to many. Its availability as a sign of a loving Spirit who cares for all life is limited. When individuals, a corporation, or a government (national, regional, or local) removes water from the common domain, reserves water for their own purposes, and allocates or withholds water to control people, to foster exclusive private development, to thwart cooperative enterprises, to jeopardize environmental well-being, or otherwise to enhance coercive power or augment profits, these individuals, commercial operations, or social institutions are seizing part of God's world and preventing it from fulfilling its purpose in the web of creation. Water is intended by the Creator to be a sign and mediation of the Spirit's immanence and solicitous care for the living. It is supposed to be the immediate provider of sustenance for all life and, for the human species, to be a means of livelihood by supporting fishing enterprises, livestock sustenance, crop irrigation, hydroelectric energy, transportation, and scenic beauty, among other community benefits. The environmental and sacramental benefits of water are negated by privatizing policies, politics, and practices and by the laws that embody and support them.

Deliberate destruction, deprivation, or denial of water, of a water supply system, or of a water treatment plant or its needed purification chemicals, whether undertaken for political, military, or economic purposes against a specific people because of their national, racial, ethnic, or religious identity, or because of their ownership or appropriate control of an Earth good ("resource") that provides an economic benefit or meets a regional or global need or that for whatever purpose primarily impacts a civilian population, is unethical and immoral, even if some legal excuse is utilized or developed to "justify" such action. It is an act of genocide to deprive a people of a necessity of life, which is their human right; during warfare, it is a war crime.

Water, then, is life, provides life and livelihood, and stimulates spiritual understanding of and appreciation for nature. Its pollution or privatization provokes death, unemployment, and underemployment and is a rejection of its natural functions, its natural beauty, and its role in nature as a mediation of the Spirit's presence and of the Spirit's provision of goods to meet life's needs.

Water availability and water quality today are pressing social issues throughout the world. Waste, drought, overconsumption, greed, pollution, privatization, and politics all have contributed to convert available fresh water—a common good in creation—into a commodity, and even into a threat to human life, health, and economic well-being. Water is diverted from providing basic sustenance for life, degraded to become unfit for consumption, and priced beyond people's means to pay for its use. Such impacts on the quality and use of water harm more than the human community. The broader biotic community is also their victim. All life needs water to survive and, beyond survival, to flourish.

Water shortages resulting from drought or overconsumption are increasing throughout the world and are beginning to impact local environments and populations. People in major urban areas are concerned whether water will be available from their faucets for drinking and cleaning, let alone for commercial, recreational, or industrial uses or for production of hydroelectric energy.

The pollution of water results from a variety of factors, including mining, agriculture, industrial plants, runoff from residential and school lawns, and illegal dumping of waste into urban systems and rural waterways. Sometimes pollution and privatization effectively, if not actually, occur in unison as ownership of bodies of water, or water rights to flowing waters, are acquired with the purchase of land, and the water is used then for commercial and industrial enterprises that will degrade the environment, divert water sources from other, often long-standing uses, and consequently harm local communities and agricultural operations. In northeastern Montana, for example, the reservation lands of the Assiniboine (Nakota) and White Clay People (Gros Ventre) are plagued by water pollution and soil contamination from the Zortman and Landusky mine, whose construction and operation required blowing off the tops of sacred mountains to extract gold. In 1998, the Pegasus Gold Corporation, which had a $25 million bond for reclamation, filed for bankruptcy after it became evident that the bond was less than half of the money needed for reclaiming Indian lands, which would be poisoned for untold generations into the future. Throughout the West, debate rages over exploration for and extraction of coal bed methane (CBM). CBM is touted as a clean energy source, but it not only would divert water supplies used by rural communities and regional farmers and ranchers (effectively privatizing them for a single use that preempts other uses) but also would directly impact their quality by raising their salinity, thereby ending prior uses of water to irrigate fields (saline water can prevent agricultural crops from growing), to water livestock, or to provide residential drinking water. While corporations and some politicians frame environmental issues as "jobs versus environment," the real conflict in this and other cases often is "energy corporations versus agriculturalists and environment."

The privatization problem is having negative impacts on water provision that match or exceed effects of overconsumption. Even a brief review of current international events, reported by the Center for Public Integrity in Washington, D.C., reveals dramatic alterations in the ownership, distribution, and use of water across the globe. South Africa, in which several cities privatized water systems in the mid-1990s, suffered the worst cholera outbreak in its history from 2000 to 2002. People who could not afford to pay for water had resorted to drinking from and bathing in contaminated rivers and water holes. In the same period, Atlanta, Georgia, which had signed a water privatization contract with United Water in 1999, terminated the agreement. The reasons that prompted the city to cancel the contract included the facts that promised repairs to the city's aging water supply system had not been done; and residents of the area had been subjected to water shortages and to brown water flowing from home faucets. In Latin America, Nicaragua and other nations that have sought economic development assistance have been required by funding organizations such as the World Bank, the International Monetary Fund, and the Interamerican Development Bank to privatize their water, commodifying it for sale to transnational corporations headquartered primarily in France and Germany. These foreign companies decide to what extent water is used for homes, locally owned agriculture, locally owned small businesses, and any other purpose. While the people within a nation ordinarily would determine for themselves what is necessary for their common good, what promotes their economic development and benefits their population, privatized water is utilized to add to international shareholders' stock dividends or corporate executives' bonuses. Citizens of a nation would certainly prioritize their people's needs over the excessive personal financial wants of others, and even more so when those others neither live in the country nor share its dreams for a better future for all, especially for the poor.

There are signs of hope in the dual struggle to prevent water pollution and privatization, and instead to protect or promote pure water as a basic right for people.

The 1972 Montana State Constitution guarantees to the state's citizens the right to a "clean and healthful environment," a provision upheld several times by the State Supreme Court as communities and environmental organizations fought to prevent pollution, particularly from mining operations. Citizens from other states (or from nations) without a similar law might explore its development, implementation, and enforcement.

On the privatization front, the city of Bogotá, Colombia, bucked a national trend when other municipalities rushed to privatize their water, guided by the World Bank, in hopes of obtaining economic benefits. Unlike dozens of its sister Colombian cities (including Barranquilla and Cartagena) in the 1990s, Bogotá turned down money from the World Bank. It improved its water and sewerage systems, including using its profits to invest in water services for Bogotá's poor; survived a national recession; and is profitable, with excellent assets. In fact, across Colombia, the public utilities of Bogotá and Medellín rank first and second, respectively, in water and sewerage system quality and provision of service; the highest-ranked privatized water system is only fourth.

Indianapolis in the United States also provides a success story about a local government's efforts to retain control of its water supplies and systems to promote the common good. When the private company that had owned and controlled the water and operated the system for 131 years decided to sell it, the city decided in turn to buy it and make it a public utility. When global water corporations tried to purchase it instead, city attorneys found that the city had first option under an 1870 law. Indianapolis bought the company and contracted a private company to manage the system, while the city retained water ownership and required the managing company to meet not only water quality and distribution standards but also customer service obligations.

The United Nations has begun to explore the relationship of water issues to other human rights issues. The United Nations Economic and Social Council (UNESCO), meeting in Geneva in November 2002, approved a draft statement on the right to water. The statement declares, "The human right to drinking water is fundamental for life and health. Sufficient and safe drinking water is a precondition for the realization of all human rights." UNESCO's statement reveals that the organization understands that it must affirm people's right to water, and advocate it specifically and strongly, because of the precarious state of people's access to pure water globally. Water supplies in some areas are becoming ever more scarce, and various forms of pollution often endanger human health even when water is available. UNESCO adds that the "right to drinking water . . . is the most fundamental condition for survival," a recognition that water as a subsistence need surpasses food, clothing, and shelter, as necessary as these are also. This right "entitles everyone to *safe*, *sufficient*, *affordable* and *accessible* drinking water that is adequate for daily individual requirements (drinking, household sanitation, food preparation, and hygiene)." UNESCO covers here several issues: water quality, jeopardized by pollution and aging delivery systems or treatment plants; water quantity, which in some populous nations or industrialized regions might be limited for local populations; water cost, which could put this "right" in jeopardy for poor segments of society; and water availability, since governments or private interests could impede or prevent individuals' and peoples' recourse to even public sources of water to provide for their needs.

The Catholic Church in its political embodiment as the Holy See (the Vatican city-state) in the United Nations became directly involved in water issues with the 2003 release of "Water, an Essential Element for Life," a note prepared by the Pontifical Council for Justice and Peace and presented at the 2003 Third World Water Forum in Kyoto, Japan. The document states that water is "a right to life issue," that water is "a common good of humankind," and that the "human right to water" should be acknowledged. The Vatican uses its familiar formulation, "right to life," to highlight the importance of the issue, to advocate distribution of water supplies to meet the survival needs of all people, and to affirm the responsibility of national and international organizations to assure that this does occur. The known and useful concept of the "common good," advocated in papal and other church teachings for a century, is helpful as well. Water is a "common good" meant for the use of all peoples, not a private resource to be reserved as "private property" by a few, which would benefit the individual owners and not the community as a whole. Water rights should be regarded as fundamental human rights, not an addition to them. The UN, which has advocated human rights virtually since its inception, should participate more vigorously in efforts to safeguard water supplies for humankind as such a natural right.

In all of the instances cited of corporate profits versus community benefit, it is evident that peoples' lives, livelihoods, health, and sanitation are threatened or already impacted by the pollution or privatization of vital water supplies and water distribution systems. Such concerns catalyzed the UNESCO and Vatican actions. Public participation is needed, in these and similar water decisions, to promote or retain water purity, public ownership of essential water supplies and systems, and public prioritization of water uses. Meanwhile, *Fortune* magazine called water "one of the world's great business opportunities," declaring it to be a twenty-first-century equivalent to what oil had been in the twentieth century.

To counteract polluted and privatized water, Earth and its life communities need living water—as a sacramental commons and in the sacramental commons—to be restored and conserved, for the well-being and even the survival of species and the planet.

LIVING WATER

Over millennia peoples have prioritized access to water. They knew that they and all living creatures needed it for nourishment and survival. They located their early settlements, walled cities, and eventually sprawling metropolises near it for subsistence, transportation, and trade purposes. They noted and made use of its cleansing effects. Eventually, they developed agriculture that utilized water provided by rainfall: directly from the clouds to their fields, or indirectly through human ingenuity when people diverted rivers into irrigation canals, or constructed drinking troughs for domesticated animals.

Peoples of the world based their claims to water on longevity in place, on conquest, or on traditions developed in their area or adapted from other cultures. They have expressed for millennia their gratitude for Earth's provision of pure water and have asserted their own right to water to meet their personal, family, and community needs. These ancient perspectives are instructive for the twenty-first century and are represented in the insights of surviving traditional peoples throughout the world. In the Americas, for example, native peoples' elders continue to teach the tradition that Mother Earth should be respected as a universal provider of benefits for individuals and communities; they reject ownership of her water, soil, and other natural goods, which are received from a nurturing Mother and should be available for the use of all who need them. Early in the twentieth century, the Mexican revolutionary Emiliano Zapata similarly linked respect for Earth's natural goods to advocacy of a common right to the use of these goods: "The land belongs to everyone, like the water, the air, and the sun's light and warmth; and those who work the land with their own hands have a right to it." Such a sentiment would serve people well for the current millennium and beyond, as an expression of their own newly formulated or revived values and practices. Land already has been privatized and commodified. Water is becoming so. Air might yet become next, the last basic natural good to fall victim to privatization. (There are already "air parlors" in some urban areas, where customers pay to breathe air unpolluted by auto and industrial emissions.)

The Bible speaks of "living water" in both a material and a spiritual sense. As a life-giving and life-providing nourishment, water that is "alive" is water flowing pure and free, and is available in surface rivers, streams, and springs, and from underground aquifers accessed through wells (usually the freely flowing surface water was the ideal "living water"). By contrast, water from pools (constructed to contain diverted flows from springs or streams) and cisterns (plaster-lined underground containers holding rain channeled from roofs, which first were developed in about 1200 B.C.E.) is stagnant and laden with the taste of minerals and of the materials used to confine it. Life-giving water might be "living" or not. That is, even the water obtained from cisterns and pools was potable, even if not pleasing to the palate, and enabled people to subsist and to thrive.

The opening verse of Psalm 42 uses living water to link bodily and spiritual needs: "As the deer longs for flowing streams, so my soul longs for you, O God." The deer in the wild, away from human habitation and in drought-plagued regions, usually has available to it only living water, not contained water, and in its thirst for survival on the land seeks this life-giving water. The human spirit, in a parallel way, seeks a living spiritual nourishment, not a stagnant accommodation to the past. The physically thirsty animal cannot survive long without water from Earth. The spiritually thirsty human spirit cannot survive long without being nourished in God's presence, encountered in ever (re)new(ed) ways and places.

Jesus reinforced the use of water as a symbol of spiritual cleansing and a source of physical sustenance. During *sukkoth*, the eight-day Feast of Booths (Tabernacles) celebrating the autumnal harvest during ceremonies in Jerusalem, water from the pool of Siloam was carried in a vessel to the Temple. During a time when prayers of gratitude for the rain that had produced a good harvest were expressed, and prayers of petition for rain in the coming season were offered, Jesus exclaimed, "Let anyone who is thirsty come to me, and let the one who believes in me drink. As the Scripture has said, 'Out of the believer's heart shall flow rivers of living water'" (John 7:37–38). Jesus dramatically offered his teachings and way of life as spiritual living water to complement the waters of Siloam representing the rains that had nurtured the fields to produce the harvest. Jesus used "living water," an actual element of the life of his people (and of all peoples), which they thought was superior to other kinds of water, to represent the purity and efficacy of his teachings: the environmental and sacramental characteristics of water flow together here as one stream of thought and a single and singular spiritual teaching. (Psalm 42 complements this Earth-related and spirit-related teaching of Jesus.) Interestingly, the water from the pool was not "living water" because it had been contained (in both the pool and the vessel); Jesus contrasted his "living water" with the ritual waters (and the Temple rituals), while he complemented his spiritual living water with subsistence living water. In a complementary incident (John 4:7–15), Jesus met an outcast Samaritan woman and offered living water to her. He asked her for subsistence living water from the community well, where it was available to all. He offered to her spiritual living water, which would also be available to all.

Living water is born as living rain. Whether consumed with cupped hands at a stream or drunk from a bucket dipped into an aquifer's bounty at a well, the water's origin is from rain clouds. Actually, of course, the cycle of water is continuous: rivers and lakes partly evaporate, the moisture rises to the sky, becomes clouds, falls as rain, replenishes the rivers, and the process continues. Whether water that is living as rainfall continues to be living for the biotic community will depend on where it falls, what enters its flow, and where it is collected and consumed.

Water in biblical narratives has a variety of functions and a diversity of symbolic meanings. Water provides life for the entire biotic community. For humans, water fulfills a diversity of needs. Water as a *subsistence* benefit satisfies thirst and houses fish needed for food. Water as a *social* benefit provides for the well-being of people as the setting for their small communities and large cities; as a natural good beneficial to agriculture's fields, vineyards, orchards, and domestic animals; and as a support for transportation and for commercial enterprises, where human livelihood is obtained through fishing or trade. Water as a *spiritual* benefit provides a sign of the Spirit's presence and loving providence, and it is used in cleansing rituals to heal body and spirit.

It is worthy of note that in the first of the two biblical creation stories (Genesis 1), water is presupposed at creation. (This parallels the earlier Babylonian creation story, the *Enuma Elish*, in which primeval waters exist, but are also the original gods in water form who bring creation into being.) In the biblical story of the "days" of creation, God creates after moving over the waters; God does not create the waters. The Temple sculpture of the primeval sea (noted in 1 Kings 7:23–26) reminded people of God's creative power and cosmic might.

Leviticus 11:32–36 declared optimistically, in a prechemical age, that since living water flowed continually, it could not become unclean.

In the biblical narratives describing a time when the Israelites wandered in the wilderness, God provided water through rain and guidance and sometimes, the biblical tradition states, in more dramatic ways. When the people complained for lack of water, Moses, with divine inspiration, struck a rock and a spring sprang forth (Exodus 17:6; Numbers 20:2–13). In another story, Yahweh provided water to the Israelites at Marah when Moses threw a piece of wood into the water to turn it from bitter to sweet so that it was potable and palatable (Exodus 15:23–25).

The book of Isaiah uses water imagery to address a variety of issues and present a wealth of teachings. God's gift of water for people in the desert provides corporeal salvation, but also represents spiritual salvation. The understanding of "waters shall break forth in the wilderness" (Isaiah 35:6) goes beyond the greening of the desert to Yahweh's solicitude for the people of Israel who follow God's ways. The message is more explicit in Isaiah 44:3–4: "I will pour water on the thirsty land, and streams on the dry ground;

I will pour my spirit upon your descendants, and my blessing upon your off-spring. They shall spring up like a green tamarisk, like willows by flowing streams." Isaiah 43:19–20 states that God will provide "rivers in the desert" that will be appreciated by wild animals and people. Isaiah 41:17–18 addresses multiple human needs: "When the poor and the needy seek water, and there is none, and their tongue is parched with thirst, I the Lord will answer them, I the God of Israel will not forsake them. I will open rivers on the heights, and fountains in the midst of the valleys; I will make the wilderness a pool of water, and the dry land springs of water." The passage exemplifies the consistent biblical teaching that God is compassionate toward the poor, concerned about the community as a whole, and committed to providing for people's subsistence, social, and spiritual needs. Isaiah 32:1–2 states that "a king will reign in righteousness, and princes will rule with justice"; they will be like a shelter from the wind, a great rock that provides shade from the sun, and "streams of water in a dry place." The just ruler will greatly benefit his people, providing them with what they require in their times of material or social need, in the way that water and formations of natural terrain, parts of God's creation, meet people's physical needs. The description of a righteous ruler is complemented elsewhere by descriptions of a righteous person in general: Psalm 1:3 and Jeremiah 17:8 state that a righteous person is like a tree planted by unfailing living water (and so they will also be unfailingly just). The deer longs for subsistence living water, and people long for spiritual living water, as seen in Psalm 42. When people find and drink of the spiritual living water and continue to use it as a source of life, they will fulfill God's requirements to "do justice," love kindness, and "walk humbly with God" (Micah 6:8).

Psalm 18:16 likens salvation to being rescued from drowning in a turbulent sea. Later, Christianity would utilize this symbolism in its baptism ritual, which signifies rescue from spiritual drowning; this parallels and reflects the flood story depiction of the function of Noah's ark to save Noah's extended family and representatives of all species from physical drowning. In John 1:26–33, Jesus is baptized by John the Baptist in the Jordan River. Baptism's role as a rite of spiritual cleansing symbolized by water's physical cleansing is presented in several passages in the Christian Scriptures. In Mark 10:38, Jesus describes his crucifixion as a baptism, and in Romans 6:3, Paul teaches that Christian baptism is participation in Jesus' salvific moment of crucifixion. 1 Peter 3:20–21 continues the analogous imagery, stating that baptism, which saves people from spiritual death, was prefigured by Noah's ark saving people from the flood. The wooden ark floating on the water is transformed to being water itself, as waters of life that rescue people from waters of death. In John 3:5–8 in the conversation between Jesus and Nicodemus, baptism is likened to physical birth. Just as the birth sac breaks and water flows from a woman when a child is born, so, too, a follower of Jesus is born into discipleship through baptism in water, and emerges as a new person. A disciple must be (re)born of water and the Holy Spirit. Jesus responds to Nicodemus's question about how someone can be born again by using the birth event itself: in both types of birth, water is the medium from which the newly born has emerged: maternal water in the first birth, then living water as spiritual water in rebirth as a follower of Jesus.

The use of an outer, physical cleansing with water to symbolize an inner, spiritual cleansing is noted in other biblical passages. Mark 7:3 describes people's practice of washing their hands before meals. Luke 7:44 observes how guests were offered water to wash their feet upon their arrival at a home. John 13:5 describes Jesus taking the role of a servant and washing the feet of his disciples. Jesus declared that this was to be an example for his followers. They were to serve one another. (Unfortunately, over time this has become, in some church settings, more a ritual in which clergy portray Jesus, rather than either a symbol of actual service or a ritual expression of the social reality of Christian conduct outside church buildings, within and beyond the community of believers.)

Jeremiah 2:11–13 and 17:13 describe God as the fountain of living waters for Israel. (Today, in the Christian tradition, that role of God is understood to be for all people and peoples.)

In Matthew 10:42, Jesus declares that giving a cup of water to a thirsty "little one" will be rewarded. The "little one" can represent a poor person, someone uneducated, or a new or vulnerable disciple, so the cup of water can mean the actual fluid needed for physical survival, or teaching needed for spiritual well-being. The text links the subsistence good and the spiritual good in a social setting. Benedict Viviano remarks regarding this passage, "It has been observed that if God will reward one who gives a cup of cold water to a disciple, how much more will [God] reward one who installs an entire city water system."[1]

Water represents both physical cleansing and spiritual cleansing in John 9:7, when a blind man receives sight after washing in the pool of Siloam as Jesus instructed.

Water can represent the Spirit, who is described in fluid imagery as being "poured out." In Joel 2:28–29 God declares, "I will pour out my spirit on all flesh; your sons and your daughters shall prophesy, your old men shall dream dreams, and your young men shall see visions." This passage is mirrored in the book of Acts 2:17–18, where in the Pentecost narrative, after the coming of the Spirit, Peter cites Joel's text to a gathered crowd of people. Similarly, in Acts 10:45, which narrates an event in Joppa, at the house of the Roman centurion Cornelius, Peter and his fellow Jewish Christians were astounded that while Peter was speaking to the household of Cornelius, "the gift of the Holy Spirit had been poured out even on the Gentiles." The Spirit comes to all people; those who are open to the Spirit will experience the Spirit.

Biblical water imagery, then, is rich in its breadth and depth of meaning. Each meaning assumes that the water used, whether for physical cleansing or during spiritual cleansing, whether regarded as living or only providing life, and whether as a sign of the Spirit or an unexpected mediation of the Spirit, is clear, clean, and potable in creation, in the Earth commons. Several of these meanings converge in understandings of the revelatory or sacramental dimension of Christianity.

SACRAMENTAL WATER

In the Christian tradition, sacramental water in religious rituals signifies a change in human consciousness and conduct, and a new or renewed relationship with the Spirit. The human spirit is enlivened in such moments, eliminating decadence and transcending depression and despair. The symbolism of the ritual would be subverted by the use of polluted water in the sacramental moment—and might well endanger the health or even life of the recipient of the sacrament. The person spiritually bathed in, blessed by, and cleansed through such water would be distracted from appreciating its spiritual significance because of its polluted material condition. The use of privatized water would have a similar impact: water intended for all would be available for spiritual cleansing only to the extent that its "owners" allowed it to be so allocated. Water would not be a sign of God's providence (to meet human subsistence needs) and God's freely given grace (to guide human spiritual needs) if its use were dependent on private whim. The waters of baptism could not signify spiritual cleansing and entrance into a new life in an inclusive, integrated community if the water used for the sacrament were polluted periodically and/or only secured sporadically from an exclusive, elitist group's restricted private source. Water used for ritual blessings would be similarly affected by polluted or privatized water, losing its intrinsic physical character and its extrinsic spiritual significance.

Throughout the world today, as evidenced by the situations cited previously, environmental degradation and water privatization have caused water to lose its nature and role as *living water*, as a bountiful source of benefits needed to provide for the common good. Water is losing also its ability to be a *sacramental* symbol, a sign in nature of God the Creator. The poisoning of waters by effluents from industrial operations and by chemicals from agricultural operations and landscaping practices has altered the life-giving nature of water. Populations of creatures of God, particularly salmon and trout but also birds and animals, have been substantially reduced and in some cases have become extinct, thereby depriving creation of some of its creatures. Surviving creatures and human communities have been deprived of sources of nourishment—water and food. Other citizens and communities have been deprived of their means of livelihood—directly as fishers and canners, for example; indirectly as merchants who depend on the latter to support local businesses, and communities that depend on their labor and taxes to support schools, parks, streets, water, and sewer systems and other community infrastructural needs. Such occurrences distract people from seeing the work of the Creator, since such harmful human works disturb the waters, divert human attention, and distort human vision. It is difficult in these circumstances for people to celebrate water as a sign of the Spirit's creative work and providence. It is difficult, too, for people to have opportunities for beneficial, community-enhancing human work that harvests the goods of the waters to provide for human needs. Earth's waters have become less sacramental, less a revelatory sign of the Spirit's presence and creativity, and more detrimental, more signs of human ignorance, carelessness, indifference, and greed.

People, as caretakers of those parts of creation with which they interact, are responsible for the restoration and conservation of living water *as* a sacramental commons, and living water *in* a sacramental commons.

Living water is a sacramental commons in itself. It is sacramental when its purity symbolizes divine being, divine compassion, and divine solicitude, and provides nourishment for all life. It is a commons when it is able to be the medium and substance that serves as the world, the habitat, for *aquatic life*—fish, birds, reptiles, crustaceans, insects, and plants; for *related life* directly dependent on aquatic life—eagles, bears, fisher peoples; and for *all life*, which needs water for survival. Living water enables and nurtures life.

Living water as a sacramental commons enables life to exist in the bioregional sacramental commons through which it flows. Living water enables and supports life on Earth, the planetary sacramental commons in which every bioregional commons is integrated into a single terrestrial whole, as it flows through Earth ecosystems and as it provides rain on Earth after its liquid form evaporates and becomes clouds. Some members of the biotic community partake directly of living water by drinking it (trees through their roots, animals with their mouths, and birds with their beaks) or by living in its oceans, seas, rivers, streams, and wetlands (fish, beavers, and otters); other members of the biotic community benefit both directly and indirectly from living water, as they drink it and as they eat the grasses, grains, fruits, or nuts whose life is sustained by living water's clouds, rain, and snow. All these beneficiaries of living water need water's sacramental character to be conserved.

The revelatory role of water can be retained by preventing chemical wastes from entering it from such human sources as agricultural fields and residential lawns in the form of fertilizers and pesticides; mining operation runoffs carrying company-sprayed cyanide or a variety of heavy metals from exposed surfaces; and paper mill effluents, particularly those containing carcinogenic dioxin resulting from chlorine treatments to brighten paper. All such inputs from human industries and communities harm and kill aquatic life, and threaten the health and life of other members of the biotic community. The sacramental commons can be enhanced and sustained by communities requiring corporations to eliminate sulfur emissions from coal-fired power plants and other industrial operations; the sulfur mixes with clouds and returns to Earth as acid rain, destroying forests, fields, and aquatic life. The sacramental commons can be restored in paper-producing areas when consumers, including commercial enterprises, demand chlorine-free paper, and when local communities demand clean water, institutionalize their demand in laws, and assess substantial penalties for violations of the laws. The sacramental commons can be maintained when water rights are established and upheld for all people, rather than appropriated into the hands of a few individuals or corporations through privatization, which eliminates living water access and use from the poor, from powerless ethnic groups, from oppressed people in general, from small, independent businesses, and from member owners of cooperative endeavors. The sacramental commons will be sustained if water sources and supplies are community based and community oriented, rather than commodified and controlled by people who are greedy for wealth and for political and economic power. Pollution and privatization harm the community of life and the waters of life, threatening the well-being of creation, communities, and the commons. Purity and public control nurture the community of life and conserve and enhance life-giving waters, benefiting the commons and communities, and promoting the common good.

Environmental and sacramental living water provide for the commons good, the well-being of the Earth home, the habitat of the biotic community; and for the common good, the well-being of interrelated and interdependent members of the biotic community. Living water also provides common goods, Earth benefits needed for the life and well-being of the biotic community. The commons needs clean water for the good of the individuals and species that inhabit its bioregional ecosystems, and to cleanse Earth periodically. The biotic community needs access to clean water for its very life, to satisfy its thirst, and, in the case of the human community, to provide those benefits and, additionally, to support agriculture and fishing enterprises and to enhance human health and hygiene. Water pollution and water privatization are an affront to the Creator Spirit, impede the universal destination of this natural good to meet the needs of all life, harm the good state of the commons, alter the character of a common good, and threaten the common good of life communities. Recognition that water is sacramental when it is not polluted or privatized should stimulate people to clean polluted water sources, to maintain the purity of pristine places, and to ensure access to water for humankind and the rest of biokind.

Appreciation for a sacramental universe and a sacramental commons, and actions to restore, conserve, and increase the availability of living water for members of the sacramental community, will prove invaluable for Christians confronting the worsening water crisis. Since living water is one of the most essential components of a healthy sacramental and revelatory commons, peoples of all faiths should be especially engaged in efforts to ensure that water is neither polluted nor privatized, and, where either or both of these violations of water's integrity and divine intentionality have occurred against this fluid common good of the commons, which is intended for the common good of all, to reverse such practices and prevent their recurrence.

LIVING WATER: A NATURAL RIGHT

People across the globe are increasingly concerned about the pollution and privatization of water. Poisoning and preemptive allocation of ever-scarcer pure water sources has the potential to catalyze a biotic community catastrophe if present trends continue. People are beginning to have a greater sense of responsibility for conserving water and maintaining its purity throughout its cycle from rain to running water and back again. They understand and affirm that natural water is a natural right: for human individuals, families, communities and nations; for individuals and species of the regional and global biotic community in all its diversity and complexity.

Community members, not distant shareholders (foreign or domestic) should make vital decisions concerning the acquisition, allocation, utilization, and distribution of essential natural goods such as water. People's needs for life and livelihood should take precedence over corporate profits in the use of this natural common good. Poor people's need to avail themselves of commons goods for subsistence should take precedence over more affluent people's desire to dispose of common goods to satisfy their wants; racial, ethnic, and culturally distinct members of communities should have the same rights as members of the dominant culture or ethnic group. Water should be carefully conserved and community owned; it should be primarily locally and regionally distributed and conserved, and shared with other communities that need it; it should not be privately, corporately, or governmentally appropriated and internationally displaced and disposed of as an export commodity.

If water is regarded merely as a commodity among commodities, as a source of profit rather than as a subsistence good, then privatization and profiteering will supplant provision of a common good for people the world over, and humans and other individuals and species will starve and die from thirst and from preventable or curable illnesses caused by water deprivation. If, by contrast, water is recognized as a natural right, and this recognition is concretized on an international scale in treaties and in national laws and policies, then humans and members of the biotic community as a whole will be able to access and utilize the living water (or at least the life-giving water, until all water is cleansed to the extent possible so that it becomes living again), that refreshes them and enhances Earth. The status of water as a natural good will be ensured because people, communities, their governments, and transnational and transcultural corporations recognize it as good in itself and as a good for others, a common good to which all biota have a natural right. Water will be sustained, then, for future generations: living and a source of life, a natural good and a natural right, an Earth good and a commons good for the common good, for the well-being of present and future generations.

BIBLICAL MEMORIES AND BIBLICAL VISIONS

In Genesis, the second creation story depicts Eden as a paradise bordered by four rivers, living waters that nourish the garden and all its inhabitants. The Spirit creates the waters and provides them gratuitously to meet the needs of Earth and all Earth's children. A Tree of Life, nurtured by these waters and the mist that results from them, provides food for humans (who are vegetarians), complementing what other plants produce for them and for all life. The first humans are instructed to serve (the same verb is used here as is used in the injunction to Adam to serve God, with obvious implications for people) and to conserve the garden, which represents all Earth. Ezekiel 36:25 speaks of dramatic changes on Earth in the future: desolate land becomes "like the garden of Eden"; in Ezekiel 47, the prophet in a vision sees water flowing from below the Temple (a vision present also in Zechariah 2:8) and becoming a river, which by its flow converts a stagnant sea to fresh water. On both sides of the river grow trees that bear fruit every month, and whose leaves are medicinal herbs. Revelation 21–22 describes a new heaven and a new Earth. In the Earth habitat, the Tree of Life that was present in the Genesis story of Adam and Eve is reborn. It bears fruit every month to provide food, and its leaves serve as medicine. It is nourished by "the river of life-giving water." The trees and the river in Revelation recall both the story of Eden and the prophetic vision of Ezekiel; in both narratives Earth transformed is Earth restored to be a paradise for all. Black Elk's Great Vision has complementary images. Below Harney Peak he sees the community circles of all peoples comprising a single grand circle of harmony. In its center stands a flowering tree that shelters "all the children of one mother and one father. And I saw that it was holy."[2]

The Earth commons is sacramental, presenced by the Spirit and intended by the Spirit to be the common ground, fed by living water, from which all of the biotic community draws the common goods needed to provide for their common good. Living water is essential for life and for the commons good, the common good, and common goods. The new heaven and new Earth, described in the visions of the seer of Revelation and Black Elk, will come closer to fruition when people respect their bioregion, responsibly care for it, justly distribute its common goods, see signs of the Spirit in its pristine beautiful places and its diversity of creatures, and walk with the Spirit on their life journey in rural or urban settings. Community property, community values, and community sharing, enhanced by water regarded as a natural right for all creatures and respected as a sacramental commons in the broader Earth commons, will lead to communion not only among humans but between humans and their biotic relatives, between this biotic community and Earth, and between all creation and the Spirit.

NOTES

1. Raymond E. Brown, S.S., Joseph A. Fitzmyer, S.J., and Roland E. Murphy, O.P., *The New Jerome Biblical Commentary* (Englewood Cliffs, N.J.: Prentice-Hall, 1990), 652.
2. Black Elk, *Black Elk Speaks: Being the Life Story of a Holy Man of the Oglala Sioux*, ed. John G. Neihardt (New York: Pocket Books, 1972), 35–36.

· 6 ·

Species Survival

$\mathcal{I}$n the northwestern United States, no species is more appreciated as a regional symbol than the salmon. In ancient native totem poles, as contemporary commercial logos, and in carvings and paintings through the centuries, salmon have been revered, respected, and represented with photographic clarity or in highly stylized artistry. Salmon have been also the traditional staple food for people living at subsistence level. Whether they caught the fish themselves or traded or bartered or paid for them, people have relied on salmon for millennia. Two centuries ago, when Merriwether Lewis and William Clark made their historic Voyage of Discovery across the northern regions of the United States, they bartered for salmon along the way in their encounters with native peoples.

During the latter part of the nineteenth century, sixteen million salmon journeyed up the Columbia-Snake rivers system each spring to spawn at their respective birthplaces. Their passage was periodically interrupted by native fishers, as it had been for ten thousand years, and by Euro-Americans whose forebears had been fishing on the river banks for less than two centuries. Salmon provided abundant food for all fishers, and were a source of livelihood not only for them but for canners and merchants who shared life in riparian communities along the network of waters.

The fishers whose lines, spears, dip nets, and seines sought a silvery harvest in that time of abundance belonged to diverse faith communities. The original native fishers wove together their spirituality and their life in society, had a profound respect for the natural world, and felt a spiritual kinship with the salmon and other free or "wild" creatures in the region's rivers. The Euro-American newcomers separated not only church and state but also their life on Earth from their expected future life in a heaven. They viewed the natural world as a treasure trove of resources to be used for human benefit, and the free creatures as a lesser form of life in a natural hierarchy in which humans were at the top of a divinely ordained, "natural law"–sustained pyramid of life.

97

The fishers' distinct worldviews were the bases for increasing conflict along the rivers. The dominant Euroculture used its political and economic power to impose its perspective in the concrete circumstances of river region life, leading to increased pollution of the waters, increased development of river shores, increased efforts to control the course and flow of the waters, and increased depletion and extinction of the salmon and other aquatic species. For more than a century the Euro-American worldview prevailed, until multiple legal decisions favoring native fishers, and an awakened sense of Christian responsibility for creation, for community, and for cultural diversity, combined to provide a foundation for an integration of perspectives. In recent years, the bridging of the cultural and religious gap has led not only to a growing complementarity of religious and ethical understandings but also, for some, to a common vision of a time when human-caused fish extinctions will have ceased and communities will be living in harmony with each other and with the salmon in their shared bioregion.

Scientists, environmentalists, Indian nations, and fishers from both native and nonnative cultures have proposed breaching four lower Snake River dams in the Columbia-Snake system to save the salmon. The dams have been a source of economic hardship, racial antagonism, and salmon species extinction. They were justified initially to provide hydroelectric power for "national security" (development of atomic and then nuclear weaponry), but then agricultural irrigation and commercial power generation became added dam functions. The salmon species had become a cultural-ecological keystone species: the life or demise of the salmon came to represent the character of the relationship between humankind and biokind.

The political, economic, ethical, and theological issues that have emerged in the salmon debate provide bases for consideration of the past, present, and prospective status of nonhuman species in a human-dominated Earth. The plight of the salmon can help focus explorations of the extent to which nonhuman species have primarily intrinsic or instrumental value; the extent to which "natural rights" should be extended to all of nature; and the extent to which species preservation should take precedence over human needs or wants. Issues of restorative justice (for fish, fishers, and fisheries; for first peoples' communities), distributive justice (among humans), and ecosystem justice (for the interwoven biotic and abiotic communities) permeate these explorations.

The focal point of the situation of the salmon in the Columbia River Watershed bioregion in recent years has been the impact on salmon species of four dams—Ice Harbor, Lower Monumental, Little Goose, and Lower Granite—on the Lower Snake River in Eastern Washington. Salmon extinctions and near-extinctions that have resulted from the dams have had adverse social impacts on the remaining Wanapum ("River People"—the people of "Che Wana," called the "Great River" in their native tongue), who trace their ancestry and presence on the river back ten millennia.

THE COLUMBIA-SNAKE RIVERS SYSTEM

In the Columbia River Watershed, the First Peoples lived a simple and sometimes harsh life as they adapted to the moods of the seasons, the vagaries of weather, and the annual migrations of salmon. In the millennia prior to the arrival of the first European and Euro-American trappers, traders, and settlers, regional native peoples fished for salmon in the rivers of what would later become the states of Washington and Oregon. They provided food for themselves and bartered smoked salmon with neighboring communities. Europeans and Euro-Americans settled in the area in earnest in the nineteenth century. A few decades after their arrival, the newcomers developed commercial fishing operations with boats and canneries, at first complementing but then competing with native fishers. The first salted salmon shipment was sent to Boston in 1830, and fifty years later regional canneries were packing and shipping some 630,000 cases of salmon to consumers across the United States. Shortly thereafter, however, the salmon stocks began to be depleted dramatically because of a combination of factors brought by nonnatives. These included overfishing; a proliferation of canneries; fishers having to dump their catch overboard on occasion when they reached port because canneries that had encouraged overfishing stopped purchasing the salmon when their plant reached capacity; and, eventually, the construction of dams to control floods and to provide electricity and to store the water behind them for agricultural irrigation systems and for use by industrial plants and railroads. Fishers lived at subsistence levels and then went bankrupt because of the loss of their livelihood when the canneries would not buy their fish, and later because of diminished numbers of available fish and the consequent closure of canneries.

While the river runs of salmon were being directly impacted by these events, the ocean migrations began to be even more diminished as mega-scale fishing operations, using large ships that served as offshore "fish factories," multiplied in the Pacific Ocean from California to British Columbia. Salmon began to become threatened, endangered, and extinct. The Snake River coho salmon were extinct by 1986, and within a decade some one hundred runs of salmon and trout in the U.S. Northwest and in northern California had joined them, while two hundred others were in dramatic decline. The loss of salmon species was an ecological tragedy and meant economic hardship for fishing-dependent communities along the web of rivers. Hundreds of commercial fishers in the river network went out of business in the last two decades of the twentieth century. Throughout the century, human-caused salmon losses cost fishers their livelihood and occupation, and provoked a ripple effect of commercial businesses' economic losses and further job cuts in riparian communities, in a downward spiral that was offset in part by the addition of new enterprises that consumed more energy and produced more pollution than fishing-related operations. The issue was not "fish versus jobs" or "jobs versus environment," as politicians and corporate managers declared when efforts were undertaken to save salmon species, but which kinds of jobs and for whose economic benefit.

Federal and state government efforts to save the salmon included construction of fish ladders on many of the dams to enable passage upriver of salmon returning to spawn; shipping young salmon downriver past the dams in tanker trucks, to aid their migration toward the Pacific; and the establishment of fish hatcheries to increase salmon reproduction and seed the rivers with the salmon offspring that resulted. Hatchery fish were not as biologically adaptable as free fish, and their interbreeding weakened the free fish genetically. When the fish continued to decline, the federal government appointed a regional body of fisheries biologists, called the PATH (Plan for Analyzing and Testing Hypotheses) commission, to analyze the causes of decline and suggest solutions to stop it. Their scientific analysis led a significant majority of the biologists to conclude in their final report (1998) that the best way to save at least several species of salmon would be to breach four dams on the lower Snake River. However, business and political leaders subverted science by affirming the minority opinion that opposed dam breaching, and demanded a new study. The federal government obliged, appointing a smaller commission of four biologists from outside the geographic area and its political and economic pressures. This commission, regarded as politically neutral, unanimously agreed with the majority opinion in the PATH report: the best hope the salmon had for survival was to breach the dams to enable the river to run freely in order that the salmon smolts swimming toward the Pacific and the adult salmon swimming upriver to spawn all would have free passage.

The proposal to breach the dams aroused the anger and opposition of some farmers who feared losing the benefit of irrigation systems because the water level after breaching would be below the entry point of pipes from pumps; owners of the barge company that shipped agricultural and other goods along the 135-mile stretch of water that was calm because of the dams; ordinary citizens who feared floods and the loss of their jobs, fears exacerbated by local politicians; and other commercial and industrial corporations that feared a diminution of profits if salmon conservation took priority over their operations, some of which included dumping effluents into the rivers. Supporters of breaching the dams included the Wanapum and other native peoples, who wanted to protect their fishing culture and livelihood; environmentalists and scientists interested in restoring and conserving salmon populations; and fishers and cannery workers, who wanted their commercial operations restored. In 2005, President George W. Bush declared that even if breaching the four dams was the only hope for salmon survival, he would not agree to it.

The current situation of the salmon and of the fishing communities dependent on them can be evaluated through an exploration of the traditional religious perspectives of a representative native nation whose subsistence and livelihood have been directly related to them and through an analysis of Christian perspectives in the Euro-American community.

WANAPUM SUBSISTENCE AND SPIRITUALITY

The Wanapum on the Columbia River are a representative native people whose lives are intertwined with those of the salmon and whose spiritual teachings relate to that linkage.

The original fishers on the Columbia River came from a diversity of native communities. Among these fishers the Wanapum have been prominent for their defense of the salmon and of native fishing rights. Populations of salmon species and subspecies had continually increased over the approximately ten thousand years that these native peoples lived and fished on the Columbia River prior to the coming of the first European explorers. But in the last decades of the nineteenth century and throughout the twentieth century, a deadly combination of mining, logging, manufacturing plants, and the construction of hydroelectric dams eliminated spawning grounds and habitat for the fish. When the Dalles Dam was completed in 1957, its backed-up waters covered over Celilo Falls, the largest native fishing site in North America, where the Wanapum and other peoples had used nets, spears, and one-fisher cable cars crossing the Columbia Gorge to catch fish they used for subsistence, trade, and sale. Water retained behind the Dalles Dam and other dams covered native villages, burial sites, and petroglyphs. The federal government had promised "in lieu" sites to replace the flooded villages and fishing places, but the substitute sites were never constructed.

The dams adversely affected salmon. Dam walls impeded the flow of salmon smolts downriver toward the Pacific Ocean and the return of mature salmon up the Columbia to their home rivers to spawn. By the last quarter of the twentieth century, overfishing in the Pacific had drastically reduced the amount of fish available to native and nonnative fishers in the Columbia-Snake system, and it also put these groups into conflict over the available potential catch. Native fishing was restricted to Zone 6, some 113 miles between the Bonneville and McNary dams. The amount of fish available to native fishers to catch was reduced by ocean factory fishing; by nonnative fishers (commercial and sport) in the five zones downriver through which the salmon swam on their way to the government-defined Wanapum area; and by conservation limitations on the Wanapum catch, limitations that were based on the initial counts of the fish after they had entered the Columbia from the Pacific, and on the count of the number remaining after they were depleted en route to their spawning grounds but before reaching the Indian fishers' region. Despite these intrusive interferences in the salmon cycles caused by the region's Euro-U.S. residents, and the fact that the River People's own numbers had diminished and they were fishing far less than they had before, the native peoples were blamed for the much-depleted salmon and steelhead runs in the Columbia River Watershed. As salmon declines continued in the Columbia River, economic hardship and racism combined in the Euro-American community and became a volatile combination against the Wanapum.

The fishing rights struggle of native peoples in the northwestern United States began in earnest in the mid-1960s with the social activism of the spiritual leader and healer David Sohappy Sr. (1925–1991). While African Americans marched for civil rights under leaders such as Martin Luther King Jr., and Chicano farmworkers struggled for justice with César Chávez, the Wanapum followed Sohappy and fought for rights guaranteed by the 1855 Fort Yakima Treaty. In that treaty, the region's peoples reserved exclusive fishing rights on their reservations and at "all usual and accustomed fishing places," as well as rights to hunt and to gather roots and berries.

Native peoples' efforts initially attracted little attention outside the Columbia River region. However, the local struggle over salmon attracted national attention because of two judicial decisions: Sohappy's successful suit against the Oregon Fish Commission and the Oregon Game Commission, which had gone all the way to, and was upheld by, the U.S. Supreme Court as *Sohappy v. Smith* in 1968; and Judge George Boldt's federal ruling in 1974 in *U.S. v. Washington* that native fishers were entitled to 50 percent of the catch on the Columbia. Sohappy's main adversaries were government officials in league with corporate members of the fishing industry, whose commercial operations took in the vast majority of the seasonal salmon catch with fish factory ships out on the Pacific Ocean netting catches whose quantity was unregulated.

David Sohappy was born near Harrah, Washington, and raised in a traditional family. His great-uncle, the noted prophet Smohalla of the Washat religion, had led a resurgence of regional native spirituality in the late 1800s. He grew up in this pacifist Washat or "Seven Drums" religion. Some Washat adherents became "Dreamers," visionaries who lived at times alone along the Columbia and were sought out for spiritual guidance and sometimes for practical advice on where to fish for salmon or hunt for deer. Some Dreamers were healers as well. During World War II, Sohappy's family and other River People were forcibly relocated from most of their lands, with little warning by the federal government, so that the Hanford Nuclear Reservation could be established for nuclear weapons development. Sohappy received a call from the Creator and became a Dreamer, healer, spiritual leader, and human rights activist.

When federal and state governments tried to restrict the rights of the River People even after his successful court cases, Sohappy used civil disobedience to fight for those rights. He fished openly and sold fish at the site of an old riverboat dock, Cook's Landing in Washington, which he and other Wanapum had occupied as their "in lieu" site and sought to have recognized as their permanent fishing village.

In 1982, David Sohappy Sr., his son David Jr., Wilbur Slockish Jr., and other Wanapum fishing activists were arrested in the predawn hours for illegal fishing and for selling the fish to undercover agents in an operation the government called "Salmonscam." They had fished openly and sold their catch, believing themselves to be under the 1855 Fort Yakima Treaty and in accordance with terms of native fishing rights contained in the treaty and affirmed by subsequent court decisions. Initially, they were arrested and indicted with great attendant publicity, accused of catching and selling forty thousand fish. The fish were missing from the Indians' Zone 6. The number of missing fish was based on the number of fish who had disappeared between the first fish count at Bonneville Dam and the count upriver at McNary Dam. By the time the case went to trial, it had been discovered that most of the fish had turned up different rivers to spawn because of effluents from aluminum plants along the Columbia and were not missing after all. However, the federal government still put Sohappy and the other Wanapum on trial. They were prosecuted under the Lacey Act Amendments, conservation laws which did not exist when they were arrested. These federal laws had been introduced into the U.S. Senate by Senator Slade Gorton (R-Wash.) whose family owned a major seafood company. Eventually, Sohappy and his companions were accused of selling only 317 fish to the federal agents, convicted in federal court in 1983, and sentenced to five years in prison. His appeal was turned down by the Ninth Circuit Court of Appeals in 1985.

During his trial and appeal, Sohappy was not allowed to use the provisions of either the 1855 Fort Yakima Treaty or the 1978 Indian Religious Freedom Act to justify his activities. He and his companions then surrendered to tribal officials, intending to be tried in tribal court to see if the result would be different. But they were taken away by federal marshals instead. Sohappy was taken in chains then, over a period of a few days, to maximum-security prisons in several states; at each stop, the sixty-year-old elder was strip-searched. He was imprisoned finally in Minnesota, thousands of miles from his family. His family found a new lawyer, Thomas Keefe, who fought successfully to have him moved to a minimum-security prison in Spokane, Washington, where he was placed in a cell with David Jr. Subsequently, the Sohappys and the other fishers were permitted to go on trial in tribal court, where they were tried and acquitted in a jury trial, but the federal government demanded that they be returned to federal prison. After he suffered a stroke in prison (which prison officials initially declared had not happened, and they refused treatment for several days, claiming that he had suffered from the "hysterical paralysis" that sometimes afflicts Indian people who have been confined), developed diabetes (and was refused access to a native diet by prison officials), and had a burst blood vessel in one eye, human rights activists around the world urged his release (including during testimony about his case at the United Nations International Human Rights Commission in Geneva, Switzerland). Senator Daniel Inouye, chair of the U.S. Senate Select Committee on Indian Affairs, was able to use his political influence to secure Sohappy's release after he had been imprisoned for twenty months. His health was poor as a result of his prison sufferings, and after resuming life at Cook's Landing with limited activity, he suffered another stroke and was hospitalized in Toppenish, Washington. He died there in 1991 after a third stroke.

In the Washat tradition, called the "Feather Cult Religion" by some anthropologists, adherents progress through four stages of development of their spiritual powers. Sohappy and his wife Myra had achieved the fourth stage. Sohappy became well known as a visionary Dreamer and as a healer who generated a special magnetic force from his hands during healing ceremonies. As is the case with other traditional healers, he could charge no fee for his services, since the healing power—which in his tradition was called the "power of the universe"—was a gift of the Creator to be used for the people. His livelihood came from his fishing, not his healing abilities. Sohappy relates that while fishing when he was in his thirties, he fell into the river. A big hand caught him and put him back up on his boat. He heard a voice telling him that he was saved because his work was not finished yet. He was said to have power over storms and other natural forces. It was said, too, that he brought rain to the area around Big Mountain, Arizona, on the Navajo reservation when he went there for an International Indian Treaty Council meeting in 1986, during a period of drought; and that while in California on another occasion, he threw into the mountains an earthquake that was about to strike a city.

When he taught about his spiritual, social, and subsistence heritage, Sohappy focused on his people's responsibilities to be faithful to their traditional spirituality and culture, and to respect the salmon, pray to the salmon spirits, act responsibly toward the salmon, and express gratitude to the salmon for providing food for the people. The salmon were special to the Wanapum. The first catch of the season was celebrated with a great feast of thanksgiving in which the whole community shared.

While he was in prison in Spokane, Washington, Sohappy communicated with this writer in 1987–1988 through letters and in-person recorded interviews. He reflected on the Wanapum way of life that integrated spirituality and sacred space:

> When a person believes in the religion he goes to Mother Earth so he can get the good teachings that the Creator gives to the believers. . . . If the Creator wants you to know something he'll tell you. We never see God, only hear him. I was asleep at one time and I heard this voice tell me "Listen to this, here is a chant you have to repeat all the time." . . . So I have been following my dream all these years.

In response to people who objected to the fishing village he and other Wanapum set up at Cook's Landing in Washington, Sohappy wryly replied, "They keep trying to tell me that we were only supposed to stay there temporarily. I told them that I'm on this Earth only temporarily, and so is everything else."

As a Dreamer, Sohappy was called on to guide his people. He stated, "We're told in a dream what's going to happen. You hold services and tell people, 'Here's what I dreamt, here's what we have to do next.' "

The Wanapum have followed an oral tradition, with its unwritten laws, since long before Europeans arrived in the region. For Sohappy, these ancient laws of the native peoples took precedence over the new, written laws of the river's newcomers:

> Lots of people couldn't understand what I was talking about when I told them that I follow Unwritten Laws. They didn't understand. I told them I follow a law that is higher than any written law. So they told me, "So you're above the laws!" I said, "I didn't say that, I said I follow a law that is higher than any written law." Their laws can't stop me. Their laws can't stop the storm.

In his role as a traditional healer, Sohappy used spiritual power rather than herbs to cure his people: "When we go to our services to help heal people we pull down the power of the universe. People that can see, can see it coming." The Dreamer, without expectation of remuneration, must use the healing power that comes from the Creator for whoever needs it:

> When you belong to the Feather Religion, you've got to do what you promised to do. If you don't, it's all over for you. . . . Once you stop, all your powers are gone. You can't heal anybody. . . . You've got to go the way you're supposed to all through your life. If your worst enemy comes over and asks you for help, you've got to help him. As long as you're asked to help, then you've got to help.

The Wanapum have a special relationship with the salmon:

> The salmon was created for the people to have for their own food. . . . We are taught that if we honor our food, it will come back. If we stop, it won't come back. They say they're bringing back the salmon. I say, "No way. Indians bring back the salmon." . . . They don't listen to me because I don't have a degree.

Sohappy notes the distinction between a right and a privilege, both of which are part of the 1855 treaty his ancestors signed: "We gave to non-Indians the *privilege* to fish for salmon to feed their families, while we retained the *right* to fish. A privilege can be regulated, a right cannot." He describes the Indian "reservation" as a place reserved by the native people when they were forced to cede the vast majority of their lands to the federal government. He states that the government did not "give" the land to the native peoples; they kept it for themselves when they were coerced into giving away most of their territory.

In the Wanapum view, not only is creation as a whole sacred, but salmon and other fish (and other species) are honored beings within creation and are sacred also. The Wanapum see themselves related spiritually and materially to a universe permeated with the presence of the holy. Because of that relationship, they have traditionally acted responsibly and even regretfully in their use of other creatures, particularly when they had to take the lives of those creatures. They view themselves as part of a web of all life, a sacred whole that is woven from spiritual, social, and physical dimensions of reality.

The traditional Wanapum people engage the essence of Earth and Earth's beings, biotic and abiotic, and come to have a sense of the sacredness of existence and existents. They engage the Spirit by acknowledging creation as a divine work; by actively seeking, or being open to, divine encounters; and by striving to walk in a spiritual way in balance with the other members of the Spirit's creation. They experience spiritual realities in a special way at particular sites, which are designated as sacred, and by recognizing the special contributions of animals and plants to the Earth; they discover the spiritual powers in the land and, participating in them, live in the multiple dimensions of reality. The Wanapum have a relational consciousness that stimulates their sense of kinship with all life, that is embodied in their unwritten laws, and that is concretized in the ethical actions that demonstrate their attitudes of caring about and being responsible for the ecosystems in which they live.

Pacific region salmon extinction and its impacts on native cultures, on native and nonnative fishers, and on regional peoples' subsistence needs, is not confined to the Columba-Snake rivers system or to the Wanapum people. In Canada and Alaska, the Haida people and their neighbors are similarly affected by the salmon's diminution and disappearance.

In the Christian culture described in earlier chapters usually people have been less concerned with this life than the next; believe that humans are at the top of a natural hierarchical pyramid; and think that nature is at humans' disposal (in both senses of the word: "use" and "discard"). In the case of David Sohappy, his people, and other native peoples, it is evident that the traditional peoples' spiritual, social, and subsistence perspectives, as embodied in their historical cultural practices, clash resoundingly with the views and actions of many Euro-Americans. By contrast, the concepts of "intrinsic value" and of "natural rights" (discussed in the next chapter), when applied to members of the biotic community, do resonate well with native peoples' traditions.

"GOING EXTINCT" AND "BEING EXTINCTED"

Scientific publications and mass media journalists report periodically that a particular species is "extinct" or "going extinct." That a species has become extinct is scientifically verifiable, given sufficient data. However, *going extinct* is an ambiguous term, scientifically, historically, and contextually. Over eons, numerous species have come and gone. They have "gone extinct" or are "going extinct" as part of evolutionary processes whereby they have been unable to adapt to nature-induced changing ecosystemic circumstances: a forest or prairie fire, a flood, glaciation, climate change, an intruding species, or a mutated and now-competing species already present in the ecosystem. The species going extinct in such contexts is the one unable to counter or alter the actions of other members of the biotic community and unable to resist, adapt to, or alter abiotic changes in its habitat.

In the past century and into the current century, numerous species have gone extinct or are going extinct because of human-caused pollution, habitat destruction, hunting, genetic manipulation, or other interruptions of nature that are part of a dynamic historical-biological process. It is more fitting, therefore, to cite the "extincting" of species in these circumstances. External human factors are causing extinction, factors that do not need to occur. Humans have alternative possible modes of action—particularly when their intrusive behavior is not needed to ensure their survival. Humans as moral agents in such humankind-otherkind contexts of interaction are responsible for their actions; other species, and components of abiotic creation, are victims of human moral and ethical failings. (When humans are not on the scene, of course, other species can be victims of nonhumans' nonmoral actions or events and go extinct.)

In the Columbia River Watershed, "salmon are being extincted" is a more accurate expression than "salmon are going extinct." Hydroelectric dams and aluminum plants along the rivers, and overfishing by fish factory ships in the Pacific Ocean at locations of salmon fisheries and along salmon migratory paths, are the primary human-caused factors in the disappearance of salmon species. Salmon are being "extincted" from the seas just as, in a parallel way, political prisoners are "disappeared" from society by repressive governments; in neither case are living beings disappearing on their own; in both cases people are not taking responsibility, nor are they being held accountable, for their harmful actions.

From within the Christian tradition, the relational consciousness would be helped in its considerations of human-biokind relationships through reflection on insights provided by representative biblical narratives describing the role played by fish to provide life for the community and to provide a livelihood for fishers, who catch them to provide food needed by their community; and by relating the roles of fish and fishers to their communities' needs for water and therefore to concerns about the conservation and provision of living water (as presented in the previous chapter).

In the Hebrew Scriptures, fish are created on the fifth day in the priestly creation story, and God pronounces them "good" along with the other creatures who will inhabit the air and the waters (Genesis 1:20–23). A big fish saves Jonah's life after he has been tossed into stormy seas by sailors seeking relief from a tempest they fear will wreck their ship (Jonah 1:15–2:10). In the Christian scriptures, as food, fish are a staple that provides life for hungry multitudes (Mark 6:34–44). As a food source, they provide a livelihood for the apostles who are fishers, such as Peter, James, and John (Luke 5:1–11) who will be invited by Jesus to be "fishers of people." As food shared, fish symbolize compassion in the story of the multitudes and in Jesus' parable of the two neighbors: no one will give a snake instead of a fish to a hungry neighbor (Luke 11:11).

People who interpret these narratives for today realize that they are instructed to share the Earth commons with salmon and all fish, among other creatures, and to share with them in the blessing and regard of the Creator. In less dramatic but no less vital ways, their life is sustained or saved by their consumption of salmon; the salmon support them as subsistence food, parallel to the big fish supporting Jonah. Salmon, some Wanapum have suggested, are like bread in the Christian commemoration of the Lord's Supper: at the community salmon feast that opens the fishing season, the salmon are shared as a sacred food much the way that communion bread is shared in Christian churches (a sharing symbolized in the story of the fish and the bread distributed to the hungry multitudes: the Wanapum share fish in their ceremonies; Christians share bread in theirs). Wanapum fishers through the ages, like the apostles who were fishers in Jesus' time, provide for the subsistence needs of their family and community. Wanapum fishers and their communities have a sharing culture: those who are in need and unable to provide for themselves will be supported by their family and their neighbors in the community. Jesus, a spiritual leader, healer, and advocate of the poor who suffered because of his ministry, recognized the importance of the apostolic fishers; he suggested that they transfer their talent of providing material food for people to a new role of providing spiritual food for people. Jesus complemented their subsistence provision role with a spiritual role, both of which are social roles, in the community. David Sohappy, a spiritual leader, healer, and human rights activist on behalf of his oppressed and impoverished people, fulfilled in the Washat religion the dual fisher role envisioned by Jesus for the apostles. He provided fish for food and communal sharing, including in spiritual ceremonies; he lived his spiritual, subsistence, and social commitment, even to the point of suffering, as he taught people by his words and actions.

If there is no living water, the salmon and the people and communities who depend on them will not survive. Humankind needs living water to drink and to serve as habitat for fish who provide them with food; fish need it in their own right as their aquatic home. Pollution of rivers and other waters, and privatization or industrial or commercial diversions of water, endanger food and drink for humankind and the rest of biokind.

RELATIONAL CONSCIOUSNESS, RELATIONAL ETHICS

A relational consciousness, a mode of thinking in which one appreciates otherkind as mutually connected beings in the cosmos, is emerging in Christian environmental thought. It is the foundation for a relational ethics in which the value and rights of both human and nonhuman creation are advocated, and right conduct toward this interdependent community of being is promoted.

A relational consciousness guides a relational community (which might be a conscientious group within a larger human community) to embrace their biokind kin, while recognizing their mutual needs and interdependence in a bioregion replete with evolutionary events. Predator-prey relationships exist. Species and individuals prioritize themselves, sometimes in dramatic conflicts over food, water, shelter, territory, and an ecosystemic niche, but they also prioritize subsistence needs obtained in collaborative, rather than conflictive, associations. The relational community recognizes both competition and cooperation in nature. The relational community, imbued with a relational consciousness, concretizes its worldview in relational ethics.

With a relational consciousness as a base, the issue of salmon extinction provides an entry into ethics via an evaluation of the relative rights of distinct species in a bioregion, and in the current discussion invites consideration of a particular species, the salmon, as an indicator species of possible human-nonhuman relationships.

The diversity of salmon-human issues examined to this point, and the insights from the Wanapum and Christian traditions, provide a base for exploring questions about intrinsic value and natural rights for nonhuman species, and the resolution of human-nonhuman conflicts over ecosystem goods and ecosystem niches. All of this can be explored within the context of seeking resolutions to the salmon-versus-dams conflict in the U.S. Pacific Northwest and in the salmon-versus-overfishing conflict in the Pacific. The proposals that follow flow from relating the issues in those social contexts to the religious and ethical understandings described earlier.

On the Columbia-Snake rivers system, alternatives should be found to meet the needs of all parties involved to the greatest extent possible. The salmon have no alternative space: they need the river as their habitat. Humans need the food provided by the agricultural lands in the region, and by the salmon in the rivers and ocean; farmers need reliable transportation to get their crops to market, as the barges and railroads have been doing, and water to irrigate their fields; area residents and industrial and commercial operations need electricity; fishers need employment; religious people need to be faithful to their belief that what the Creator creates is good; all creatures need their natural rights to be expressed in laws for their protection.

Similarly, in the Pacific fisheries and in their related riparian communities, salmon conservation and restoration must be accomplished, and linked to the economic, social, and spiritual well-being of regional peoples. (Floating fish factories in the Pacific have nets that stretch for miles, do not discriminate between species of fish, and entangle and kill unwanted species indiscriminately. This is irresponsible predation and an exercise in speciesism.)

Human choices for courses of action to balance or meet the needs of people and salmon (and, by extension, the needs of humans and members of nonhuman nature) should be based on the integration of available scientific and social data, and of human spiritual insights and ethical considerations. The relational consciousness, aware of conflicting needs, seeks to integrate them one with another; relational ethics in this context is ecosocial ethics, seeking the good of the ecosystem and its species and individuals, and of the social milieu with its communities and individuals.

Ecosocial ethics, as a basis for human conduct, acknowledge that salmon and all creatures have intrinsic value, whether that is seen as flowing from their status as creations of God, from their contributions to the integrity of a holistic ecosystem, or from their unique individual or species nature; that value must be recognized and respected. Salmon and all creatures are good, and their natural rights, based on their intrinsic value, are egalitarian rights. In order to properly understand and respect the foregoing, humans need to reject anthropocentric perspectives and develop a relational consciousness as they ponder intricately interwoven interspecies interactions. In human-nonhuman conflicts, people should use their greater overall knowledge and the responsibilities of their moral agency to develop, where possible, equitable resolutions of the conflicts. They must relate to other creatures as their kin rather than as their conqueror. The Ice Harbor, Lower Monumental, Little Goose, and Lower Granite dams on the lower Snake River should be breached to promote the salmon's intrinsic value, natural rights, and species survival.

Thousands of jobs have already been lost—and many could be restored—because commercial fishers went bankrupt, taking with them canneries and related enterprises engaged in processing, marketing, and distributing fish. The issue is not flood control. The dams do not serve that purpose. The real issue is how people see themselves in relation to each other, to other species—in this case, to a disappearing species—and to their commons home, and what sort of responsibility they choose to take for these relationships.

Working people have the right to support themselves and their families with their labor. Jobs should pay a living wage, pose no threat to the worker or their loved ones, provide basic health and retirement benefits secure from company interference, have long-term security, and enhance, rather than endanger, the ecological and community settings in which they are located. Social and environmental impacts should be considered when siting or closing commercial and industrial enterprises.

The needs of regional workers and entrepreneurs do not have to conflict with the needs of the salmon. Just as the salmon make sacrifices—in their case with their lives—to meet human needs, so, too, must people make sacrifices for the common good, understood in terms both of human needs and the integrity of creation. This common good can be promoted in resolving the divisive issue of dam breaching.

The breaching of the Snake River dams cited, most scientific studies suggest, would result in increased fish populations and increased fishing-related jobs, and help to conserve one of God's creatures. However, agricultural, shipping, and industrial enterprises would need to make adjustments to the new environment, and residential and industrial energy users might be faced with higher utility rates, if they do not conserve electricity voluntarily.

The salmon must be saved for their intrinsic value and for their instrumental value. The current dams on the lower Snake River must be breached, and further dam construction must be prohibited, to effect the salmon's salvation. Factory ships along the Pacific routes of the salmon must be carefully regulated, to ensure not only salmon species' survival but ongoing employment for commercial fishers and related offshore and onshore enterprises that employ or could employ thousands of working people. Irrigation pipes should be extended down into the lowered river so that crops still might be watered. Railroad cars, which already transport most of the grain to market, should be increased in number to provide space lost when the barges will not be running. Working people from the barges should be retrained and provided jobs on the railroad. Native peoples should have permanent in-lieu fishing sites on the Columbia. State and local governments should recognize the expertise and the value of local fishers and other community members when developing species survival and restoration laws and policies. Solar and wind power, and other energy alternatives, and energy conservation, should replace the hydroelectric power currently generated by the breached dams. In Canada and in the United States, adjacency should be a principal factor in the allocation of fishing rights, so that local communities' subsistence needs and economic well-being could be maintained. Fisheries should be comanaged by government entities—including native peoples' governments—and local citizen organizations. Corporate power and economic hegemony should be curtailed.

The sacrifices people would have to make should be ameliorated by government (federal, state, and tribal) action. In brief, this action might include continued monitoring of and limitations on salmon catches, to enhance species survival; low-interest loans for extension of agricultural pipes to lowered river levels, and for pumps to bring the water to irrigation lines; subsidies to farmers to ship their goods by rail and truck to keep these shipping rates comparable to current barge rates; conservation of energy by governmental, commercial, industrial, and residential customers; low-interest loans to utility companies and cooperatives to explore and implement alternative energy sources, such as wind power and solar collectors and cells (the construction and operation of such sites could provide rural communities with jobs, and placement of windmills and solar collectors on farms would increase agricultural income); a moderate reduction of ocean fishing for salmon for a decade, to promote salmon reproduction and recovery of threatened and endangered species; riparian habitat enhancements; granting greater decision-making authority to joint committees of community stakeholders educated about scientific, social, and ethical implications of diverse courses of action; ongoing objective scientific and sociological studies; development of alternative employment possibilities; designation of the Hanford Reach area as a Wild and Scenic River; and cleanup of the extensive pollution of the Hanford Nuclear Reservation. These are not the only possible remedies for overcoming conflict and saving salmon, jobs, and rural communities, but they can serve as starting points for community discussion and action.

The intrinsic and instrumental values of salmon species are being debated still in the Columbia River Basin—while salmon species are being extincted. Where natural waterfalls exist, people are thrilled by the drama of salmon hurtling upward to return to their birthplace to spawn. People enjoy satisfying their hunger with a variety of salmon-centered meals. Native peoples have a spiritual relationship with salmon, and in special community feasts, they share together the gift of the salmon's life. Peoples of diverse ethnicities and cultures have earned their livelihood through salmon-based enterprises. Despite the debates and despite all of these peoples' regard for salmon, extinction continues. People with relational commitments should be prompted to participate in projects to conserve salmon populations.

The breaching of the four dams, and fisheries policies and practices based on the centuries-old experience of local Wanapum fishers and residents of other area communities, would be practical steps to take to save the salmon from extinction. They would be symbolic and practical steps illustrating human regard for other creatures and for creation. They would be revelatory of a newly developing relational community consciousness as humans acknowledge the intrinsic value of salmon as creatures of Earth and creations of a loving Spirit, as well as their instrumental value to meet human needs. This relational consciousness concretely expressed would promote social justice—particularly restorative justice and distributive justice, in the context of ecojustice—and help strengthen the strands of the web of the biotic community and safeguard its Earth home. Saving salmon as a representative species means, to a great extent, stimulating human consciousness of the intrinsic value of all species and abiotic nature, and catalyzing human conscience to translate that into committed efforts to benefit Earth and biokind.

III

COMMUNITY

In the Earth commons, species and individuals in the biotic community have collaborative and competitive relationships and depend on abiotic nature for survival. All creatures have intrinsic value, and some creatures come to have instrumental value in another creature's perspective, particularly in predator-prey relationships. Intrinsic value is acknowledged and accepted, not assigned; it inheres in a creature by virtue of its material existence. All of nature, not solely humankind, has natural rights, which are best maintained when codified into laws. A relational consciousness perceives intrinsic values and natural rights; distinguishes between harm that results from human injustice, and harm that results from natural catastrophes; and formulates projects to promote the commons good and the common good, through an equitable sharing of commons goods and common goods.

· 7 ·

Nature's Natural Rights

$\mathcal{T}$he sacramental commons is visible today in few places globally. It will be more evident when Christians, who comprise the majority population in the nations contributing most to global warming, global pollution, and global privatization of Earth's land and goods, *reappropriate* the spiritual, social, and subsistence dimensions of their biblical and historical traditions; *reflect* on them in the light of twenty-first-century realities; and *respond* to the needs of Earth and of the biotic community as a whole. Within that community of life, people must be especially attentive to meeting the needs of poor people victimized by racism, sexism, and oppressive economic and political structures, and the needs of endangered species brought almost to extinction by commercial and industrial processes and products and by the political policies that support them. Christians' fulfillment of their responsibilities in creation can stimulate a greater sense in humanity as a whole of its role in creation, and catalyze humankind's interrelated integration in the biotic community, care for the Earth commons, and efforts to ensure that commons goods are distributed for the common good. In order to promote and protect a sacramental commons, Christians will have to experience a change of consciousness from an anthropocentric domination of nature to a relational interdependence with creation, and act accordingly. They will have to acknowledge the intrinsic value of creation and respect the natural rights of nature.

CHRISTIAN TRANSITIONS

Since the time of early Christianity, anthropocentrism has dominated Christian perspectives about nature, Earth, and the extended universe. In the anthropocentric view, "man" is the center of creation in several ways. "He" was the primary focus of God's creativity, and not only above all other creatures (including women) in God's concern and in Earth's perceived hierarchy

117

of creatures but also the center of the universe—all the heavenly bodies revolved around "his" planet and therefore around "him" as Earth's central being. Moreover, God had become "Man" in the person of Jesus, thereby elevating not only the status of "man" as a species but also "man" as male, and had brought salvation and eternal life to humans alone. In the patriarchal social, religious, and intellectual context of Christianity, "man" held the principal political positions, religious leadership roles, rights to property ownership, and family authority. Sacred and secular laws maintained this privileged male position.

Beginning in the sixteenth century, the myths about the preeminence of man-ness and maleness began to be challenged, particularly by scientific findings. Nicolaus Copernicus (1473–1543) and Galileo Galilei (1564–1642) came on the scene and announced that not only was Earth not the center of a cosmic system, but it was not even the center of a local part of the universe; Earth was part of neither a geocentric universe nor even a geocentric local region of the universe; Earth was but one of several planets in a heliocentric solar system within a vast universe. Johannes Kepler (1571–1630) added that the perfect circular orbits that Aristotle, Copernicus, and Galileo described because they believed them to be elegant and appropriate for heavenly bodies, were not accurate scientifically; actually, the planets followed elliptical orbits around the sun. Charles Darwin (1809–1882) displaced humans farther from their Western-perceived central position in creation and the universe with his theory of evolution, a process of natural selection rather than individual creature creation. Georges Lemaître (1894–1966), a Belgian priest and astrophysicist, in 1927 proposed a theory about a dynamic universe that complemented Darwin's theory of evolving biota: he suggested that the universe originated in a singular explosion. Initially, Lemaître's idea was ridiculed as the "Big Bang theory"—the name by which it is referred to most often today, but now with respect. As a result of these scientific developments, the ideological male-centered universe became reduced to an orbiting planet (within an immense, expanding universe), inhabited by human males and females living in a biotic community whose member species had evolved over billions of years.

In the United States meanwhile, the dominant culture and race were being confronted by efforts to promote social justice for all peoples. The abolitionist movement, Harriet Tubman's Underground Railroad, and the Civil War led to the abolition of slavery. Consequently, some civil rights for African Americans were codified in constitutional amendments (which were to be extended later due to the efforts of the martyred Malcolm X and Martin Luther King Jr., among others). Activist women suffragettes such as Lucretia Mott, Elizabeth Cady Stanton, Susan B. Anthony, and Sojourner Truth (who represented both African American and women's struggles for justice) catalyzed complementary changes in the status and roles of women. Their efforts would later be supplemented by the development of feminist, woman-ist, and *mujerista* theologies. Then social activists and deep ecology advocates raised further questions about androcentric, anthropocentric, and ethnocen-tric ideas and practices.

The results of these philosophical and political changes were that oppressive social conditions and ideological presuppositions were ameliorated or even eliminated in some cultures. Respect for Earth and the biotic com-munity, and concrete efforts to effect an equitable distribution of Earth com-mons goods (in both their original state and as materials in products resulting from human work) to meet human needs, began to be more evident in reli-gious and humanist contexts. Within some religious traditions, scholars and leaders came to respect other faith commitments, and shifted away from belief in the Spirit's engagement in creation exclusively with humanity, a per-spective which had reserved divine communication to one tradition, one sacred book, one species, and a few tradition-limited and -limiting individuals.

As a result of all of these transitions in thought and politics, "man," and more specifically (in terms of social and environmental control) "white Chris-tian man," experienced the trauma of the loss of biological, familial, species, psychological, and spiritual preeminence and dominance.

The four basic Christian cultural perspectives that developed through these centuries with regard to the human species' status, position, and role in creation were *domination, dominion, stewardship*, and *relation*.

The Latin roots of *domination* and *dominion* mean "lord" or "property." *Domination* is the excessive use of power to control lives, social structures, and events in order to benefit unjustly inordinate individual, family, group, nation, or species desires. The domination attitude toward creation expressed in religion, politics, economics, and science asserts that people have a sover-eign right to control and use Earth, and Earth's goods and creatures, as they see fit. *Dominion* is the responsible, privileged exercise of authority over lives or land, so that they might serve the purposes that the one with authority understands them to have. In the dominion worldview, people essentially believe that the world is created for humans. People are to be responsible lords over a creation which has been developed for them and is oriented toward them. In much the manner of the lord of the manor, people are to govern their Earth domain judiciously and fairly.

Stewardship means that humans responsibly take secondary charge of Earth, Earth's goods, Earth's creatures, or human goods fashioned from Earth or Earth's goods, on behalf of and in trust from the Spirit, their pri-mary owner. People are God's stewards, and as "images of God" they care for and manage Earth and living creatures. The term has been viewed as positive, overall, in that it reminds people that Earth and Earth's goods are the creation of God, to whom belong Earth and all the goods or natural capital of Earth. The Creator Spirit regards these as good and intends them to be used to meet the needs of all creatures, for whom the Spirit is solicitous—as expressed in biblical texts such as Job 38–41 (where God provides food for birds and animals) and Matthew 6:26–30 (where Jesus states that God cares for birds, lilies, and people).

The stewardship understanding has been a corrective against those who regard "private property" as an absolute right, and Earth's goods as private benefits for personal or corporate profit. Stewardship has fostered a sense of intergenerational responsibility, too. However, despite its utility in fostering some care for creation, at its core "stewardship" is still an anthropocentric concept with cultural and practical shortcomings. While it might safeguard Earth and Earth's creatures and abiotic benefits from exploitation in some cases, it retains humans in a hierarchical managerial role over lesser living creatures and abiotic components of Earth. Eventually, some people might suggest that human management means primarily to safeguard those aspects of creation that have instrumental value for humans, although human management could come to be animated by recognition of creation's intrinsic value, and respect for all creatures. Stewardship retains a hierarchical structure, nonetheless: God > humans > nature. In the hierarchy, humans are closer to God and serve as a bridge between God and nature. Humans mediate God to nature; nature does not mediate God to humans. The steward is viewed as having been placed over nature by divine appointment (according to the stewards' self-description and self-affirmation of their role, which includes some element of self-interest), with responsibility for or control of nature; has a higher status than other creatures in the natural world; and has from all of this a preeminent and controlling role in creation. Such human hubris can inhibit human interrelatedness with creation. Members of stewardship traditions might not explore the depths of their connectedness to all creation, and become conscious of their relatedness to all creatures, both physically (e.g., DNA commonalities) and spiritually (sharing in common in the immanent presence of the solicitous and creating Spirit).

Relation is an attitude of reciprocal responsibility for Earth, Earth's goods, Earth's creatures, and Earth's places, in a context of human species' engagement with and interdependence among other Earth beings. In the relation perspective, people see themselves as one part of a dynamic biotic community, living in ecological systems where competition and collaboration interdependently characterize the interaction of species, and where the immanent presence of the creating Spirit permeates all being. In the relation perspective, nature mediates God to humans. A relational consciousness, a way of thinking in which one appreciates all biokind as mutually connected beings in the cosmos, guides participation in a relational community and is the foundation for relational ethics in which the value and rights of both human and nonhuman creation are advocated, and right conduct toward this interdependent community of being is promoted. The relation perspective reveals a *creatiocentric consciousness*. This creation-centered understanding expresses a renewed traditional perspective for humankind. Within this perspective, people recognize an integral relationship among the Spirit, humankind, and all biota. Human-divine engagement positively affects human-nature relationships. Humans mediate the Spirit to nature. Similarly, the Spirit's immanence is mediated by nature to humans. Humankind will relate positively to nature, recognizing both its intrinsic value and its spiritual instrumental value as a revelation of divine Being and Becoming. In addition to the Spirit's own relationship to other-than-human creatures, there are two other flows of Creator-creation engagement: God > humankind > nature; God > nature > humankind.

Despite new religious understandings, scientific and sociological theories and data, and social thinking and activism (which can inspire a sense of wonder about the intricacies of the universe, and a belief in and practice of intrahuman and interspecies egalitarianism), within Christian religious thought some still describe "man" and "humans" as the focal point of creation and of the Spirit's solicitude. Christian belief is professed to be the exclusive and excluding requirement for salvation; nationalism, ethnocentrism, capitalism, and political hegemony are allied to it. Androcentric domination continues to be exercised by a few, especially in the United States and other Western nations and in countries that they control or unduly influence.

As a consequence, Earth has continued to be seen by many Christians as a planet to be dominated and exploited, and as a temporary place of trial and suffering which serves as a prelude to the real reason for humans' creation: an afterlife (blessed or damned) in a world to come. People believe that the Creator intended nonhuman creation to serve humans; actually, this is a form of idolatry: humans are as gods served by the created world. The goods of Earth continue to be designated "resources" to be extracted and used primarily for human benefit. Anthropocentrism still finds its cultural expression in pronouncements and practices that foster human domination or dominion over the rest of the created world.

By contrast, when a relational consciousness permeates the community, humans affirm their unique place in creation as the reflective consciousness of Earth as a whole; acknowledge their kinship with all life on Earth because they share genes in common, and with nonliving creation because of their common origin in the transcendent Spirit's creative power and in the primordial explosion; and appreciate their common, intimate engagement with the immanent creating Spirit.

INTRINSIC VALUE AND
INSTRUMENTAL VALUE

The universe reveals the divine origin and assignment of, and the divine ordering of and appreciation for, all being and beings. Intrinsic value is imparted by the Creator of the universe, a cosmos-chaos ever forming from the interplay of law and chance, of necessary and contingent events.

Intrinsic value is a being's inherent worth in itself. It is self-regard or self-worth, whether or not a creature is self-conscious. Living creatures express this sense of self-worth when they deliberately or instinctively strive to survive in perilous circumstances; when they seek food, water, and shelter in the ordinary course of living; and, for humankind, when people work to improve their personal, familial, or professional well-being. Even when a creature is unaware of its intrinsic value it is still inherent in them by virtue of their existence. Other, conscious beings might acknowledge it to be present in them, a valuation based on their membership in the evolving biotic community or, for those with a theistic perspective, because they are the creation and the mediation of divine being. Intrinsic value, then, is not only asserted by or acknowledged in oneself (by oneself or another); it can be discerned and accepted (by oneself or another).

A creature's *instrumental value* is its worth to another creature. It is the regard of external beings for a particular benefit that a being would provide for them. Both conscious and not-conscious beings can have instrumental value. Both conscious and not-conscious beings can appreciate or benefit from the instrumental value of another being, and be aware or unaware that they are experiencing that benefit. (A tree, for example, had it the consciousness to do so, would "regard" a river or rainfall as instrumental to its survival as its roots absorb water's nourishment.) Instrumental value is always discerned and assigned, usually by another being (sometimes one might recognize, even if only instinctually or intuitively, one's value to another: e.g., a construction worker to a suburban developer or to a construction site; an elk to a wolf pack on the hunt). Intrinsic value is internally active and adhering in an independent subject because of the subject's be-ing. Instrumental value is externally assigned, acquired by an objectified subject from another subject, in a particular place or time. Instrumental value can be based on relational interdependence within the ecosystem commons. Water has instrumental value to a salmon. A salmon has instrumental value to eagles, bears, and humans.

Humans have individual and species biases, and a tendency in some cultures to consider all beings' existence to be anthropically designed (by divine intention) or anthropically oriented (because of increasing complexification). Therefore, humans in the Earth commons are not appropriate judges or grantors of intrinsic value; this value exists a priori in the being ("thing") observed. Humans accept it and respect it in other species, in their individual members, and in abiotic Earth. Humans acknowledge intrinsic value in others but assert it for themselves. Humans are able, through scientific study, to determine instrumental relationships in an ecosystem. Such relationships do not diminish the intrinsic value of the beings studied and classified, even when humans judge a living or nonliving being to have instrumental value for themselves. Intrinsic value and instrumental value coexist, cohere, and inhere in a being. To some extent, all aspects and entities of creation have instrumental value, based on such divergent roles as their contributions to an ecosystem or their integrality in cosmic dynamics.

Scientific reductionists and religious fundamentalists alike—and people whose perspective lies somewhere in between—can conclude that creatures have intrinsic value. For the former, it would follow from their research findings on the complexity and uniqueness of species. For the latter, it would follow from their belief that God created all species (directly or indirectly), and so species and their individual members must have some inherent value as God's creatures. Scientists and fundamentalists alike are aware of the instrumental value of creatures: for the integrated and interdependent role they have in the biosphere, for the goods they provide for humans, or for their utility to each other.

A "detached" observer passing over or journeying throughout Earth could recognize interrelated, interdependent, and integrated good and valuable beings who have intrinsic value specifically as members of the Earth commons (e.g., a spring whose crystal waters flow into a river that nourishes all life) or more generally as component entities of the universe (e.g., humans as the reflective consciousness of a local manifestation of cosmos-chaos-cosmos dynamics).

The *intrinsic value* of one creature is changed to *instrumental value* in the perspective of another creature whose survival need for prey takes precedence, in the view of that predatory creature, in a specific situation and locale for a specific historical moment. A predator might volitionally or instinctually act to meet its subsistence needs and thereby prioritize and preserve its own intrinsic value. An individual salmon, for example, has intrinsic value which endures while it is in its protective habitat; in a more vulnerable locale, in the eyes of a member of another species—a grizzly bear, a golden eagle, or a human fisher, for example—it would be viewed as having instrumental value. Similarly, huckleberries with their own intrinsic value would come to have instrumental value for a grizzly bear or a human fisher in the same ecosystem; the human fisher might come to have instrumental value for the same bear, who otherwise might seek nutrition from the fish or the berries. Competition might arise over such conflicts of interest: between rival members of a single species over territory, between different species over an ecosystem niche, or between individual representatives of different species over a specific space or role in an ecosystem. Each conscious creature regards its own intrinsic value and natural rights, essential to its survival, as primary in those respective circumstances, even if it lacks the intellectual capacity to express its needs in ethical or moral terms.

Species have instrumental value (and intrinsic value) in creation's ecosystem, as long as they find and fulfill a needed niche. Individuals ordinarily would be less essential or instrumental. Something that is needed for the "working of the universe," or the "integrity of the ecosystem," does not thereby have solely *instrumental* (utility) value, and no *intrinsic* value. It has both. Creatures simultaneously have intrinsic and instrumental value in creation.

Species and their individual members become extinct when they no longer have instrumental value in fulfilling a particular niche among evolving forms of life in an ecosystem, unless (as with humans) they are able sufficiently to control their environs rather than be limited by them. Each species is good in itself and during its life serves the common good, the commons good, and overall biotic evolution. It has a role in evolution and on Earth during its particular time and place(s) of existence.

Individual intrinsic value is related to species intrinsic value and environmental intrinsic value. Intrinsic values are autonomous, not anthropogenic; they are present whether or not humans are present to acknowledge them, whether or not humans acknowledge them when humans are present, and whether or not humans think that they assign them. Places, too, have intrinsic value as creations of divine being, as the locus of divine immanence, or as parts of the integrated Earth commons. When the force of a strong wind causes a tree to fall in a forest, the sound of its impact occurs, even if no humans hear it, and the wind's invisibility makes it no less real; when a forest burns because of a lightning strike, trees burn even if no humans see them afire. Intrinsic value and natural rights should not be limited anthropocentrically to those with moral consciousness and moral agency, just as natural realities are not limited anthropocentrically to human aural or visual perception. The deer that jumps in fright at the sound of the tree falling, or that flees from the forest fire, reacts to real events even without thinking words like *noise* or *fire*, and if its escape path takes it through a nearby farmer's fields, it retains its intrinsic value and is not morally or legally culpable for crop destruction.

Not every individual, or even their species, has solely an instrumental value in a bioregion. Individual members of a species retain their intrinsic value until their life ends. Some individuals might not subjectively and consciously experience a change in value until they die from sickness or old age, and they come to have instrumental value as food. Consider an elk in a forest. Not every individual elk is killed to provide food, and not all elk reproduce. Ecosystemic integrity requires that some be killed by predators for survival consumption and that others have offspring. Not every species has instrumental value on a continuing basis, since species do become extinct. All living beings at the end of their life have instrumental value as carrion or otherwise as nutrients that provide a source of biotic survival for others (unless their remains are infused with chemicals and sealed in a coffin).

NATURAL LAWS IN NATURE

A "natural law" is a law inherent in nature. It might be discovered by a person individually or by a people collectively. An individual human person within a community (or communities), in or for a specific situation, who seeks to discern the natural law(s) bearing on the situation, uses their intellect, traditions (for the Christian: biblical and historical), and the exigencies of the situation itself. The extent of an act's (un)ethical character is based on the volitional freedom, intentionality, and competence of the reasoning subject; the subject's capacity to reflect on possible and available courses of action; the inherent character of the act; application of previously learned principles; and the potential and actual consequences of individual or communal courses of action.

Natural law does not evolve; people's understandings of it and of its principles or rules for natural conduct do change sometimes as new information (e.g., scientific, social scientific, or spiritual) comes to light. Human awareness and understanding of the extent and complexities of natural laws do evolve. Native peoples' elders teach their people to follow the natural laws "that were given to us by the Creator." It is an intergenerational "us" to which they refer, including distant ancestors, present people, and descendants yet to come.

The interaction between natural laws and human perceptions of what is "natural" in nature in general and for the human species in particular can lead to conflicts between people who respectively view contradictory courses of action as "natural." Each decides that their perspective is "truth," based on the Bible or their specific tradition. An inherent weakness of many natural law theories and systems is that their proponents tend to freeze for all time the understandings and principles developed in one particular time period, and within one particular culture (e.g., among the ancient Israelites of three millennia ago or from medieval Christianity less than a millennium ago; consider, for example, current discussions of whether homosexuality is inherently a "sin" or is "natural" to humanity or for individuals within humanity). Slavery was considered in past ages to be "natural" (Aristotle) or biblically endorsed (Colossians); women's biological and intellectual "inferiority" and subordinate familial and social position were considered "natural" or affirmed by "tradition." Over time, and after much suffering, these misanthropic and misogynic attitudes have, among individuals and in some cultures, been altered or eliminated, and practices and laws based on them have been diminished to some extent, although not entirely.

What might be helpful, here, is a post-postmodernist perspective. Considerations in that regard would be that first, some but not all norms concretize enduring values and truth, not all are merely expressions of cultural biases or of the dominant and dominating voices of a place and time; second, not all norms should be discarded as ephemeral and culture limited, nor should all situational suggestions for appropriate conduct be affirmed because "my opinion is as good as yours," or "that's just how you see things" (the latter is, of course, important to recognize and assert when "opinions" are being expressed—this is not helpful, though, when scientific or historical data are under discussion); and third, data or ethical principles suggesting right conduct are not to be dismissed in a new absolute situational ideology that declares emphatically and absolutely that "there are no absolutes" (scientific theories, e.g., while not asserting an "absolute" claim to truth, do come to have over time a substantial body of knowledge to support them, as does simple arithmetic; current debates over creationism versus evolution occur because creationists, while claiming absolute truth for their "scientific" perspective based on a religious text, ridicule the theory of evolution as "just a theory").

A difficulty in all of these discussions is the attempt to absolutize perspectives into a single manifestation of the "natural," rather than acknowledge that it might be possible for different individuals to have "natural" (according to *their* "nature") orientations or modes of behavior that contradict each other, one of which is accepted within and the other rejected by, the bearers of a current "norm" in a culture or religion. Gradually, over time, where people and peoples have the humility and courage to acknowledge that some of their "principles" are culturally based and time limited, they are able to accept that distinct modes of behavior, none of which are harmful to the common good (specially or broadly conceived), might be natural to those embodying and actuating them.

Thomas Aquinas taught that all people can discover the natural law through the use of reason, without revelation. Some scholars, limited by their religious parameters, teach that only the Bible teaches truth and ethical principles and, more important, that only the Bible presents doctrines of faith needed for "salvation" in a world to come. People who accept that there are natural laws in nature and acknowledge simultaneously that while these laws do not change, people's understanding of what they are might change, should strive to discover or formulate natural rights that flow from natural laws and also natural laws that flow from natural rights. Such developments should occur without freezing historically the ideas, laws, theories, and ethical principles of one time and place. When "natural laws" are discerned, then "natural rights" to promote or realize compliance with those laws of nature should be legislated; when "natural rights" are situationally or theoretically developed, then laws based on nature should be developed and codified to ensure those rights.

When people are conscious of the intrinsic value of the whole, they will come to recognize their value as part of the whole. The biophysical world as a whole is the place of necessary interdependent, instrumental activity of integrated, intrinsically valued beings, sometimes influenced by contingent events. Similarly, the scientific world is the locus of theories, some of which will be altered or discarded over time; and the religious world is the locus of doctrines, norms, and rituals—some of which are core and will be retained, others of which are peripheral (even if not so understood initially or over an extended period of time) and will be modified or superseded.

Humankind can recognize, and formalize in law, the right to life of all biokind—while bearing in mind at the same time the exigencies of survival for all creatures, including themselves, in an evolutionary setting with limited space, in which predators need to consume prey. While intrinsic value and natural rights should be acknowledged for all creatures, a "right to life" cannot rationally be absolutized for all members of the biotic community. People who restrain predators from consuming prey whose rights have been absolutized would, of course, jeopardize an equivalent absolute right to life of predators who need to consume their prey; a salmon's absolute right to life would negate an eagle's right to life where the eagle depends on the availability and accessibility of salmon to be its food. The absurdity would be eliminated if every creature were acknowledged to have a right to life based on both its intrinsic value and its instrumental value in creation as a whole and in the specific ecosystem of which it is a part. In specific circumstances, a creature would prioritize its own intrinsic value over another's, to the extent possible.

The fact that the biotic community needs an ample species gene pool, diversification, and even complexification to survive is another argument against absolutizing the right to life of particular species or individuals. In human communities, of course, people's and peoples' rights to life and to other human rights should not be denied on this account by despots or other sociopaths. The Holocaust, genocide as "ethnic cleansing" or under another name, massacres, the cavalier dismissal of human rights by designating civilian deaths as "collateral damage" during warfare or by advocating, authorizing, or practicing torture: all demonstrate why a right to life and personal integrity should be promoted as human rights.

If lives did not end, then evolution, the passage of generations, and the equitable distribution of Earth's goods would not be possible. Every creature has an initial and continuing right to life (which could extend over its entire natural life span), based on its intrinsic value in creation as a whole and in the specific ecosystem of which it is a part. The right to life could be challenged and denied by another individual creature (or, in extremely rare circumstances, a species, such as a smallpox virus) if it is perceived as a threat by that creature or has some instrumental value for the survival or well-being of that creature or a member of another species who is prioritizing its own survival interests. The tension between natural rights and natural realities, and the balancing of values and rights, are part of the competition and collaboration that are characteristic of life in an evolutionary world. As sometimes happens in moments of moral decision making by responsible humans, when conflicting principles have to be prioritized in specific contexts, one value or right supersedes another.

BIOTIC EGALITARIANISM

All creatures, including humans, should exist in egalitarian relationships. All have unique and complementary capacities, though not, of course, on the same intellectual or moral plane. Some, including humans, are predators. But since humans alone have moral agency, they alone have the capacity to be *responsible predators*—thoughtful, conscientious, taking and using only what they need, compassionate, and trying to conserve creatures' lives or Earth's abiotic goods—rather than *reckless predators*—thoughtless, irresponsible, driven by wants more than needs, wasteful of commons goods, callous, and without regard for the well-being of biota. The conduct of a wolf pack in nature is instructive here. Ordinarily, wolves are social and familial among themselves, and responsible predators in their predation. However, a rare pack aberration occurs sometimes. Near Yellowstone National Park a few years ago, where wolves have been reintroduced to restore the balance of the ecosystem, a wolf pack ran wild among a flock of sheep, killing far more than they needed for food at that moment or in the foreseeable future. A collective blood lust turned these responsible predators into reckless predators. The pack was found and its members were killed so that there would not be a recurrence of the event. While wolves do not have moral agency, they were held accountable for the slaughter of the sheep, not because of the flock's intrinsic value or natural rights but because of their value as property to the sheep rancher.

The consideration of natural rights—moral and legal—for nonhuman nature raises the issue of whether species should have equal rights or egalitarian rights. Humans might acknowledge that all creatures are equal in essential ways since they have intrinsic value and have emerged from the creativity and power of the Spirit of the universe, who regards them as "very good." *Equality* means that rights should be the same for all beings; *egalitarian* means beings have rights that are equivalent. In either case, rights (e.g., the rights to life or shelter) might be lost or taken away. In real bioregional contexts, an essentially equal relationship, contextualized in creatures' competition and collaboration in an interwoven web of life in a particular habitat, might shift to an egalitarian relationship. Two creatures could not occupy the exact same niche at the same time, but they might be able to live in balance in equivalent niches. The egalitarian relationship might evolve into a confrontational one because of changing occupants or conditions of the ecosystem, or because one species came to view another instrumentally.

Nonhuman creatures within biokind could exist in egalitarian relationships with humans. They, too, have unique capacities, complementary to those of humans, though not, of course, on the same intellectual or moral plane. Humans are predators. Humans also have the moral consciousness to carefully exercise predation, limiting it to their needs out of respect for other creatures and the ecological integrity of a bioregion, or at least because of their own self-interest (e.g., if all the salmon are extincted today, a source of food and livelihood would be eliminated from the future). If humans (individually or as particular communities or as a species) do not live up to their moral capabilities and are reckless predators, then other species might rightfully react against them because of perceptions of the harm they are doing or might do to other creatures or to the ecosystem.

An interesting question here would be whether or not a nonhuman species that in a particular ecosystem did more good for, or less harm to, creation should displace the human species at the top of the moral significance grading scale in this context. This might be particularly true if the other species had greater operative respect (even if not consciously) or at least neutral regard for other fauna, more acceptable motives for predation, and a better ecosystem "fit" with a more sustainable niche; and the humans there were irresponsible and were harming the ecosystem's abiotic setting and its living inhabitants, acting as reckless predators. Humans, although they have the scientific knowledge, technology, and tools to adapt almost any Earth context to themselves, rather than or in addition to adapting themselves to it, do not thereby have the right to do so other than primarily to satisfy human spiritual, social, and subsistence needs, or to elevate the well-being of the community as a whole, using appropriate technologies and sustainable rates of consumption of commons goods and common goods.

If humans, who are respectful, morally responsible predators in theory, become reckless, immoral, irresponsible predators in fact, then humans such as hikers in a forest might be treated as threats by those members of biokind who have the physical capability (e.g., teeth and claws) and assertiveness to respond fiercely and protectively in their territory. The nonhuman individuals and species would be acting defensively, even if aggressively, to thwart actual or perceived threats to their survival. This might result in harm to a responsible, respectful, and peaceful hiker or family intruding innocently and amiably in a place where other humans have intruded arrogantly; the bear does not distinguish personality types of individuals or human individuals from the human species.

People who understand that other creatures have equitable intrinsic value still would have a moral, social, and psychological preference for their own species. Humans' concern for human needs and rights is a biological, psychological, or social preference—or all of these, depending on the context. This perspective is not *speciesism*, a belief in one's own species' preeminence and an attitude of dominance over other species, leading to careless or intentional harm against other species. It is a natural impulse to prefer one's own species' survival vis-à-vis that of other species. Concern for one's own species is an appropriate moral preference; speciesism is an inappropriate immoral preference. Speciesism suggests dominance over another, not concern and respect for the other; it engenders immoral practices, intentional or unintentional. The status ranking of other species does not have to be regarded as speciesism. All species have a right to moral consideration, even if they are believed to be of differing moral significance (some people would not accept this and would advocate egalitarian moral significance). The moral consideration and ranking of other creatures is not speciesism. All species (even those without advanced intellectual capabilities or moral agency) favor their own kind and might be either neutral toward other members of biokind or competitors with or predators on them, and act accordingly. *Racism* means the attitude and practice of racial domination, *sexism* means gender domination, and *speciesism* means species domination; these are all immoral preferences that promote immoral acts. Just as a bear would not be accused of "species-ism" (recognizing, of course, that bears would not think about the term) when killing and eating a salmon or when protecting its territory from intrusions that threaten its own or its species' survival, neither should a human be so accused for seeking to preserve his or her own life or the lives of other members of the human community or species.

In an integrated and interrelated ecosystemic whole, biological reality and a sense of ecojustice should be integrated by humans with their faith perspectives and the sociological exigencies of their species, communities, and individuals. It is not species self-hatred for humans to acknowledge the contributions and benefits from other species—for example, trees cleanse the air and provide oxygen for all life—just as it is not unpatriotic to acknowledge that a nation other than one's own is more just and does more for the human community and for human cultural history. This is not meant to be a justification of the misanthropy of some members of groups such as EarthFirst! who question whether humans contribute anything to Earth, and assert that nothing would be lost if humans were to disappear. Rather, it means that humans, who have filled some niche(s) in evolution over millennia, should strive to be creation's integrating and caring consciousness, and live up to their own inherent creation-affirming capabilities in the context of meeting their needs in balance with others' needs.

NATURAL RIGHTS FOR NATURE

"Natural" rights are held by all of nature. Earth in its intricate interplay of energies, elements, entities, and events, and the biotic community in all its diverse and complex forms, share in these rights. All abiotic and biotic natural beings should have ongoing natural rights in nature to conserve their natural condition. On a planet with an evolutionary tree of life, that natural state includes collaborative and competitive interdependent relationships within the biotic community. Primary natural rights reside in the biotic community; secondary natural rights are recognized for abiotic nature.

Currently, the term *natural rights* is used anthropocentrically. It is reserved exclusively for human rights, particularly human political rights. (Thomas Paine did write, however, that the right to the necessities of life is a "natural right" for animate beings, thereby providing an opening toward recognizing natural rights for all living creatures, all of whom need and seek a suitable habitat and necessary nourishment.) Reserving "natural rights" solely for humankind is extreme anthropocentrism. It expresses the assumption that the human embodies to a greater extent than any other single creature, and more than all nonhuman creation combined, what is "natural." It thereby heightens the anthropocentrism that already has been enhanced by scientific and religious sentiments that humans are at the peak of creation by evolutionary chance or evolutionary inevitability, or by divine choice and design. For some, this means that all other creatures and Earth's goods belong primarily to humans for their use (and abuse), and can be exploited unconditionally to meet human needs and even human wants.

The anthropocentric position that "rights" pertain exclusively or primarily to humans is based on a circular reasoning. Humans define "rights" to refer solely to themselves, then intellectually justify reserving "natural rights" only for themselves, and finally legislate natural rights that apply only to their own species, since only humans have rights. Such "natural rights" are in actuality "human natural rights," a subset of "biotic natural rights." In order for the common good to be promoted and the value of living beings to be acknowledged, "natural rights" should be recognized for all nature.

The "natural rights" focus in philosophy and political science is at heart a focus on human "personal integrity rights" (individual human *in se*) or "civil rights" (individual human as citizen with social rights) or "human rights" (humans aggregated as a species, global organism, or specific member of the biotic community). Humans are not objectively outside nature, able to determine objectively (without bias and without a stake in the outcome) who or what has "natural" rights. Definitions of rights have been formulated in such ways (for example, the requirement of "moral agency" in philosophy, or "self-consciousness" in science) that only humans can be covered by them or conform themselves to a mutuality-based reciprocal observance of them. This remains the case even though scientific experiments have demonstrated, among other things, that not-human primates can experience social pressure and feel ashamed for not sharing food with the rest of their community, and that dolphins have a reflective consciousness. Sometimes people use theology, based on the biblical phrasing that humans are created in the "image of God," to assert human status and power over a divinely ordained hierarchically stratified nature, and to state that the universe is created for, or oriented toward, or designed to lead inevitably to humans. Other people with equal fervor have advocated human supremacy on the basis of human cerebral development and imagination that have enabled their hegemony within the biotic community; or on philosophies abstracted from real-life engagement with nature in historical moments, concrete places, and ongoing relationships.

Humans define the rights that safeguard human individual and social existence in human societies, in relation to other species, and on Earth as planet; codify those rights into laws; use laws to govern their relations with each other, other species, and Earth; and deny those rights and the protection of those laws to other living beings and to Earth. A strong attitude of anthropocentrism is attached to the claim that such definitions of rights and promulgation of laws are based on rational, objective reasoning and moral or ethical considerations, rather than acknowledge their human self-serving and species-serving origins, development, character, and impacts.

It is ironic that while religion and theology often have been accused (rightly) of anthropocentrism, philosophy (when it restricts definitions of "natural rights" only to humans) and science (when it places humans atop a pyramid of life because of their complexity within the biotic community, or their control over abiotic and biotic existents) display a marked anthropocentrism as well, sometimes even while condemning the trait as expressed in religious beliefs or practices.

It might be argued that *value* is assigned by humans, and that *rights* require moral agency and a political system to be acknowledged and enforced. But where a person or culture believes that the Spirit creates the universe, or that the universe is unfolding, in an interaction of cosmic laws, autopoiesis, and contingent events, they can accept the divine affirmation in Genesis that all creation is "very good" or a scientific discernment of the universe's necessary diversity and complexity, and decide that biota beyond humankind, and their abiotic habitat, have intrinsic value and natural rights. In this way, the common good of each and all might be served.

People who argue that only those with "moral agency" should have rights declare that rights are embedded in reciprocity. However, the conservation and restoration of the natural world will be difficult to promote if humans asserting absolute "rights" to property ownership and use are granted higher standing in all circumstances. So-called takings laws, for example, ideologically (but not inherently) reduce the intrinsic value of members of the biotic community, and of aspects of abiotic nature, to instrumental value. Recognized legal, ethical, and moral rights for nature would diminish and, over time, even eliminate the anthropocentric exercise of the coercive power of the state that currently favors those having greater political power and economic well-being, and that promotes an exaggerated human species sense of self-importance and right of domination. Natural rights should be seen in the context of an evolving universe and evolving biotic community, and should include the right to seek a new niche in nature, or even to go extinct if no appropriate place is available for adaptation.

NATURAL RIGHTS:
PRIORITIZATION IN CONTEXT

In a relational community, interspecies regard means forgiving threats or even harms from nonhuman creatures who have no moral awareness or agency. A human fisher, for example, might forgive a hungry bear who chases her away from the salmon she has so arduously brought to shore. A human hiker might forgive a sow bear with cubs who chases him up a tree and consumes the rations he brought along for his wilderness trek. Animals' acts to satisfy their hunger or to defend their territory in the face of perceived danger to themselves or their offspring are forgivable acts, even when they cause harm. On several occasions, U.S. Forest Service employees have relocated bears or wolves from locales where their predation of human food sources or livestock caused financial hardship; on other occasions, hikers who had been attacked and wounded by bears have implored the Forest Service not to kill the bear involved because the latter was doing what was instinctive to them to protect themselves, their territory or their offspring from perceived threats to their life or well-being.

If a hungry bear meets a man in a forest and eats him to survive after finding no other food, the bear (and any other nonhuman animal in a similar situation) would neither be conscious of nor culpable for violating the rights of other living beings; the bear is not a moral agent (a human concept expressing a human role within a human context). The common denominators here are that the human and the bear each has intrinsic value and the right to survival, to life, enabled by its consumption of food, as would be the case of a bear eating a salmon or of a salmon swallowing an insect; and that an ecosystem (albeit unconsciously) has the right to be sustained in balance. The human-bear, bear-salmon, and salmon-insect encounters are moments when each one's respective rights to life are in conflict, and each seeks to prioritize its existence. Rights are prioritized by the creatures involved, and the one most adapted to the situation will prevail. A hiker encountering a bear will become the bear's food; a bear meeting an armed hunter will become her clothing and perhaps her food. An agile salmon or athletic hiker might escape the swiping paw of an aged, weakened bear. An insect might fly beyond the salmon's leap. In all of these circumstances, the inherent rights and intrinsic value of the creatures involved continue for themselves even while they strive to survive as prey or when they succumb to being prey, even as they are regarded as having solely instrumental value by their respective predators.

Similarly, in intraspecies situations, a parent or other adult would forgive a child who unknowingly damages property or inadvertently hurts a sibling. Forgiveness as an expression of love need not require that the one forgiven be morally culpable for the wrongdoing experienced by the one forgiving. The "forgiveness" has to do with neither punishing, nor seeking redress for, another creature's taking of what a human person would see as their own rightful possession: food, freedom to travel responsibly, even life. "Forgiveness" in this sense does not imply that the other has done something objectively wrong, but rather has done something ordinarily wrong in human society. The human as moral agent is saying here that she will not use human understandings (e.g., of property rights), human laws, or human power (exercised by an individual with a gun, or by the state on behalf of the individual) to judge and punish (or have punished) nonhumans who are acting appropriately according to their species nature and the natural world context in which the event(s) occurred.

Biotic nature should have primary natural rights to meet natural needs. If a biotic community prioritization according to complexification becomes operative, humans should acknowledge and control the anthropic bias in such an ordering (which is based on satisfaction of needs, in promoting human individual and species survival in an evolutionary world in which predator-prey relationships exist) and recognize and control the potential of a creeping anthropocentrism or even anthropolatry present in such an anthropogenic ordering. Humankind must be mindful also that microorganisms far simpler than human organisms are necessary for human survival (e.g., to break down food that was consumed; to heal an illness that was contracted). Abiotic nature should have secondary natural rights. Otherwise, foxes could not have dens, birds could not have nests, and humans could not live in houses constructed of lumber made from trees, use computers made with metal components, or use irrigation systems to divert rivers for agricultural irrigation.

NATURAL RIGHTS

Natural rights apply to all individuals and species.[1] Recognition of this inclusive context of natural rights would enable humans to appreciate balance and interdependence in nature and to act accordingly. The current base for human natural rights should be developed to provide a foundation for a more inclusive understanding and application of nature's natural rights. In this spirit, philosophers who require moral agency as a criterion for natural rights might formulate basic criteria that are less exclusive and more universal.

Species and individuals should have *natural rights*:

- *the right to live a natural existence* according to their dynamic species characteristics in the niche(s) they occupy in an evolutionary Earth context;
- *the right to reproduce their species* in responsible relation to their local and, where applicable, global setting, and in natural balance with other species;
- *the right to nutrition and bodily sustenance* from Earth's bounty; for humankind, this right includes *the right to medicine and health services*;
- *the right to shelter* in Earth habitats, in natural competition and cooperation with other life;
- *the right to appropriate outer body covering*, which for biota would mean fur, skin, hide, scales, or feathers, and for humans might take the additional form of clothing for themselves and regard for the physical integrity and needs of biota with whom they come in contact (including free animals, and domesticated animals who provide wool, milk and other food, and other goods needed by humankind);
- *the right to be free from human intervention* in their lives and environment, except as necessary when humans, as other creatures do, struggle competitively and responsibly to meet their own needs (note the focus on "needs"); humans, as other creatures, can satisfy some needs only by preying on other living creatures or by altering the environment (eagles, bears, and humans eat salmon; foxes build dens; birds build nests; humans build homes and places of business); and
- *the right to habitat integrity and restoration*, the former to conserve the context for the other rights, and the latter as appropriate and feasible when humans have destroyed or altered these contexts unnecessarily.

If these rights were to be accepted and activated by people then nature as a whole and in its component parts, and not just the human part of it or human-favored parts of it (e.g., scenery and exotic biota), would have natural rights.

Conservation and preservation of select forests, fields, and fisheries are needed to assure natural rights, since such places provide food and habitat for all creatures, respectively as wood, agricultural land, and food for biota, and are sources of human livelihood.

The basis of human assignment of secondary rights for abiotic nature is "inanimate" nature's instrumental value to flora and fauna, and so the necessity of preserving its integrity for biota. When this ecosystemic instrumental value is not recognized, and only their instrumental value for humans is taken into account, the biotic community and the ecosystem suffer. The intrinsic, natural, and legal rights of abiotic nature actually are incorporated into the rights of living organisms. Biotic nature could not exist without benefits provided by abiotic nature. Abiotic rights are extensions of biotic (natural) rights in this view. Abiotic rights are operative to support organic beings, but these rights are not absolute "rights," since they are related to living creatures as they meet their needs, and they are related to all creation to protect living and nonliving creatures from human despoliation, and thus become subordinate to the primary natural rights of the living. In other perspectives, abiotic nature's rights are intrinsic or ecosystemic regardless of the actual or self-perceived requirements and rights of individuals and species in the biotic community.

Abiotic creation is natural when its basic components—air, land, and water—are pure, or are "living," metaphorically (or, actually, in some traditions). Living water, living soil, and living air are natural and become for Earth and biota life-giving water, life-giving soil, and life-giving air. They have intrinsic value and instrumental value. The integrated, interdependent, and interrelated species and individuals of the biotic community are the natural inhabitants of Earth habitats, which contain life-giving water, air, and soil.

Abiotic nature has natural rights because of its intrinsic value in nature. Since it is difficult for most humans to acknowledge such intrinsic value or rights, people with a relational consciousness and a sense of a relational community, who believe in the commons good and commons goods, will have to appeal to self-interest in the wider human community until its members acquire a similar relational consciousness. The appeal would be to protect abiotic nature because of its instrumental value and to advocate derived natural rights for abiotic creation. Earth goods as abiotic nature are needed by the biotic community for survival and material well-being.

People establish and acknowledge rights, and codify them in laws to protect the values they hold dear. Without natural rights, natural values would be disregarded or disdained, and the intrinsic values of creatures and creation would be reduced to instrumental values. If each creature and all creation were regarded as having an intrinsic value, the amount and extent of environmental devastation and species extinction would be reduced.

"Legal rights" are, in effect, codified human, civil, and natural rights. If nonhuman nature has none of these, it is without legal standing as well as without moral standing. "Legal rights," even if specified for different categories of being, are related most often to human ownership or control. However, in some times and places, humans are not alone in having legal rights. For example, cows are sacred in India; endangered species are protected by law in the United States. Legal rights formalize moral rights and concretize intrinsic value. Extending natural rights to all nature, and legalizing that extension, would provide some measure of protection not otherwise available to nonhuman nature. Laws, then, can and should be enacted, as necessary, to conserve the natural rights of natural beings who comprise "nature." The establishment of legal rights for nature would be a practical political tactic to protect and conserve creatures' intrinsic value from unneeded human predation, by recognizing and codifying their natural rights—even if a creature or part of creation cannot conceptualize "rights." Humans would thereby incorporate all creatures into an all-embracing legal system, acknowledging the standing of each among all.

Extension of natural rights to include all of nature does not diminish inclusion of humankind among those to benefit from that extension. Humans are a part of nature, with their own intertwined role within nature, and therefore have the same natural rights as all members of the biotic community. Because of their relational consciousness, informed conscience, and conscientious balancing of commons and community needs; their moral agency; and their greater ability than most biota to adapt nature to their own needs, humans must exercise their natural rights reflectively and responsibly.

All that exists—biotic and antibiotic being, and cosmic energies—ultimately has natural rights as part of *integral being*, the continuing, changing, and complexifying original existent. Integral being has integral natural rights from which all natural rights are derived. For the believer, integral being is the dynamic cosmos as a whole—existing in, engaged with, and sacred because of—divine presence. It originates in the creating transcendent-immanent Spirit who is Being-Becoming. For the humanist, integral being is the complex cosmos in itself, with all its diversity of being.

Conservation of species diversification and of the Earth commons requires that people acknowledge natural rights in nature as a whole rather than reserve them exclusively and anthropocentrically to humankind. These natural rights should be codified in human laws, not just in "natural laws" as understood in the Christian tradition and in indigenous traditions, in order to protect the world of nature. When humans accept that nature has natural rights, and strive to protect them, they will be acting not only for their own self-interest but in the interests of evolving life in an active planet in the dynamic universe.

NOTE

1. For complementary and, at times, contrasting views on natural rights and intrinsic value in nature, see James A. Nash, *Loving Nature: Ecological Integrity and Christian Responsibility* (Nashville, Tenn.: Abingdon, 1992); and Holmes Rolston III, *Conserving Natural Value* (New York: Columbia University Press, 1994) and *Environmental Ethics: Duties to and Values in the Natural World* (Philadelphia: Temple University Press, 1988). Their writing and my conversations with them have stimulated my own thought.

Commons Good, Common Good, and Common Goods

Spirit-transcendent is Spirit-immanent. The Spirit presences the cosmos and is in intimate communion with creation as a whole and with all creatures: humankind and all of biokind, and abiotic being. This communion is reciprocal, relational, and realized to the extent of species', individuals', and abiotic beings' capacity for openness to it and awareness of it.

As people become conscious of divine presence in, and discern their own relationships to, the broader natural world of which they are a part, they discover and are distressed by devastation in creation. They note that Earth is treated poorly and Earth's goods are distributed inequitably. They wonder why Earth's abundance is not meeting people's needs, as the Creator intended; why Earth is being exploited for human wants, to the detriment of its ability to provide for human needs; and why people who are called to image a loving, creating Spirit instead are ignoring the Spirit and destroying creation. Their conclusion that Earth (and the universe as a whole) and Earth's living creatures are permeated by a loving and creating divine presence leads them to recognize and affirm that Earth is a sacred commons and shared common ground. Their awareness of pressing community and individual needs leads them to consider how Earth's lands and goods might provide necessary space and needed goods, to be shared in common by members of the human family and by its extended biotic community.

An ecological vision derived from theistic and humanist sources would imagine Earth renewed, with globally extensive and accessible clean air, potable water, and unpolluted soil. The proponents of such a vision would propose practical projects to care for creation and care for community. People striving to live this vision live in a way that expresses their consciousness that in the Earth commons they share common ground and should promote the common good by sharing common goods.

In the teachings of their respective faith traditions, religious leaders across the planet find insights for educating their constituencies about their responsibilities, as both communities and individuals, for their local environments and for engaging people in practical projects to reflectively experience and responsibly care for creation. People of faith, with a relational consciousness expressed in a relational community, recognize that nature is revelatory of a Spirit who elicits human regard for Earth. On the macro level, they see a sacramental universe to be contemplated with awe and humility. On the micro level, they see a sacramental commons in which they are called to promote the commons good and the common good.

THE COMMONS AND THE COMMONS GOOD

The *commons* is the shared space or place that provides the context and goods needed as home and habitat by biokind. It is replete with integrated (through necessary and contingent events) abiotic dynamics and the interaction between the biotic and the abiotic. A commons has varied expressions in distinct types of physical space or levels of human understanding.

The *Earth commons* is the planet as a whole, whose orbital location and physical setting enable life to emerge, diversify, and complexify, and whose lands and goods, its soil, waters, air, and energy sources, provide for the subsistence and well-being of the biotic community.

The *human commons* is the present or future aggregate of social values acknowledged by most or all people and peoples. Ordinarily, humans are by nature social and communal beings. People as individuals gather into communities and share place, time, and goods with other individual community members. Culturally, self-interest might come to predominate as a basic (but not inherent) human trait. Before the primate became specifically and specially human, it was individual and communal according to its genetic coding and its interactivity. Its survival needs might, on occasion, foster either independent self-interest or interdependent relations with a heightened group interest and interaction. The survival instinct in some cultures came to be writ large and extended to become selfish. Individual wants were prioritized over community needs. *Selfishness*, which is a negative, acquired individual or cultural flaw, should not be confused with *self-interest* (the legitimate quest for survival or betterment), *self-regard* (an appreciation of who one is, and of what abilities one has), or a sense of self-worth (an understanding of how one relates and contributes to community), which are needed for survival, social interaction, and spiritual development. Neither is *individuality*, which is a sense of and affirmation of one's uniqueness, identical to *individualism*, an affirmation of egoism and a step toward egocentrism. People come to have community-regard when they integrate their own self-regard with an other-regard and when they interact with each other—to the extent possible—as intrinsically related and relating subjects rather than as instrumentally valued separate objects. Martin Buber's understanding of two fundamental types of relationships, the subject-to-subject "I-Thou" and the subject-to-object "I-It," has some bearing here. People might personalize (regard as persons) or objectify (regard as objects) other people and peoples.

The *cosmic commons* is the aggregate of goods that, beyond their intrinsic value, have instrumental value in universe dynamics or as providers for the well-being of biotic existence. In the cosmic commons, goods that will eventually be accessible on the moon, asteroids, meteors, or other planets should prove useful to humankind and, by extension and secondarily, to biokind collectively. Acceptance of the idea and ideal of a cosmic commons becomes ever more important as nations and corporations (now transnational; potentially trans-stellar) reach out into the universe through space probes, orbiting space stations, and possibly, in the future, satellite colonies on other worlds. The business and government intent of such activities ordinarily is to derive some commercial benefit or military advantage. The acceptance of the cosmos as commons would become even more important should other advanced life forms, seeking the same goods or interested in exchanging human-desired goods for human-discovered and human-developed goods, be encountered in cosmic explorations.

COMMONS GOOD AND COMMONS GOODS

Each type of commons must be safeguarded on behalf of humankind and biokind, or even, should such be known, for the well-being of its abiotic components, including its forms of energy, which are needed for ongoing cosmic or Earth dynamics. In the Earth commons, for example, destruction of an apparently "useless" form of life might have catastrophic impacts on more valued forms of life, and thereby on humankind and biokind. In the human social commons, rejection of a social good (such as equitable distributions of property and goods) or dismissal of beneficial social values (such as protection of the innocent and weak), besides inflicting immediate personal and social harms, might result in the loss of the intellect and creativity of people who would benefit a community or humanity as a whole, civil or global conflict, and a spiraling escalation of violence. In both the Earth commons and the human social commons, carbon emissions can impact human health and can alter the climate with catastrophic results, such as hurricanes that destroy coastal regions' ecosystems and agriculture, and ice melts that eventually raise coastal waters to heights that destroy coastal cities worldwide.

The *commons good* is the good of the commons as a whole. Earth has terrain and tectonic plates subject to unexpected movement, such as earthquakes, and unexpected forces, such as tornadoes and hurricanes. Over recent centuries, the use of explosives for mining and other purposes, the release of industrial effluents, clear-cutting of forests, diversion of rivers and pumping of aquifers, and nuclear weapons use and testing, among other human-introduced impacts, have jolted Earth and impacted its local terrain. People rarely think in terms of how their way of life and military and industrial effluents and emissions harm the commons as a whole. Recent concerns about the loss of extensive areas of the Amazon rain forest, the "lungs of the Earth," are one exception. Unfortunately, not even that devastation has prompted citizens or their governments to be sufficiently concerned to take the regional, national, and international measures needed to slow or stop forest devastation. Greed and actual or feigned innocence or ignorance outweigh compassion for those living in the present, and overcome a sense of intergenerational responsibility toward those yet to come. Conservation of the commons is necessary for the well-being of life and for the integrity of Earth as a whole.

Commons goods are Earth's global or ecosystemic benefits that are needed by living beings. Individual goods exist in balance because of their stability in place or their interactivity across places and time. These goods include healthy soil, pure water, clean air, coal, oil, wind, and elements in the form of useful metals and minerals. Interspecies interactions in the evolutionary commons, as seen earlier, require some living beings to be the prey of others in whole (lion and gazelle), where the organism might be consumed in its entirety, or in part (chimpanzee and fruit), where the food-providing organism's integrity remains in place.

THE COMMONS AND COMMON GROUND

Humankind is an integral part of the Earth commons within the context of creation. People are called to relate to each other and to their extended biotic community not as superior beings but as kindred beings. In the local commons that they share as a common habitat with other living members of the ecosystem, humans come to understand the complex common ground they share. All are interdependent and interrelated on *spiritual* common ground, *social* common ground, *scientific* common ground, and *spatial* common ground. Humans, alone among living creatures, have the ability and the consciousness to know and understand the realities common to all life.

The commons is *spiritual* common ground. Christian insights about the Spirit develop from the Bible; doctrines, ethical principles, and theological reflections emerging over the course of church history; and a living faith shaped by engagement with and relation to the Spirit in sacramental moments that transcend time and place. In complementary spiritual traditions, peoples of different faiths acknowledge that all creation flows from the creative vision and loving power of the Spirit-transcendent and is graced by the Spirit-immanent. Creation, therefore, is intrinsically and ultimately very good. People realize that the Spirit cares for all creation and that they have their own distinct role in creation. In biblically based traditions humans acknowledge that as images of a caring Spirit, they are to provide responsible care for Earth's land and other goods entrusted to them to provide for human material, social, and spiritual needs, now and into the future. People of faith acknowledge and celebrate the sacramental character of the commons as they see signs of the immanent and loving Creator and as they experience divine presence in creation.

The commons is *social* common ground. People are individual members of the human species and part of a human community. As social beings, people cluster in communities in which they can contribute their knowledge and skills to help meet community needs while providing for the needs of themselves and those close to them. In the process, people realize that in the relationships within their immediate community and between that community and the regional biotic community in their shared ecosystem, cooperation and collaboration, more than competition, will enable them to provide mutual support for each other in social settings and biotic contexts that are ecologically and economically sustainable.

The place in which a community is situated influences human interaction and livelihood. Interaction is based on occupation of a place—residence in a particular location—and an occupation in a place—work in that location that generates livelihood. Both types of occupation are directly or indirectly related to commons goods (soil, water, wind, solar) or common goods appropriated as instrumental goods (oil for heating homes, metals for manufactured goods, soil for food production, trees for wood to build shelter) of a place. The social common ground and common good are intimately based on and dependent on the spatial common ground and common goods. Degradation of natural places and excessive consumption of natural goods ultimately harm the social commons in the short- or long-term. Conservation—humans' reasoned use and responsible distribution of natural places and goods—helps sustain the social commons for humans, and the Earth commons for all life.

The commons is *scientific* common ground. People discover and understand the intricacies of interwoven commons laws of biology, chemistry, and physics. They can know about the dynamic cosmos and evolutionary life on Earth. Educated members of human societies understand, at various personal and professional levels of sophistication, that fundamental laws of physics, chemistry, and biology interact in the universe, and that scientific investigation provides data, or at least formulates theories, to describe interactive cosmic and commons processes and what results from them. People with a spiritual consciousness realize that the freedom and the dynamics of the cosmos are not eternal, nor did they suddenly emerge from nothing. The Spirit-transcendent envisioned and created the initial form, essential characteristics, and guiding (but not absolutely constraining and limiting) parameters of the energies, elements, entities, and events comprising existence in the dynamic universe and, eventually over time, in the evolutionary commons. Their being and becoming are permeated by Spirit-immanent, who grants their ongoing interactive creativity the freedom to explore and experience varied possibilities with multiple potential outcomes. Cosmos-chaos-cosmos results in the cosmic commons; diversification and complexification emerge in the Earth commons.

People ranging from academic scholars and religious leaders through ordinary citizens concerned primarily with day-to-day existence and working to acquire needed goods carefully consider scientific data and theories, including some with ecological implications, that seemingly contradict religious beliefs. Religious reason ("faith seeking understanding") probes for truth in these circumstances. Jews and Christians believe that the creation of the universe and the inspiration of the Bible have God as a common source; therefore, scientific and religious truths ultimately are compatible. In contrast, biblical literalists juxtapose faith and reason, find the Bible and science irreconcilable, and advocate "creationism" and "intelligent design." Mainstream Christians and Jews understand that the Bible is a sacred text, not a science or a history text, although it includes elements of early scientific thought, and contains aspects of human cultural history. Christians recall that Augustine declared earlier in church history that where science and the Bible conflict, the Bible should be taken allegorically. Augustine and other Christian leaders from the fifth century and into the twenty-first century of the Christian era have taught that biblical and scientific truths ultimately are complementary, not contradictory. The Bible describes divine creativity and divine *kenosis*; life in the process of evolution reveals it.

Life exists in a dynamic, evolving physical universe analyzed by scientists in depth and to the extent possible given existing data; personal interests, biases, and limitations; accessible funds; professional responsibilities and expectations; and available instruments. Simultaneously, human life is part of a dynamic, evolving cultural universe, an interactive exchange of insights that developed in or are emerging from distinct social and religious traditions. The overlap of the scientific and the spiritual is seen in developing human understandings of the sun. In ancient Egypt, Greece, and Mexico (and in other cultures), the sun was a god: Aton, the sun disk, in Egypt; Helios in Greece; Tonatiuh in Aztec Mexico. People in these cultures worshiped this "divine" being that provided Earth and its inhabitants with light and warmth. Over time, as new data and insights resulted from human explorations at the ideational and technical levels, people's scientific knowledge and perceptions changed. The divine circle became a sphere and then a star, which came to be known to be a mass of flaming gases. The god became an entity of the universe, a cosmic being and (for the person of faith) a creature, not a Creator. The depth of its being came to be analyzed scientifically rather than theologically. Science helped religion to gain new understandings about the sun's being and activity. Scientific common ground enhances understandings of spiritual common ground.

It has been also (and for some people lacking basic scientific knowledge, still is) an "obvious" scientific and religious "fact" that the sun, no longer a god but a heavenly body, revolves around Earth. The most casual glance at Earth's horizon in the morning notes that the sun is "rising" in the east, and will cross the sky and "set" in the west. But once the theories of Copernicus, Galileo, and Kepler became everyday knowledge, then prior "common sense" or common knowledge, and biblical and Aristotelian cosmic constructs, were similar to "stars" that "fell" from the heavens coming to be known as meteorites burning in Earth's atmosphere as Earth's gravitation brought them toward Earth's earth. The realities of heavenly bodies and their movements and journeys became known to a greater extent.

What is actually "true" or the fullness of a being's "reality" is not solely what is seen by our eyes, even when aided by telescopes or microscopes. Human insight surpasses human eyesight. The sun went from circle to sphere, and more of its complexity and depth of being became known through this conceptual (but not actual) transformation. It became known even more fully when its gaseous, exploding yet bonded unity was discovered. Similarly, initial perceptions of other aspects of the material universe become the basis of, but not a limiting edifice for, human awareness and knowledge of material and metaphysical realities. The dynamic universe and evolving biotic community and the autopoietic Earth are known now to be in *process*, not in *stasis*. In that process, cosmos is cosmos-chaos-cosmos in apparently random ways, moments, and spaces.

Fundamentalist theists seek to reduce ancient sacred texts to secular scientific texts. They offer the Bible's metaphors and expressions of prescientific understandings as a contemporary "science" that rejects current stages of Christian belief and human knowledge. So, too, reductionist scientists try to describe the totality of reality solely as energies, elements, entities, and events that can be quantified, replicated, and verified, and they try to limit acceptable theories solely to those that are "falsifiable," essentially by physical experimentation. For both fundamentalist types, it is easier to simplify reality, whether physical or metaphysical, material or spiritual. It is easier to believe or "know" that a simple disk circling Earth's sky is a divine being, who can be described and worshiped, and analyzed and explained, than a celestial sphere that appears to the naked eye to be the largest object in the sky but, when the eye is assisted by a telescope, is found in actuality to be dwarfed by distant stellar bodies. Similarly, the commonsense explanation that the sun revolved around Earth was displaced by knowledge, derived through mathematics and the telescope, that Earth revolved around the sun as one of the planets of a heliocentric system. But those who engage and relate to the Spirit-immanent, and those who have had glimpses, "indistinctly, as through a mirror" (1 Corinthians 13:12) of that divine Presence, realize that some simple explanations of "reality" can be merely simplistic explanations. Just as a flat disk can be intellectually transformed into a spheroid gaseous star, and in the process its true being and function as the center of the solar system and a light among lights in the Milky Way galaxy and in the extensive universe can be understood, so, too, if people look carefully into reality and are open to new existential possibilities and surprising complexities, a more complete understanding of the totality of reality is given to them. Dreams and visions, and engagement with the Spirit, take place in a spiritual dimension of reality; they cannot be measured or detected by tools, however exotic, manufactured to detect and evaluate material reality. Sometimes, dreams become realities; sometimes spiritual experiences transform reality. Eventually, the literary reverie of Jules Verne became material reality through Neil Armstrong; it became possible to go from Earth to the moon and to stand on the moon, as Verne had imagined a century earlier. Similarly, some of the scientific speculations of Leonardo da Vinci became verified; the artist depicted reality with more than his paint brush. Similarly, also, the visions of Black Elk and the dreams of David Sohappy become historical realities, and the dream of Martin Luther King Jr. might yet become a reality. Similarly, too, spiritual realities are intertwined with and affect material reality. Spiritual insights inform rather than contradict scientific facts and theories. Spiritual common ground enhances scientific common ground.

The commons is *spatial* common ground. People depend on Earth's goods in their local Earth place to meet their essential needs, to the greatest extent possible. Their individual and community human needs must be integrated with those of species and individuals of their biotic community who share the same home and habitat. The spatial commons provides vital air, land, water, and other benefits that make it an appropriate and viable locus for human life and a base for human livelihood. When people become truly native to their place, they appreciate both its natural beauty and its practical benefits. They come to regard other members of the biotic community as relatives, kindred beings in shared space, with whom they share in common much of their DNA. They share, too, a common ancestry traced back not just 3.5 billion years to the earliest life form that emerged from terrestrial waters, but beyond to common primordial origins in energized cosmic dust that was envisioned in divine imagination, emerged some fifteen billion years ago, and continues to express divine creative power directly or indirectly. In spatial common ground humankind is integrated, interrelated, and interdependent with other members of the biotic community to a greater extent than in other types of shared common ground. In their bioregional ecosystem and its interconnected ecosystems, species and their members interact most beneficially when they live in a balanced and sustainable relationship with each other.

A healthful natural environment is the context, the spatial common ground, of the community. It is a place of clean air, potable water, and healthy soil. It is the ambience within which the web of life is woven. It is the place that provides for community needs. The understanding of the "common good" is extended in this environment to incorporate other living creatures to be members of the "common" sharing in the "good" as species and individuals of an extended family that shares the commons in common. Then the common good of humankind and biokind, in their integrated web of Earth lives, can be sought and secured.

THE COMMON GOOD IN CREATION

The term *common good* has two distinct meanings. First, it describes the collective well-being of a community, whether solely human in constitution or including the biotic community as a whole. Second, it delineates an Earth benefit that is or should be shared to some extent exclusively by humankind or inclusively by all of biokind.

The community *common good* has three integrated components: the sum total of individual intrinsic goods; the aggregate of potentially instrumental goods from which all the community's individuals might select those they need to reinforce and enhance their own individual intrinsic good; and the collective well-being of the community as a whole. An ecological common good is evident in the Earth commons when the shared and interdependent well-being of individuals and species is integrated into their own communities, the biotic community, their bioregional ecosystem, and the global commons. The human common good is the aggregate of needed subsistence, social and spiritual goods required for individual and community well-being. Community well-being might require individual sacrifice of individual wants and superfluities and even individual goods and apparent individual self-interest in the interests of all, to meet community needs. Sometimes an individual or community might seek or hold a perceived common good (e.g., gold to be utilized in computers that would be used in turn in hospitals to aid in the diagnosis or treatment of illness or injury) that actually is not a needed common good (gold could be obtained by recycling existing gold products) and might in fact ultimately be harmful to an individual, to individuals, or to the community as a whole (gold mining usually poisons streams and rivers and consequently kills animals and birds and pollutes drinking sources and agricultural lands needed by humans).

The well-being of the biotic community implies and requires the well-being of abiotic creation as its home and habitat. The common good includes and requires the commons good.

An Earth benefit is a *common good* when it is needed for subsistence, security, or enhanced well-being by a species or by individual members of a single species or of competing species. A common good promotes survival (subsistence needs met), social well-being (interdependent relationships, just societal institutions—medical, educational—and just societal structures—political, economic, and religious), and spiritual well-being. The common good should promote personal and societal, individual and communal development. Justice and peace, compassion, sharing of common goods, care for creation, and love of God and neighbor are essential for the common good to be promoted and sustained.

The idea of a "common good" emerged as people came to understand that there are certain community benefits and individual benefits that become operative in society only when individuals commit themselves to promoting the well-being of the citizenry as a whole. With this understanding, and actions that follow, communities are better able to meet their most basic needs for adequate, life-sustaining food, clothing, shelter, medicines, water, and energy.

It is difficult for some individuals to advocate or accept a "common good" rather than or in addition to their individual good and wants. The contexts for their resistance include situations where, and times when, survival concerns are paramount, and there are insufficient reserves of needed goods; or, when the places where necessities for life previously had been gathered have since been depleted of these goods or have been privatized and prevent access to needed goods. In other circumstances, insecurity about the future might prompt people to hoard what they have in the present. For some people, greed is a factor: they want to maximize their own possessions or the ostentatious quantity, complexity, or value of their possessions. They believe (and are reinforced in that belief by their culture or by some members of it) that their worth or status is dependent on the number and quality of their "toys," the extent of their holdings in land, or the size and diversity of their stock portfolio.

To promote the common good, community and individual needs must take priority over private wants. The right to own and use private property is not an absolute individual right. It must be related to aggregate benefits for the individual owner within, and as part of, a human community. People should remember that private property, although secured through civil law, is really held in trust from God primarily for the community and must be used wisely and justly. Public property is a good that should be carefully conserved while being equitably shared by the community. Conservation of both private and public property requires that humankind as individuals and communities be ecosystemically interrelated and integrated.

While some people might reject the idea of a "common good," other people find ample reasons for accepting it. They recognize that acknowledgment of a common good and practices to uphold it can result in social stability, mutual respect, reciprocity, and continuing efforts to live justly and in harmony with others.

The purpose of government is to promote the common good and, today more than ever before, to promote the good of the commons so that it might provide common goods for the common good. Local, state, regional, and national governments within a country will promote the well-being of their citizens as a whole when they seek to provide for those most in need, and take steps toward an economic democracy and a mutual regard that transcends distinctions of color, race, ethnicity, religion, sex, political affiliation, culture, and economic class.

The aggregate of national responsibilities toward the environment is embodied in international treaties, documents, and laws, and in the vision and projects of the United Nations. Pollution does not respect national boundaries, nor is it confined solely to the national territories of polluting nations. The aerial aftermath of the eruption of the Mount St. Helens volcano in Washington State in the United States in 1980 demonstrated how nature's airborne ashes, and humans' industrial smokestack emissions and artificial mushroom clouds from exploding nuclear missiles, can launch airborne pollution that is carried transglobally by wind currents, and impacts the lives and health of Earth's peoples. Sulfur emissions from coal-fired power plants and industrial enterprises in the Ohio Valley come to Earth as acid rain in Canada and in the northeastern United States; mercury from coal-fired power plants harms children's health throughout the world; carbon emissions from these same plants and other industrial operations contribute greatly to global warming, which threatens to melt polar ice that will in turn raise global sea levels, which will flood coastal cities and their food-producing regions, and imperil the lives, livelihoods, and well-being of millions of people world-wide. The Kyoto Accords, not yet fully implemented because of U.S. government intransigence and transnational corporation greed, set a minimum standard for nations to alter their pollution of the air and to diminish thereby global warming. Similarly, heavy metals from mine operations, sewerage from urban areas, and pesticides from lawns and agricultural operations poison water across state and national boundaries. Meanwhile, overfishing of Earth's open oceans is threatening fish populations in regional fisheries by jeopardizing their ability to reproduce and to provide food for the world's peoples. In addition, land throughout the world is being poisoned by legal and illegal industrial dump sites, and is being diverted from responsible agricultural or residential use to commercial and industrial ventures and to recreational preserves. The impacts are evident, in all of the preceding scenarios, of human population pressures and excessive consumption patterns. The continuation of such irresponsible attitudes and harmful acts jeopardizes the commons good, the common good, and common goods.

THE COMMON GOOD IN HUMAN COMMUNITIES

Since the human common good requires that the subsistence and social needs of all be met, and that distributions of Earth's land, air, water, and natural goods ("resources") beyond those needs be equitable, justice must pervade human consciousness and human communities. Contradictory concepts of "justice" promote such principles as to each the same thing; to each according to their merits, skills or status; to each according to their needs. Since the focus of a common good orientation is that the well-being of all should be sought and secured, beginning with provision of sustenance goods, the understanding that justice means distribution of goods equitably to each according to their needs is most appropriate. *Equitable* means appropriately and approximately equal. In a cold climate, for example, the burning of some type of fuel is essential for heating homes. To conserve fuel needed for energy production, a community might establish a target upper limit of 68 degrees

Fahrenheit for a thermostat setting. But elder citizens need warmer homes (and hospitalized people need warmer rooms) because of their physical condition. Since the object of heating homes is for people to be warm and healthy, an equitable setting for an elderly or ill person might be 76 degrees Fahrenheit.

The common good requires that there be an equitable distribution and redistribution of Earth's land and goods. Dispossessed people and peoples throughout the Earth, who suffer from political and economic oppression and the lack of a land and resource base, can better meet their subsistence and livelihood requirements if they own (especially communally or cooperatively) and have control over their own lands and can initiate and maintain responsible economic development. Steps such as these toward economic democracy and justice for the world's poor oppressed of every color and ethnicity would establish a firm foundation for political democracy and for world peace. Poverty and ecoracism are overcome by ecojustice. Without justice, there will be no peace.

The common good also calls for the elimination of intrahuman political and economic oppression, which negate community and communal sharing of commons goods and common goods; and racial, sexual, and ethnic oppression, which negate intrahuman personal and community acceptance and affirmation.

COMMON GOODS IN CREATION AND IN HUMAN COMMUNITIES

In order for the common good to become a reality, people must recognize that there are common goods. These are Earth-provided benefits and human-produced benefits that should be communally held and utilized in perpetuity, or community prioritized and made available to each and every person as needed individually. People have a right to land to produce their food, clothing, shelter, or fuel; to air that is clean in their lungs; to unpolluted water to satisfy their thirst and irrigate their fields; and to sunlight for agriculture and for gardens and to be converted through solar heating, hot water, and electrical generation systems into usable energy. Earth goods should be common goods, even when, to provide community benefits, they are used privately for people's homes and places of business. All property is, in some sense, a social trust, whether it is publicly owned as a community park or privately held to meet individual needs or to provide a livelihood.

Just as there are goods that are common to the human community, so are there goods common to the biotic community as a whole. Humankind must learn to share such goods more equitably with all of biokind, at least out of self-interest (polluted soil poisons human food and plants not used by humans; polluted water is unfit for salmon habitat or human consumption of water or salmon) if not from a sense of general regard for other species who have evolved, diversified, and complexified on Earth in the Spirit's creation. Primordial stardust has become planets, paramecia, plants, platypuses, penguins, primates, and people; all are related.

INTERGENERATIONAL RESPONSIBILITY

Intergenerational responsibility is an inherent component of seeking the common good. Human responsibility across generations is not solely linear into future time, and not solely for forthcoming human offspring, but also horizontal, toward the multiple diverse generations of different ages existing simultaneously in any time period, and inclusive of concern for the well-being of all members of the community of all life. Earth at any single moment, and Earth in its extension through time, is home to an interrelated intergenerational community. This community is linked by the continuity of life and the transfer of genes within species and their members in the biotic community, and by the creative complexification of cultural history within the human community.

Intergenerational concern must also include regard for the continued availability of components of abiotic nature—air, water, soil, minerals—for all members of the biotic community in their Earth home.

The intergenerational interrelatedness of a biological community, as a species and in its individual members and families, has been innovatively and eloquently expressed by John Trudell, an American Indian poet and a social activist. In an impassioned speech at a Montana meeting of the Indigenous Environmental Network (IEN) several years ago, Trudell addressed the dangers of biotechnology. He offered a new rendition of the meaning of DNA, declaring that it meant "Descendants 'n' Ancestors." Each human person is a life in a present moment that comprises the genetic matter developed over millennia of ancestors during the past and, simultaneously, is the ancestor who contributes genes to descendants of millennia yet to come. Each is, in his or her moment of time, a bridge between the characteristics that they received from past generations down through the ages, and those that they will pass on through their own offspring to generations yet unborn. Each person is responsible to his or her ancestors and personal descendants, and to the future community as a whole whose members will be the recipients of the collective genes of multiple individuals and families. (Trudell's insights are informative also in their implications about the dangers of bioengineering other species of animals and of plants.)[1]

Human rights abuses and territorial injustices committed against native people throughout the world are of particular concern. American Indian nations in the United States, First Nations in Canada, and indigenous peoples across the globe still have their traditional lands and Earth goods stolen from them—whether or not these are guaranteed by treaty rights—and their traditional beliefs, stories, and prayers suppressed. Cultural and physical genocide are extant. In the United States, the fishing rights case of David Sohappy attracted international concern, including from the United Nations International Human Rights Commission (which appointed an investigator—a *rapporteur*—to travel to the United States to evaluate the condition and oppression of Indian peoples). Native spiritual leaders and activists who object to human rights violations sometimes are imprisoned or murdered. The human common good requires that native peoples' territorial sovereignty, and rights to land, goods, and culture, be restored and retained.[2]

AN *EARTH CHARTER* FOR
THE EARTH COMMONS

The United Nations Conference on Environment and Development, held in Rio de Janeiro in 1992, was organized to address and ameliorate environmental degradation and devastation. Maurice Strong from the UN Environment Programme advocated an *Earth Charter* to complement the UN's *Universal Declaration of Human Rights*. However, nationalistic interests linked to transnational corporation pressures prevented government leaders gathered at the Earth Summit from promulgating policies to protect the planet. Consequently, Strong sought to keep his vision viable by forming an Earth Council in 1994 to foster sustainable development. The following year he linked with Nobel Peace Prize laureate and former USSR leader Mikhail Gorbachev, founder and president of Green Cross International (a global environmental organization), to continue *Earth Charter* development. Funding for their efforts was provided by the government of the Netherlands under the leadership of internationally respected Prime Minister Ruud Lubbers (later the director of the World Wide Fund for Nature). Over the following two years, numerous international consultations, which included sessions with scientists and representatives of environmental organizations, gradually developed foundational principles promoting care for Earth, concern for the biotic community, and consideration of the needs and rights of humankind. The Earth Charter Commission (ECC), an international (six-continent) representative body, resulted from these activities in 1997. The ECC assembled an international drafting committee that wrote and issued the first draft, Benchmark I, the same year. Discussions of that draft in diverse venues, including at the World Council of Churches Ecumenical Center in Bossey, Switzerland, in 1999, led to Benchmark II. After additional input from around the world, the *Earth Charter*[3] was released in 2000 at UNESCO headquarters in Paris and then launched at the Peace Palace in The Hague shortly thereafter.

The *Earth Charter*'s principles—sixteen in number—and subprinciples—an additional sixty-one guidelines—promote an encompassing vision of human communities that are characterized by justice, integrated with biokind as a whole, and respectful of their shared Earth habitat. The *Earth Charter* contains insights and principles complementary to Jubilee requirements, sacramental commons ideals and principles, and Christian ecological ethics formulations. It suggests alternative ways of being and acting in the Earth commons.

The *Earth Charter* preamble declares that "in the midst of a magnificent diversity of cultures and life forms we are one human family and one Earth community with a common destiny. We must join together to bring forth a sustainable global society founded on respect for nature, universal human rights, economic justice, and a culture of peace." The preamble recognizes cultural diversity and biodiversity, but it states that since all life is integrated into one community with a common future, people must coordinate their concerns and commitments to effect global community sustainability. It declares that Earth's peoples are responsible "to one another, to the greater community of life, and to future generations." Humans should have a spirit of "solidarity and kinship with all life."

The *Earth Charter* offers a holistic vision of interdependent and intergenerational Earth communities: among humans, across species, and through time. The charter's principles promote realization of that vision. They integrate the common good of humans with the common good of all species in the Earth commons they share as their home and habitat.

Earth Charter principles advocate community consciousness, promotion of the common good, and realization that Earth is common ground shared by individuals and intergenerational species in the community of life. On this foundation, human communities in distinct bioregions or clusters of bioregions might build a more intensive and extensive elaboration of principles to promote realization of the charter's holistic vision of transglobal and transgenerational consciousness, and to stimulate concrete local, bioregional, intergenerational, and global projects to conserve and renew bioregions. Collaborative thought *and* action, globally *and* locally, would universalize care for Earth: across cultures, beyond national borders, and through time.

Principles and subprinciples relating to community, the common good, the commons good, and intergenerational responsibility call people to "respect Earth and life in all its diversity," since "every form of life has value." The practice of "care for the community of life" leads to "responsibility to promote the common good." People should "promote social and economic justice," work to "eradicate poverty as an ethical, social, and environmental imperative," and "affirm gender equality and equity." These attitudes and actions are not merely to benefit the people and places of a current evolutionary moment and historical era. Humankind must "secure Earth's bounty and beauty for present and future generations" and remember that the "freedom of action of each generation is qualified by the needs of future generations." Taken together, these principles offer a holistic vision of intergenerationally integrated, interdependent, and interrelated human and Earth communities sharing common goods in common places.

The diverse component principles of the vision should be assessed in terms of their potential to effect environmentally beneficial impacts on communities and the commons, both as these principles are currently presented and as they might be elaborated more intensively and extensively in particular local, regional, and national contexts.

The *Earth Charter* proposes a twofold focus of human engagement with the environment: recognition of integrated community relationships within the human family, and between people and other members of the biotic community; and respect for their common ground, the Earth home shared by a biokind that is interdependent within and across bioregions and generations.

Earth Charter principles promote respect among members of Earth's human community, toward members of Earth's biotic community, and for Earth as their common ground, their home and habitat. In this regard, it reflects humanist and religious understandings of peoples' relatedness to the world of nature, to biokind as a whole, and to the global human family. The charter evidences teachings from Judaism (respect for God's creation), Islam (obligations to Allah's creation), and Hinduism and Buddhism (their reverence for all life), and it includes insights compatible with the religious traditions of the first peoples of the Americas and of indigenous peoples throughout the world (their respect for all creation, living and nonliving). The document's principles complement contemporary developments in faith communities—such as Christianity's long-overdue reappropriation of a sense of divine immanence to complement the churches' teachings on divine transcendence, its awareness of the sacramental nature of creation as a whole or in part, and its advocacy of social justice for all peoples.

The *Earth Charter* speaks in general terms of the spiritual dimension of reality, without limiting itself by reference to a particular faith tradition. It notes the "spiritual potential of humanity," the "spiritual wisdom in all cultures," and the right of all to "spiritual well-being." It offers ethical principles and a vision for the future that link ecology with economics, and nature's rights with natural rights. Although the charter does not represent the ideas of a particular religion, traces of all religions permeate the document. Since it is not specifically faith based, it has the potential to be acceptable to people of all faiths or of a humanist perspective. It provides hope for people around the world that they will be able to live within a just social order, with a healthy environment, and sustainable employment.

Humans and their biotic community live in a sacramental cosmos and a sacramental commons, a vast universe and a local place permeated by the loving presence of a creative and creating Spirit. The *Earth Charter* provides a concrete transcultural and transspiritual expression of fundamental environmental ethics that flow from the spiritual understandings of diverse peoples. It provides a basis, therefore, for intercultural and interreligious discussion of an environmental vision for the present and the future, and for the formulation of concrete measures for realizing that vision. The charter's promise is that it will help humankind responsibly chart a course for a better future for Earth in all its complexity and for the biotic community in all its evolving diversity.

Earth Charter principles complement goals proposed by the United Nations Development Programme (UNDP). The UNDP formulated eight Millennium Development Goals to stimulate responsible economic development that would be related to social development and integrated with environmental sustainability. The Millennium Development Goals are as follows:

- Eradicate extreme poverty and hunger.
- Achieve universal primary education.
- Promote gender equality and empower women.
- Reduce child mortality.
- Improve maternal health.
- Combat HIV/AIDS, malaria, and other diseases.
- Ensure environmental sustainability.
- Develop a global partnership for development.

Member nations are encouraged to implement target steps toward achieving these goals, in the hope that by 2015 they will be realized or at least that there will be significant progress toward their realization.

The integration of a relational consciousness, recognition of the intrinsic value and natural rights of creatures and creation, *Earth Charter* principles, Christian ecological ethics, and United Nations Millennium Development

Goals would have a significant impact on resolving current environmental crises and meeting human needs. It would help promote and realize the commons good, the common good, and an equitable distribution of commons goods as common goods.

When human consciousness and human activities are oriented toward the commons good and the common good, and when humankind shares common goods with all of biokind, then social justice among humans and ecojustice among all living beings will become possible. Earth will not groan in unison with the fading cry of the eagle and the mournful cries of the poor, oppressed racial and ethnic minorities, and other oppressed peoples. Swords will be beaten into plowshares. Food will be provided in greater abundance when instruments of death are changed to implements for life, missile silos become grain silos, and killing fields become fields of crops to sustain life.

Policies and projects to promote the commons good, common good, and common goods are more visions than realities in these early years of the twenty-first century. There exists still a tension between what is and what might be, between the *topia* (place) of today and the *utopia* (no-place; envisioned future; ideal place to be achieved; goal inspiring action) that is the human dream.

Realizations of the commons good, common good, and equitable distribution of common goods are absolute utopias that can be reached over time by the realization of relative utopias. The latter stages on the way to absolute utopia can be stimulated by humanist ideas, religious teachings, transcultural ethical principles, or international documents, and they can be expressed in realistic and realized projects that concretize the ideals they express.

NOTES

1. Insights from American Indian activist and poet John Trudell are presented in Paola Igliori, *Stickman: John Trudell* (New York: Inanout, 1994), and in CDs of his music and readings: *Bone Man* (Daemon Records, 2002), *Johnny Damas and Me* (Rykodisc, 1994), and *AKA Graffiti Man* (Rykodisc, 1992).

2. American Indian spiritual and historical perspectives are explored in depth in Vine Deloria, *Custer Died for Your Sins: An Indian Manifesto* (Norman: University of Oklahoma Press, 1988), *God Is Red: A Native View of Religion* (Golden, Colo.: Fulcrum, 1994), and *The World We Used to Live In: Remembering the Powers of the Medicine Men* (Golden, Colo.: Fulcrum, 2006); George E. Tinker, *Missionary Conquest: The Gospel and Native American Cultural Genocide* (Minneapolis: Augsburg Fortress, 1993) and *Spirit and Resistance: Political Theology and American Indian Liberation* (Minneapolis: Augsburg Fortress, 2004); Jace Weaver, ed., *Defending Mother Earth: Native American Perspectives on Environmental Justice* (Maryknoll, N.Y.: Orbis, 1996); Oren Lyons and John Mohawk, eds.,

Exiled in the Land of the Free: Democracy, Indian Nations and the U.S Constitution (Santa Fe, N.M.: Clear Light, 1998); and Winona LaDuke, *Recovering the Sacred: The Power of Naming and Claiming* (Cambridge, Mass.: South End, 2005) and *All Our Relations: Native Struggles for Land and Life* (Cambridge, Mass.: South End Press, 1999). These works are complemented by the music of the singer-actor (*Dances with Wolves, The X-Files*, and *Hidalgo*, among others) Floyd Red Crow Westerman in his CD *Custer Died for Your Sins/The Land Is Your Mother* (Trikont, 1993).

3. Information about the *Earth Charter*, and the complete text in numerous languages, is available at www.earthcharter.org. Other key figures in *Earth Charter* development have included Steven Rockefeller, who claimed the international drafting committee and is a member of the Earth Charter Commission; and Mirian Vilela, executive director.

·9·

Job, Injustice, and Dynamic Nature

$\mathcal{H}$urricane Katrina became the worst natural disaster in the history of the United States in August 2005. It caused substantial damage in Florida before going west across the Gulf of Mexico and flooding New Orleans, killing more than 1,300 people (most of them poor African Americans) and causing billions of dollars in damage. In October of the same year, a massive earthquake that registered 7.6 on the Richter scale struck the Kashmir region between India and Pakistan. More than ninety thousand people were killed, millions became homeless and hungry, and roads, homes, schools, and hospitals were not rebuilt for months because international aid was not provided at the level needed to address the catastrophe. Ten months previously, in December 2004, a 9.0 Richter scale earthquake in the Indian Ocean caused a massive tsunami that swept across coastal Asia. This catastrophe killed almost two hundred thousand people and destroyed homes, businesses, and places of worship. Arguably, this ten-month period, in which hurricanes and earthquakes in other parts of the world complemented those mentioned already, had a greater diversity and intensity of destructive storms than any similar period in human history.

Natural catastrophes have afflicted humankind throughout human history. In the fourteenth century, the Black Death (probably the bubonic plague) swept through Eurasia, killing an estimated two hundred million people, about one-third of the region's population. The deadliest earthquake on record occurred in Shaanxi, China, in 1556: 830,000 people died. Volcanic activity has harmed people locally and globally. When Mount Vesuvius erupted near Pompeii, Italy, in 79 c.e., thousands perished. The spectacular eruption of Mount St. Helens in Washington State in 1980 killed only fifty-seven people locally, but Krakatoa's explosion in Indonesia in 1883 killed thirty-six thousand—and both eruptions sent ashes around the world, disrupting lives and livelihoods.

Some people might regard Earth's periodic cleansing through wildfires and hurricanes, volcanoes and floods, and sickness and death as beneficial. In an evolutionary context, these occurrences catalyze circumstances in which life can diversify and complexify, allowing for new life and new forms of life. For others, natural events in Earth's geologic history that have caused millions of deaths in the course of human history have been viewed as natural disasters because of human suffering. In past centuries, people assumed that natural catastrophes were divine punishments, and they sought to propitiate their gods by performing penitential rituals and reforming their personal and collective conduct. Similar religious responses resulted when people were attacked and subjugated by their political, economic, or ethnic enemies.

Natural disasters rarely have been as frightening or as harmful to life and limb as have been social disasters in which people inflicted horrendous evils on other people or peoples. The Nazis and their collaborators murdered six million Jews and uncounted Gypsies, communists, the mentally ill, and others in gas chambers during World War II; the Holocaust was unmatched in savagery, depravity, intensity, and intentionality in human history. The atom bombs dropped by the United States on Hiroshima and Nagasaki in 1945 to end World War II killed hundreds of thousands of Japanese civilians, some immediately and others over decades as they succumbed to radiation-induced cancer. The Khmer Rouge murdered a million or more people in Cambodia in the 1970s. In the score of years that included the last decade of the twentieth century and the first decade of the twenty-first century, U.S. bombings in Iraq during the course of two wars killed about one million people, some when the bombs fell and others, particularly children and the elderly, as a result of the deliberate destruction of potable water sources and water treatment and delivery systems, and the subsequent denial of funds and materials for their repair. Thousands of Africans died during the slave trade era. Thousands of black Muslims were killed by Arab Muslims in the Sudan at the beginning of the twenty-first century. On September 11, 2001, almost two thousand people were killed when terrorist-commandeered airplanes crashed into the twin towers of the World Trade Center in New York City. Through the course of the history of European contact with and conquest of peoples of the Americas, tens of millions of native peoples have been killed, a genocide that continues into the current century. Throughout history, unnatural evils perpetrated by humans have caused millions more deaths than have natural disasters (except for the Black Death).

Natural catastrophes result from the dynamic processes of a world experiencing geological and biological changes, and from human activities that either precipitate them or augment their extent and impact. Major Earth events unconnected to human activity might or might not be able to be avoided, but they might be ameliorated. Earth events that result from humans' actions can be avoided and sometimes ameliorated. Unnatural evils result from the clashes of individuals, cultures, classes, and nations at conflicting stages of political, religious, and economic development. These social-based events can be prevented or can be diminished in their impacts through national and international laws based on justice, which promote peace based on justice; and through acts of compassion, contrition, forgiveness, and restitution.

Reflection on the meaning of a sacramental commons in the midst of such havoc stimulates consideration of the meaning and role of suffering in the cosmos and the commons. Rainbows, beautiful sunsets, and the graceful flight of an eagle stand in stark contrast to televised news stories in which weeping survivors of war or natural disasters await relief from international agencies to alleviate their hunger, homelessness, and despair.

Even though there is no permanence for or on Earth, people are called to conserve and care for the biotic community's home, to be compassionate toward people who suffer, and to try to diminish causes of suffering. It is possible to prevent (un)natural disasters that result from irresponsible human-caused or human-exacerbated global warming and pollution of air, land, and water. Future generations will suffer irrevocably if present generations do not alter their conduct.

Creation, even as a sacramental commons, is not benign; it is not immediately and continually beneficial to creatures. Catastrophic events such as earthquakes, floods, droughts, tornadoes, and hurricanes—and human susceptibility to suffering and death—remind people that both the universe and those who inhabit it are part of a dynamic creative process, continually emerging from its primordial origin, whether the origin be viewed as divine or fortuitous. Such events give humanity a "reality check."

Two sources of suffering afflict humanity: natural disasters and human evil. Since "evil" implies moral agency, it is inaccurate to speak of "natural evil," because the suffering that people experience as a result of natural forces originates in Earth dynamics, which occur independently of human agency and which would occur even if humankind did not exist. Earth has no moral agency in causing earthquakes, volcanoes, tsunamis, tornadoes, hurricanes, droughts, floods, and so forth. It might be possible to view such events as evil in some cases because of a secondary factor of human moral agency. Humans are responsible for Earth events that result from irresponsible human acts, such as nuclear detonations that cause shifts in geological formations and carbon dioxide emissions that contribute to (or cause) global warming and weather pattern shifts. The natural events themselves would not be "evil" because events have no agency; the human acts that caused or contributed to them or worsened their impacts would be regarded as evil.

Even just people experience undeserved suffering from human evil and natural catastrophe. Illness could result from either or both sources. A lack of personal hygiene might cause suffering through one's own fault (from ignorance or from presumption of exemption from consequences); through society's fault (because water is privatized or polluted; because adequate medical care is not available); or from the migration of a harmful microorganism (because companies or countries prioritizing profits did not take precautions adequate to protect public health and safety, nationally or internationally; or because of the microorganism's chance migration).

The biblical book of Job presents an account of a man who suffers greatly from Earth's natural disasters and humans' evil acts. It reflects on the relationships of the Creator to creation, and of humans' relationships with and responsibilities to God and to each other in community.

JOB'S SUFFERING AND FAITH

The story of Job, a just man subjected to diverse forms of suffering, is well known. When the book was written, people generally assumed that only sinful people—or those whose parents or earlier ancestors were sinful—suffered from dramatic natural catastrophes, accidents, sickness, or human evil. The theological understanding was that Yahweh afflicted the wicked to punish them. A person who suffered as much as Job did would have been viewed as a great sinner who managed somehow to keep his transgressions hidden from friends and neighbors.

Job suffered evil at the hands of people: the Sabeans attacked his tenant farmers and killed them, and they stole Job's oxen and donkeys; the Chaldeans stole his camels and killed his servants. Job also suffered from harmful natural events: lightning consumed his flocks of sheep and the shepherds caring for them; his children all were killed when a strong wind destroyed their eldest brother's home while they were dining there; and sores covered his body from head to foot. Job, then, lost his heir and the rest of his children, his servants, his livestock, his wealth, and his health. After all these events, Job curses the day he was born and wishes he had been stillborn, but he does not blame Yahweh. His friends do "blame" Yahweh, however, in that they assert that Yahweh only punishes the guilty, not the innocent. Their logical conclusion seems to follow irrefutably: Yahweh is punishing Job because of his sins. But the reader and Job know that Job is innocent.

While afflicted, Job wonders how his divine friend could have allowed his suffering to occur and then permit it to continue. The harms he experienced provided an opportunity for his adversaries—those who spoke with him and those who mocked him from afar—to call into question his virtue and his good name. He seems to accept the initial devastations from natural disasters and human evil as merely unfortunate, unexpected, unwanted, and even inexplicably divinely ordained events. He declares, "Naked I came from my mother's womb, and naked shall I return there; the Lord gave and the Lord has taken away; blessed be the name of the Lord" (1:21). He knows that he has acted justly, and accepts what has happened as part of the normal events of the time, even though the coincidence of all harms being compounded and coming in such a compressed time would be remarkable (and in the understanding of the time, questionable—given his just conduct and previous divine blessings). He is grateful that God has blessed him in the past; he understands his losses to be God's will, even if he does not know the rationale for the divine reversal. But as the suffering continues and his good reputation is ever more pressingly called into question, he becomes less accepting. He debates aloud a hidden and silent deity.

The story raises questions of theodicy—why do bad things happen to good people if God is loving, just, and omnipotent?—and of justice—why do good things happen to bad people if justice is God's concern? At times the just suffer from natural disasters, economic hardship, and political oppression; at times the wicked evade natural disasters, prosper financially, and dominate politically.

In the view of Job's contemporaries, these are senseless questions. His friends, Eliphaz, Bildad, and Zophar, and a stranger, Elihu, all believe that bad things do not happen to good people. If someone suffers because of natural disasters or wicked people, it must be because they are guilty of sin. Conversely, good people are blessed by God.

Job's adversaries are ideologically frozen into their position. They stubbornly cling to tradition, which holds that God is just and acts justly, that God punishes the wicked, and that a suffering person (or their ancestor), therefore, must be guilty of having done evil to deserve their affliction. Job's adversaries do not note the flaws in their position: there are wicked rulers and wicked wealthy people who remain unpunished and even prosper, who are heartless in oppressing the poor. They profit from the labor of the poor while denying them food, drink, clothing, and shelter. So, while God might punish some wicked people, it is obvious that God does not punish all wicked people. It might also be the case, then, that God might not bestow abundant blessings on all good people and that good people might suffer. Job will not curse God, nor will he admit to wrongdoing that he did not commit, as his adversaries suggest. He will not lie to reinforce their smugness in their traditional religious perspective that the world is governed by a coercive deity.

Therefore, in contrast to what some (self-righteous) people prefer to think of as moral "common sense," the story teaches that the poor cannot be blamed for their poverty. The greed of some powerful people prevents Earth's commons goods and humans' common goods from being equitably distributed. Correspondingly, the concentration of Earth property and goods into a few hands is not, then, a "blessing from God" or a "favor from God" bestowed on a particular person or favored nation. The inequitable distribution of commons goods is not "God's will," or God's doing. Neither the powerlessness, poverty, and suffering of some, nor the power, prosperity, and security of others, can be declared to be the result of a divine dispensation of punishments and rewards. In fact, as Job indicates to his adversaries when he lists among his virtuous acts that he defended the poor from the powerful, often the two conditions are linked: the powerful subjugate the poor.

Job's adversaries believe that they have absolute moral truth in their "wisdom," and that they speak on behalf of God, when they voice their traditional teaching that suffering is a punishment for sin. Job horrifies them when he declares that God destroys both the blameless and the blameworthy and gives land to the wicked (9:22–24) and that robbers are safe in their tents (12:6).

In the Christian Scriptures, centuries after the Job narrative's origins, Jesus teaches that God's sun shines alike for just and unjust people, and God's rain falls equally on the fields of the righteous and unrighteous (Matthew 5:45); and before healing a blind man, Jesus tells his followers that the man he is about to heal is not blind because of his sins or his parents' sins; rather, his presence presents an occasion for God's power to be revealed (John 9:1–3). In his Last Judgment story (Matthew 25:31–46), Jesus warns people to express compassion toward the poor by providing them with life's necessities derived from the Earth commons and from human labor in the commons. The community as a whole should benefit from Earth's goods and from human goods made from them, such that no one is in want.

The moral and ethical implications of these ideas of Job and Jesus are multiple. Poverty in the local or global commons and the hunger, thirst, nakedness, homelessness, and ill health of the poor are not the fault of the poor. These conditions result from powerful sinful individuals and prevailing sinful social structures; people and policies prevent the equitable distribution of commons goods as common goods for the common good.

The Job narrative is very direct in stating that oppression in human communities is the work of the wicked (24:1–15). In graphic detail, the story describes how evil people remove property markers; steal flocks of sheep; deprive orphans of their donkeys and widows of their oxen (the widow and the orphan, here and in the biblical prophets, represent both actual widows and orphans and, symbolically, all poor people). The theft of domestic animals that help people earn a livelihood deprives the poor of opportunities to support themselves economically. Evil people also push the poor off the road when they are traveling and drive the poor away from their homes and communities. In order to provide food for their children, parents who are poor must scavenge in the wilderness, work as hired hands, and glean in the properties of the wicked. The poor are forced to sleep in the mountains, shivering and wet, and without clothing or shelter. The wicked even callously take infants from the poor in pledge for their debts. Ironically, the poor who are hungry carry harvest sheaves of wheat, from which they cannot make bread, and press out cooking oil that they cannot use; the poor who are thirsty press out wine that others will drink. In various ways Earth's fruits are denied to Earth's peoples; the commons is productive for the few and not for all.

Job has a moment of empathy for the hardships experienced by the working poor, noting that his condition, and his anxious wait for vindication and assistance from God, are like the longing of slaves for death to end their harsh lives, and the longing of laborers for wages delayed them (7:2–3). As a result of his suffering he is able, as most other well-to-do people are not, to understand hardships that unprivileged people endure.

The Job narrative is explicit in its teaching that an indication that a person is just is their attitude toward, and treatment of, the poor. In defending himself against his friends, who continue to accuse him of wickedness, Job declares that he rescued the poor who cried for help; assisted the orphan and the widow; was blessed by the poor for his righteous acts; helped the blind, the lame, and the needy; supported the stranger; confronted and overcame the power of the powerful who were preying on the powerless (29:12–17); did not turn away from the needy who required help, cried with those experiencing hardship, and suffered in spirit with the poor (30:24–25); and provided for the pressing needs of the poor by giving food and shelter to the orphan, clothing to the naked poor, and shelter to the traveling stranger (31:16–19; 32).

The story describes the responsibility of the prosperous toward the poor. Much as in Jesus' later parable of the Workers in the Vineyard (Matthew 19:16–30), in the Job story, a wealthy leading citizen expresses in concrete ways his compassion for those in need. In fact, as the debate between Job and his adversaries suggests, this is required of Job if he is to be a just person. The contrast between Job's just action and the unjust inaction of which he is accused by his opponents, resonates with Matthew's contrast of the vineyard owner's action and the rich young ruler's inaction (Matthew 20:116). Job helped the poor, as does the vineyard owner in the parable; the unjust person limits his support for the poor, as does the rich young man in the gospel, or rejects the poor, or oppresses the poor. Both stories suggest that some wealthy people have a conscience and are compassionate; the rich class does not merit condemnation in its entirety. Indeed, as the experience of Jesus with the rich young man indicates, God provides opportunities for the wealthy to help the poor. The number and extent of wealthy people's positive responses to the Spirit's invitation might be rare and limited, but they do exist.

Job suffers from dynamic nature and human oppression, much as have other good and just people through the ages. If the suffering poor identify with him in some way—while realizing also that he began among the prosperous and returns to being prosperous—and note that in the end the Spirit vindicates him and brings him to a better life, they might find in this story, as they do in the parables and life of Jesus, a message of hope while suffering from economic deprivation.

Through all his suffering, Job remains hopeful and faithful. He continues to obey God's laws as he understands them, even though it seems that this has no bearing on whether or not he will prosper or suffer. He hopes that God will vindicate him eventually, perhaps after he dies.

But finally, an exasperated Job demands a debate with Yahweh, surely a scandalous request (Job is questioning divine action and inaction) and an uneven match (human versus deity), to raise these issues and to protest his innocence and his loss of respect in his community. For the reader who hopes that, at last, the age-old question of the suffering of the innocent will be answered, probably the story disappoints. Yahweh tells Job that Job lacks the ability to understand the workings of creation, that everything has a reason, however hidden. Yahweh's response to the suffering issue basically is no response: Yahweh does not answer the "Why?" of Job's question; Yahweh only suggests, in essence, "Trust me." The inquisitive reader who is compassionate and possessed of a sense of moral responsibility might be frustrated and dissatisfied with the divine response that the cosmic evidence of divine creativity and power, and the commons revelation of divine compassion for all creatures, should be sufficient reasons for humans lacking the ability to comprehend divine works and intentions to accept what they cannot understand, including the suffering of the just and the innocent.

In the story, Job suffers because God permits the evil spirit to test Job's fidelity to and friendship with Yahweh. The underlying question that prompted the test and is its continuing rationale is whether or not people would be faithful to Yahweh and Yahweh's commandments if they were not coerced by fear of divine retribution for infidelity, or were not enticed by hope for a material reward for their fidelity: a spiritual blessing or enhanced community status. Job provides an affirmative answer. At the story's end, Yahweh's confidence in Job is validated. During his trials, Job taught that suffering is not always a punishment from God. Job remained faithful to Yahweh even when there seemed to be no hope of being vindicated or blessed again. God blesses Job, rejects the arguments of his adversaries, and instructs the latter that they will be forgiven for their erroneous opinions (traditional though they might have been) and their claim to be speaking for God (Job reprimanded them for this in 13:7) when they stated these positions, if they bring offerings to Job to be sacrificed to God. The story teaches that a knowing God permitted Job's test so that the Satan, the culture of the time, and, eventually, Job's adversaries all would learn that just people who suffer can and will remain faithful to Yahweh. Moreover, they would learn that human suffering might be a test of human faith in God and fidelity to God's commandments.

Job's conflict with his friends presents the historically recurring conflict between tradition and innovation in a moment of potential transition to a new way of thinking and acting. Job suggests innovation: God does not always protect the just; suffering is not always the result of sin. Job's adversaries want to maintain tradition: God rewards the just with good health, prosperity, and long life; God punishes the wicked with illness, poverty, and a shortened life span; suffering indicates where one stands with God. In this conflict, there is some common ground: both Job and his adversaries state that an indication that a person is just is their attitude toward and assistance to the poor. Job's opponents claim that a reason he is being punished is that he has ignored the poor; Job provides numerous examples of his compassion, in thought and deed, toward those less fortunate, including protecting the oppressed from their oppressors. Here is an area where tradition and innovation agree: justice means to succor the poor. When one considers that traditions more easily go into transition when what are seen as their core beliefs or core moral values are maintained, while their more "negotiable" secondary beliefs and values are altered, it is evident in the Job story that both the traditionalists and the innovator agree that compassion for the oppressed poor is a core value.

The story's central question and problem are presented through multi-level debates. The question of whether or not there is a relationship between human conduct and a system of rewards and punishments that promote good and deter evil involves a debate between God and the Satan, between Job and his adversaries and, at the end, an implied, unvoiced debate between God and Job's opponents when God affirms Job's position and condemns that of his adversaries. The problem of innocent suffering in the presence of a loving and powerful deity involves a debate between a vocal Job and a silent God, and then a vocal God and a silent Job; and, a debate between a silent God and the questioning reader who is drawn to and reflects on the narrative (as evidenced by the way it has been interpreted over millennia by people of diverse cultures and distinct eras). The reader is not distracted from their own concerns about evil because of the framing of the Job story by the heavenly realm discussion between God and the Satan, which implies that Job's suffering results when God allows the Satan to test him.

God finally participates in the debate. God tells Job that it is beyond his human intellectual capability to understand the reasons why he has had to suffer. God, therefore, neither explains divine reasoning to him nor gives him some consolation by responding to the question of innocent suffering. God does state that God is aware of the needs of creatures in the sky's heights and the seas' depths and provides necessities of life for them.

Job's understanding—divinely affirmed at the story's end—that God is not coercive is complemented by the teaching of Rabbi Abraham Joshua Heschel in *The Prophets*.[1] Heschel reflects on divine pathos in times of human suffering and wrongdoing. He states that the prophets do not proclaim justice. Rather, they proclaim God's pathos, they speak for "the God of justice, for God's concern for justice."[2] The prophets' passion for justice is "rooted in their sympathy with divine pathos."[3] Heschel observes that for the prophets, God is "in a personal and intimate relation to the world,"[4] and thereby is "moved and affected by what happens in the world, and reacts accordingly. Events and human actions arouse in [God] joy or sorrow, pleasure or wrath." Human deeds move, affect and grieve, or gladden and please God.[5] God is "personally involved in, even stirred by" human "conduct and fate."[6] God experiences what creation experiences: "God is concerned about the world, and shares in its fate."[7] Within the world, God is particularly concerned about humanity. The human predicament "is a predicament of God Who has a stake in the human situation."[8] Indeed, "Whatever [a person] does affects not only [their] own life, but also the life of God," to the extent that God's life is directed to people.[9] In the Bible, people encounter Yahweh not as "Wholly Other" but as "transcendent relatedness."[10] The Spirit's life "interacts with the life of the people. . . . Biblical religion is not what [people] do with [their] solitariness, but rather what [people] do with God's concern for all [people]."[11] God, then, is transcendent being and immanent becoming, engaged with and experiencing creation, including with creatures who suffer in the Earth commons.

The thought that God suffers with them might or might not comfort people who experience or observe suffering in the Earth commons, who wonder how the commons can be sacramental in such times. While recognizing that the Spirit suffers but does not cause suffering, they wonder still why God permits it, and allows it to continue. While acknowledging that God does not constantly use the carrot and stick to control people, they ask still why God does not use divine power to help them when they are in need, whether from nature-caused or human-caused harm. The Spirit's absorption of suffering, sympathetic incorporation of it into divine being-becoming, and use of it toward its transformation into nonsuffering in future generations might alleviate the experience of suffering intellectually and spiritually, if not actually and materially. But it is still a hidden God who does this, and the suffering remains visible, disruptive, and painful.

An altruistic person might hope that suffering is in some sense redemptive, that what they or someone beloved to them endures will be personally or socially transformative, and perhaps in some way promote greater divine-human, divine-creation, or people-to-people communion. The suffering of one or several people might effect a better future for self, family, or community, however broadly conceived. God allows evil in order to effect an ultimately positive result; or, God eventually derives from evil an ultimately good outcome. In these scenarios, an evil action comes to have a good final result. In Genesis, Joseph taught his brothers, decades after they had sold him into slavery, that he would not otherwise have come to power in Egypt and been able to save them from the drought afflicting the region (45:4–15). Good ultimately emerges from evil over time, due to the Spirit's corrective intervention either directly or indirectly, through the use of people or of natural forces, or due to processes in progress in the interplay of cosmos and chaos. Other acts or historical events that represent the understanding that innocent or unjust suffering leads to a good (or at least acceptable or endurable) outcome include religious interpretations of the use of the scapegoat in Israel; Jesus' acceptance of the consequences of his just life in an unjust context; and, for some rabbis after the Holocaust, the suffering of Jewish innocents to atone for human evil on a global scale and to promote a subsequent transformation of human conduct. Here again is altruism: suffering on behalf of others. Complementarily but on a smaller scale, a parent with limited income might sacrifice having some goods that they would like to acquire, deciding to provide instead for their children's needs or reasonable wants, as understood in the present or as projected for the future.

Another response to theodicy issues flows from the final chapters of the Job story, from God's response to Job. In the vast, diverse, and complex universe, where cosmos and chaos, order and contingency interact, events in cosmic microcontexts are in some way an integral part of a dynamic cosmic macrocontext and an evolutionary Earth commons (with its abiotic turbulence, its biotic predator-prey relationships, and its human evil). The current creating process is to be viewed as the best way, in divine understanding, for events to progress (at times with Spirit's loving guidance toward unity and harmony, and toward a relational community). If there had been a better way for creation to unfold, the Creator would have initiated it.

In none of the preceding, however, is there a definitive and universally satisfying answer to the question of theodicy, of divine nonintervention in a divinely initiated world in which the innocent suffer harm. It remains the human task, beyond philosophical and theological speculation, for people to adjust their lives and respond to natural disasters, and to work to promote justice to overcome human evil in its individual and institutional forms.

The secular version today of Job's adversaries' position would be to blame the victim, to declare that poor people should "pull themselves up by their bootstraps," because "anyone can make it if they really try." This assertion sometimes has racial overtones, which in the Earth commons and the human commons are expressed as ecoracism. Regions with politically powerless, racially distinct poor people are subjected to toxic incinerators, polluting trash sites, or poisonous effluents and emissions from industrial plants. Additionally, when natural disasters afflict these areas, people do not receive the sympathy, prompt response, or necessary assistance from the dominant culture that they would have received had they been members of the dominant culture in such a plight. The assumption is that the poor, especially the ethnic "others," are lazy; in countries where there is some form of social assistance to the poor, they are labeled "welfare cheats" or the equivalent. Such an attitude on the part of the relatively better-off reinforces individual self-righteousness ("I'm good because I'm doing well") and ethnocultural indifference; both are linked to greed as well as to lack of compassion. If their poverty is poor people's own fault, then the affluent do not have to enact laws and promote policies that aid the poor. Consequently, tax monies should be returned to the more affluent, advantaged taxpayer so that they might purchase more consumer goods rather than be used to assist needy, disadvantaged people who seek community assistance. People advocating these courses of action will vote for politicians whose campaigns proclaim they will lower taxes, even though both candidate and voter know that that means cutting "social programs" that aid the poor who need them; but, after all, "they could make it if they really tried."

For the biotic community in the Earth commons, the Job narrative affirms God's concern and provision of necessities for a range of creatures, from hawks in the mountain heights to fish in the ocean depths (38–41). In a passage reminiscent of the perspective of St. Francis and of teachings in Psalms, Sirach, and Wisdom, Job suggests, "Ask the animals, and they will teach you; the birds of the air, and they will tell you; ask the plants of the earth, and they will teach you; and the fish of the sea will declare to you. Who among all these does not know that the hand of the Lord has done this? In his hand is the life of every living thing, and the breath of every human being" (12:7–10). Creation is a mediation of the Creator, but also has a role and sacredness in itself. In the passage, creatures have the capacity to pass on insights from God (doing so consciously seems to be implied; doing so unconsciously is the traditional interpretation). Creatures are (consciously or unconsciously) sacramental beings who reveal the Spirit-immanent in the commons. This role becomes operative in the Earth commons when humans emerge in the course of biotic evolution, and become Earth's reflective consciousness.

GOOD AND EVIL IN THE
EVOLUTIONARY COMMONS

Cosmic dynamics began with a singular, explosive event some fifteen billion years ago. Earth in turn was formed about 4.5 billion years ago, and primitive life emerged a billion years thereafter. The basic laws of the physical universe had begun to be operative after the singularity, and they interacted from that moment on with contingent events in the extended universe and in local solar systems. Humans evolved on Earth physically, but with a distinct spiritual consciousness created by and related to divine consciousness. Later in the course of biological and cultural evolution, the Bible would call humans "images" of God. In their early historical moments people were integrated with other members of the biotic community and adapted to their Earth commons and bioregional commons. They gathered roots, nuts, fruits, and vegetables; they hunted animals for their flesh and skins, to provide food, clothing, and shelter. They shared their local environment with herbivores, with carnivores, and with other omnivores.

In some religious histories, humans in the distant past turned away from a unique relationship with the Creator and creation, and disrupted the integral biotic community. They "fell from grace." Other, more contemporary traditions (religious and other) dispute the "fallen" nature of humans. They view stories of an idyllic past as really a vision and a hope for the future, when humans will be interrelated, interdependent, and integrated Earth inhabitants. In this view, humans are rising apes, not fallen angels.

People in the Christian tradition believe that Jesus came to guide humans to live in harmonious relationships within their own communities while they are related to other communities, and while they live in communion with God. The "reign of God," the relational community or creation commons community that Jesus proclaimed, parallels within human history the evolutionary unfolding of God's continuous creation process in biotic history. The implications of Jesus' teachings are that people should integrate both histories as responsible members of human communities and as responsible caretakers of the broader biotic community and abiotic creation. People who envision a unified creation, operating as a relational community, and who strive to bring it into being, seek to effect the realization of a time when God's will is done "on Earth as it is in heaven." In this Christian understanding, the Spirit incarnate redeems people from their disunity with their Creator, with each other, and with creation as a whole, liberating them through grace to assume their biblically envisioned role as "images of God."

In the Christian tradition, divine incarnation is divine intervention and divine immersion, both in time and in the course and projects of human history. Other divine interventions are plausible from a Christian perspective, which raises again the question of why God does not intervene to prevent evil. Perhaps what might be considered here are grades of evil, or the degree of severity of particular evils. Some types of evil or deviation from a divine plan or sensibility require some form of direct divine intervention, others indirect, and yet others will work themselves out in human or evolutionary or geologic history. The epistemological problem is that while people impacted by them view them as extremely important at this moment in this place, they are ultimately only fragments of time and space in the overall course of cosmic time and cosmic expanse.

One way of responding to the problem from within the tradition is through a deepened consideration of the scriptural understanding of God's voluntary relinquishment of divine power. In his letter to the Philippians, Paul teaches that Christ Jesus, although he had a divine form, "did not regard equality with God as something to be exploited, but emptied himself, taking the form of a slave, being born in human likeness. And being found in human form, he humbled himself and became obedient to death—even death on a cross" (2:6–8). The original Greek word for God's self-emptying is *kenosis*. If the concept of kenosis at the time of the Incarnation is considered as a divine characteristic, expressed also during cosmogenesis, the existence of evil can be understood better by considering its emergence and existence in cosmic and commons contexts characterized by freedom. Through kenosis the Creator Spirit allows creation to participate in divine freedom by having its own freedom. God rejects the use of divine coercive power to set up a system of rewards and punishments, to make the universe conform to some kind of preconceived design, or to deny creative cosmic freedom. The Creator is free; creation is free. The cosmos as a whole, in that regard, and not just humankind, is an "image of God." Creation and humans within it have freedom to act, to make choices. Christians believe that God in Jesus is born powerless in a stable, to poor people in an oppressed nation, rather than to the family of the powerful Roman emperor. His eventual crucifixion demonstrates God's acceptance of the fullness of kenosis, allowing humans power even over God incarnate; and describes God's direct experience of suffering, parallel to what Heschel expressed as the "divine pathos." Kenosis as God's *cosmic* self-emptying occurred when God imaginatively conceived the universe, when the universe was born, and as the universe continues through time; and kenosis as God's *commons* self-emptying occurred in the conception, birth, and death of Jesus. The Spirit's self-emptying in the Jesus event resulted in the conceptualized divine-human being assuming concrete form. The Spirit in both events gives birth. Both the cosmos and Jesus are offspring of divine love. Cosmic kenosis complements incarnational kenosis. Paul's teaching in Philippians contradicts the beliefs of Job's adversaries, and complements the beliefs of Job and the book's author. Paul teaches that God does not use divine power coercively, but empties divine being of that power in relating to humanity compassionately. Paul teaches, too, that innocent people suffer—including Jesus, in whom God dwells. In both narratives an innocent just man suffers, is disparaged by his contemporaries, and through divine power has his well-being restored: Job in material ways, Jesus in material and spiritual ways.

All the good work that people do as God's images relates human history to biotic history and geologic history, and brings creation closer to its fulfillment. The Creator's primordial vision, incrementally concretized in the creation process in the cosmic commons and the Earth commons, becomes realized at the end of time as a new heaven and a new Earth.

Liberation theologies rightfully have pointed to sinful social structures, as well as sinful individuals, as the sources of evil and harm to people and peoples. Such social structures are human constructs and violate the responsibility of governments to ensure, to the greatest extent possible, the societal and physical well-being—the common good—of members of their society.

In Brazil, the *favelas* of the poor are situated on the mountainsides around Rio de Janeiro and other cities. In other nations, the mountain mansions of the wealthy hold commanding positions over the modest dwellings of less affluent or impoverished people. But the dangers of torrential rains and massive mudslides mean that in Rio the shantytowns of the oppressed poor will hug the perilous high places. While the harm done by rain and mud in such circumstances might seem to be a "natural disaster," in reality it comes from social control, from sinful structures that confine the poor to dangerous places to live.

The goodness of creation is in its correspondence to the Creator's intent that it have the freedom to develop over cosmic eons in the presence of a patient and eternal Spirit (Psalm 90:4 declares that "a thousand years are like a day in God's sight"). Human impatience with the pace of developing goodness rightfully might be, given an oppressive human condition, an expression of frustration from waiting expectantly over generations for divine vision to be realized. People need intergenerational hope as well as intergenerational responsibility. Human hope is realized to the extent that human responsibility is fulfilled. Divine vision and divine expectation are realized while divine patience bears with and guides, on occasion, developing human social responsibility as it interacts with biotic evolution and abiotic dynamics. Creation is "good" when natural disasters occur, or during other types of violence in nature (e.g., predator-prey relationships), including evolutionary events, because it reveals and expresses cosmic freedom and creativity in process.

If the process is very good overall, in that it leads to the betterment of the *whole* (or partial "wholes": the biotic community, Earth, cosmos), where the community takes precedence over the individual or species, then individuals and species in an evolutionary process are contributing to this process and participating in the overall evolution of the cosmos, perhaps with the hope of participating in some beneficial end result in the distant future.

People who respect the process as very good should consider the extent to which they are interfering in it unnecessarily, and destroying or diminishing its goodness, when their actions directly or indirectly devastate habitat or eliminate entire species. The cosmos, Earth, the overall evolutionary process, and human self-interest are negatively impacted by their actions. People cannot expect a miraculous intervention of a deus ex machina or a *deus ex caelum* to rectify human errors, nor can they assume that the Creator has inserted into physical laws a corrective to offset harmful activities of aberrant individuals and species. If human destructiveness toward nature or oppression of human and not-human creatures continues, some creatures (or genes within creatures) that are essential for some type of evolutionary development later in Earth's history will disappear before their time arrives to contribute to biotic and cosmic development. Disappeared or extincted species, or some of their individual members, might have possessed genes or gene combinations needed for adaptive purposes, genes that are possessed by no other creatures or individuals. This will impact the possibility of existence of other species that might have existed, or of currently existing species that might have adapted to available niches necessary for continuing evolution or for the well-being of the biotic community. Needed new medicines, foods, and other potential developments will be postponed or never come to be. An *un*natural "natural" catastrophe might result from irreversible alterations of the environment and of ecological relations, because of human impacts in and on the commons. Natural catastrophes and social evils will disrupt the intention and activity of cosmic freedom.

The second creation story (and the flood story) in Genesis state that humanity brought (and brings) evil into a good creation and that death and suffering came into the world with human sin (a historically inaccurate understanding). Today, the story's meaning might be that humans have altered ordinary evolutionary processes for selfish ends and that they strive to extend and deepen anthropocentrism so that they will "become like gods." They seek to orient creation toward themselves and use it solely instrumentally. This is idolatry. Creation already groans for relief from the impacts of human failings. Creation itself is not "fallen." It suffers from human failings or "fallenness" throughout history, not solely in the distant past.

In the spirit of Job, people uncomfortable with religious descriptions of violent divine power who believe in a loving and merciful—and just but not judgmental—deity, might question the extent to which attitudes or acts purported to be "God's punishments" are really human cultural descriptions versus human attributions of divine action. (Sometimes, rather than seeking to be "images of God," Christians and others project God as an "image of man" and follow the false god they created in their own image.) Elsewhere in the biblical Wisdom literature, the book of Wisdom states (1:13–14) that God did not create death; God does not "delight" in death; God wants life to exist.

In Job, Yahweh's response to Job about innocent suffering is one possible formulation about theodicy from that period of biblical history that might be found insightful today, millennia afterward, in the current moment in evolutionary history. The story teaches, as seen earlier, that God cares about creation and creatures and even solicitously provides food for free or "wild" animals. There are cosmic and evolutionary processes and events that humans cannot understand or can only partially understand. People might have to accept natural disasters as part of the way the world works when divine kenosis gives it freedom, but recognize at the same time that the same divine love that brought the cosmos into being still works in the world without eliminating its freedom. These responses are not universally acceptable. But perhaps, like Job, ordinarily people in the commons are able to see only fragments of the whole. Their individual microcosmic moment and place is within a macrocosmic process that encompasses past, present, and future through cosmic time and throughout cosmic space. In the meantime, God suffers with those suffering in creation. The Spirit-transcendent conceptualizes and gives birth to the universe, directly or indirectly. The Spirit-immanent participates in the continuing creation of the universe, and absorbs and transforms, in time, its pain and suffering.

People might develop more of a teleological perspective, then, and have confidence in an ongoing process initiated and continued by the Creator Spirit, even when they cannot see the whole for the transitory and transitional parts. Initial creation and ongoing creation might actually be doing what they are supposed to be doing according to their created capability to evolve and organize and go from "emerging" to "emerged." John Muir reflected along these lines: "Storms of every sort, torrents, earthquakes, cataclysms, 'convulsions of nature,' etc., however mysterious and lawless at first sight they may seem, are only harmonious notes in the song of creation, varied expressions of God's love."[12]

The Spirit brought the universe into being and by kenosis grants it freedom to develop. This includes freedom for abiotic Earth with its turbulent hurricanes and tornadoes, and its violent earthquakes (some of which generate tsunamis) and volcanoes, but also with its gentle rains that promote plant life and growth for farm and forest, and its living waters that nourish creatures of the land, air, and water: plants, animals, birds, and fish. The divine Spirit gives evolutionary freedom to biotic Earth with its predator-prey relationships but also with its collaborative relationships among distinct species. Job notes both the power of God to create and the prerogative of God to care for creation. God reminds Job that Job was not living when the universe initially began to come into being; God further instructs Job that God provides food for birds and animals. The abiotic commons, then, is turbulent, and its activity at times will harm humans and their interests. But its Creator is compassionate toward the biotic community and alleviates some of the impacts of abiotic restlessness and biotic competitive relationships. The divine pathos is both an experiential and an expressive mode of divine being-becoming. Compassion counters cosmic chaos and commons conflicts. The Spirit's creating power is complemented by the Spirit's mercy and love. The Spirit teaches people, through Job, about divine creativity and divine solicitude. The Spirit provides food for hungry living creatures in the skies, mountains, and seas.

The story of Job offers insights for considering how human evil operates to oppress the powerless, and why natural disasters occur in dynamic nature. Humans are the integrating reflective consciousness in creation. As people reflect on the harms that they and other creatures experience they might discern, nonetheless, ultimate meaning in the vast and dynamic cosmos of which they are a part. Insights about the cosmos and the commons might come from other creatures, or from the Spirit who speaks with and through them: "Ask the animals, and they will teach you; the birds of the air, and they will tell you; ask the plants of the earth, and they will teach you; and the fish of the sea will declare to you." The sacramental commons instructs people who are open to its teachings.

NOTES

1. Abraham J. Heschel, *The Prophets: An Introduction* (New York: Harper Torchbooks, 1969), 2 vols.

2. Heschel, *The Prophets*, I: 219.

3. Heschel, *The Prophets*, I: 218.

4. Heschel, *The Prophets*, II: 3.

5. Heschel, *The Prophets*, II: 4.

6. Heschel, *The Prophets*, II: 4.

7. Heschel, *The Prophets*, II: 5.

8. Heschel, *The Prophets*, II: 6.

9. Heschel, *The Prophets*, II: 6.

10. Heschel, *The Prophets*, II: 7.

11. Heschel, *The Prophets*, II: 10.

12. Edwin Way Teale, *The Wilderness World of John Muir* (Boston: Houghton Mifflin, 1954), 169.

IV

COMMON GROUND

$\mathcal{O}$ver the centuries since the biblical Christian era, people who identified themselves as Christians have focused on Spirit-transcendent almost to the exclusion of Spirit-immanent so that they have forgotten or neglected social teachings of Jesus that relate to compassion for the poor, except insofar as they have practiced works of "charity" to those in need. They have not addressed or sought to eliminate structural injustices and social problems in the commons. The biblical Jubilee Year, adapted to contemporary contexts and issues, remedies this omission. New Jubilee principles complement principles of Christian ecological ethics. When people live in or strive toward a relational community, these combined principles provide common ground for the interrelation of engagement with the Spirit, conservation of the commons, and care for community.

· *10* ·

Jubilee in the Commons

The Spirit is immanent in cosmos and commons. The creative power of the Spirit is incorporated into cosmic dynamics and evident in biotic evolution and commons dynamics. In the dynamic commons, humans are invited—as individuals and as communities, as the integrating consciousness of creation—to care for Earth, the biotic community, and each other. Throughout history, people have rejected or misunderstood this caring responsibility. As a consequence, Earth has been harmed and the goods of Earth have not been distributed equitably. The relational community initiated by Jesus has yet to become coextensive with creation and community. The integration of the human common good within and in balance with the broader biotic community is incomplete. Anthropocentrism and individualism essentially and extensively have displaced creation care and community collaboration.

In the past and to some extent yet in the present, people have been imbued almost exclusively with a sense of God-transcendent. In Christianity, this continues even though Jesus, when his disciples asked that he teach them to pray, told them to call God "Abba," a term of intimate love and relationship, and despite Jesus' teaching that God cares about creatures other than humans, such as birds and flowers. Still, many if not most Christians tend to view and to relate to the natural world of their human lives as solely a place of passage, a short-term dwelling site about which they are to have little concern. They have separated creation from incarnation and redemption, negating the integral relationship between these complementary aspects of the creating and loving Spirit's relation to the universe.

Cosmic creation and social transformation are inextricably linked. The Spirit in whom all creatures live and move and have their being continues to bring the universe into existence. The Spirit calls people to care for their niche in creation, to care for each other, and to care for all life. In the Christian tradition, doctrines of divine creativity and divine incarnation are woven together in the biblical Jubilee Year, which serves as a periodic reminder for

181

people to acknowledge and actuate their responsibilities to God, to each other, and to all creation. In the Jubilee Year prescriptions, people are reminded to care for the commons as a trust from God and to distribute equitably commons land and commons goods as common goods, so that the needs of all might be met and the common good ensured.

The Jubilee Year presents the Spirit-transcendent relationally engaged with creation as Spirit-immanent. The Creator Spirit's care for the biotic community as expressed in Genesis and Job, among other biblical books, is expressed in Jubilee teachings. People are taught four practices of ecojustice to transform the way they live in community and in the commons, so that their creation care will complement the Spirit's solicitude for the biotic community. As with other biblical texts cited previously, the Jubilee passages emphasize that the Creator is not concerned solely with humankind and did not intend Earth and the extended universe to be viewed and used solely or even primarily as merely a setting for human life.

Reflection on the Jubilee Year offers people an opportunity to focus anew on a vision presented first in the Torah and then affirmed by Jesus. It gives humanity a moment to envision and explore how Abba's will might be done "on Earth as it is in heaven." The Jubilee principles for social and planetary transformation are outlined initially in Leviticus and later recalled by Jesus in Luke. Analysis of the Earth commons, the situation of the biotic community, and relations among human communities reveals that such a vision is even more imperative today than in past ages. People who recall the vision are prompted to ask how the biblical Jubilee might be revived and implemented in current social contexts. The Jubilee is understood not just as an ideal presented in and for a past age; it is accepted as a challenge and an invitation through the ages. People should take responsibility for recalling the vision and restoring its application, as appropriate for their own place and time.

THE JUBILEE CALL

Yahweh instructs the people of Israel to proclaim a Jubilee, a "sabbath of sabbaths," every fifty years. The Jubilee Year included the sabbath year provisions regarding care for the land, care for free and domesticated biota, and compassion for people, and added land reform to them. The Jubilee expressed ecological teachings that ultimately Earth is God's creation and ultimately God's possession; and that the Spirit expects people to care for Earth and to provide equitably for the needs of the human community and the broader biotic community.

The Jubilee should implement four practices (see Leviticus 25; Deuteronomy 15; Exodus 23):

- Rest for the land
- Release of slaves
- Remission of debts
- Redistribution of the land

These Jubilee observances were designed to rejuvenate Earth and the community. The Jubilee teachings promote recognition of divine dominion in creation and relate human trusteeship of Earth both to care for the land with which humans work and to justice for the poor. People are called to use Earth's land and commons goods responsibly. Property in land, and in goods from the land, is to be used by those who have civil ownership of land and those who work for them to benefit the community as a whole, with a particular regard for the landless poor.

Rest for the Land

The Jubilee prescription of *rest for the land* was intended to remind the ancient Israelites about several fundamental biblical teachings. First, God is the ultimate and only absolute owner of the land: "The land shall not be sold in perpetuity; for the land is mine, and you are but aliens who have become my tenants" (Leviticus 25:23). Second, the land needs periodic rest from the impacts of human work: "You shall not sow, nor shall you reap the aftergrowth or pick the grapes from the untrimmed vines" (Leviticus 25:11). Third, all God's creatures have a right to the land's produce: "You shall let the land lie untilled and unharvested, that the poor among you may eat of it and the beasts of the field may eat what the poor leave. So also shall you do in regard to your vineyard and your olive grove" (Exodus 23:10–11); and "While the land has its sabbath, all its produce will be food . . . for your livestock and for the wild animals on your land" (Leviticus 25:7). All of these practices enabled the land to rest, and humans, animals, and birds all were entitled to be nurtured by its "volunteer crops," which grew from seeds sown or trees grown in past years.

The practice of rest for the land reminded the people that Earth is God's and that they should respect and care for the Creator Spirit's creation and creatures. It required that the land not be sown or harvested during the Jubilee Year, which would result, apparently, in economic hardship for farmers and their families and in food shortages for the general populace. It reminded people to have faith that Yahweh would care for them as Yahweh had done in the wilderness years, when Earth and divine power provided for their needs. Now that the people were settled on the land, they were to cooperate with Earth and Yahweh as they did their planting, cultivating, and harvesting in the sixth year, and rely on that cooperative work to provide for their needs for the next two years: from the end of the sixth year's harvest until the harvest at the end of the first year of the next cycle of years. Domestic and free animals were not to be chased from the farmer's fields, for the farmer has no exclusive ownership in land, and all creatures have a right to provide for their needs from Earth's bounty. The prescription meant that Earth should periodically rest, as people do. In a practical sense, this meant that farmers would not overwork the land, which would be detrimental to their material survival and their economic self-interest. It meant also that they should recognize that God calls Earth and all creatures "good" in themselves, not just because they provide goods to meet human needs and wants. The Earth commons, including air, water, soil, and biota, has intrinsic value, not just instrumental value.

Release of Slaves

The Jubilee Year required *release of slaves*: "This fiftieth year you shall make sacred by proclaiming liberty in the land for all its inhabitants" (Leviticus 25:10). Slavery was an important economic benefit for the slaveholders, who had to compensate their workers with little more than food, clothing, and shelter for their survival and reproduction. There were two categories of slaves: fellow Hebrews who had voluntarily become slaves during times of economic hardship, when they feared that they might not be able to provide for themselves or their families; and foreigners who had been captured in battle or bought from slave traders. In Israel, both types of slaves were to be treated with respect, but that did not eliminate the demeaning nature of their social status, nor their lack of opportunity to have a family and an occupation of their own choosing. In the Jubilee Year, Hebrew slaves who had provided economic benefits solely for others had the right to be free and to use their labor to provide for themselves. Throughout the years leading to the Jubilee, the community as a whole was to help their neighbors both by ameliorating the circumstances—health, natural disasters, personal shortcomings—that had pushed some of their members into slavery, and by amending economic policies and social practices that maintained them there.

Remission of Debts

The Jubilee Year, as with other Sabbath Years, required *remission of debts*: "At the end of every seven-year period you shall have a relaxation of debts, which shall be observed as follows: every creditor shall relax his claim on what he has loaned his neighbor" (Deuteronomy 15:1–2). This principle implements a minor redistribution of wealth. Those who had benefited most from the combination of their own talents, their family position and inheritance, and operative economic structures were to give to those who had experienced economic hardship an opportunity for a financial comeback and a renewed stake in society. The remission of debts stimulated members of the community to practice economic compassion and to promote economic renewal. People with the least financial resources, who had little or no hope of ever paying their creditors, would benefit most. Freed from their immediate economic burden, they would be enabled to start over and use their abilities to provide a better life for their family.

Redistribution of the Land

The Jubilee Year required *redistribution of the land*: "It shall be a jubilee for you, when every one of you shall return to his own property, every one to his own family estate" (Leviticus 25:10). People were to receive back, from those who had bought their family homestead, their ancestral property—free of all encumbrances. The intent of this requirement was to prevent the land base of Israel from being consolidated into the hands of one or a few large landholders. If the land were not periodically redistributed, social and natural wealth would be controlled by a wealthy minority, to the detriment of the community as a whole. The controlling landholders decided how the land should be used and how much of it was to be dedicated to the (sometimes selfish) interests of property owners and how much to the needs of the people as a whole. Concentrated ownership would violate Israel's religious understanding that Earth is primarily and ultimately God's, secondarily a community good, and last of all a private benefit. The Jubilee taught that individual families were to earn their livelihood by working with Earth and for the human community. The redistribution of land every fifty years would mean that even those whose family had owned the agricultural land that was least productive and therefore least economically viable would receive it back if it had been sold, and they would have an opportunity to start over again with their restored land as their economic base. Those with the most productive land would not be able to use its natural wealth as a source of power to control the lives and future of all the people by buying and retaining other families' lands when natural disasters, accidents, or ill health prevented a family from working diligently to receive a financial return from their labor on the land.

The Jubilee Year, then, was to be a time of starting over for the Israelite poor: their debts were cancelled, their slavery was ended, and their property in land was to be redistributed to them. The descendants of the original Hebrew settlers, according to the original boundaries that had been determined at the time of settlement, would receive back their family inheritance. The land would be renewed as well, since the Jubilee Year was also a Sabbath Year, a year of rest for the land so that it might restore itself. Yahweh, the ultimate owner of the land, entrusted the land to the entire community to be used as a common good, even when it was divided by property lines. The Jubilee requirements represent an effort to ensure that land remained a community benefit as a source of life (food production) and a source of livelihood (added value from agricultural labor).

The Jubilee expresses concerns that if the land of Israel were not periodically *redistributed*, a few families might eventually own it and determine its future—and the future of the people of Israel—according to those families' *wants* and not the people's *needs*. If the land were not *cared for*, it would become unproductive, unable to provide for the people. In either case, the needs of the community would not be met.

The basic criterion for land ownership and use, then, was quite simple: will this ownership and use benefit the entire people as a community, or only enrich a segment of that community? The understanding that there were three levels of ownership—divine, community, and private, in descending order—reminded people of their responsibilities as landowners. Private property in land, the third level, was subordinate to the needs of the community and ultimately to the dominion of Yahweh, on whose behalf people were trustees of the lands they held as families and individuals within a community.

JESUS AND THE JUBILEE

In Jesus' time, land consolidation into the hands of a few, and poverty and exploitation of the many, were pressing social issues. The Roman occupation and oppressive subjugation of Israel hindered Jewish farmers' observation of biblical requirements for land use and for compassionate care of the poor; the collaboration of some Jews who benefited economically from the occupation exacerbated conditions for the vast majority of Jews. Jesus preached a radical sermon on land ownership, use, and distribution when he was invited as an itinerant rabbi to teach in the synagogue in his home town of Nazareth.

Luke (4:16–21) narrates how Jesus called for observance of the Jubilee Year. The text that Jesus read, on which he would base his sermon, was a passage that describes a time when Yahweh's anointed one (Messiah) would proclaim "good news to the poor." Captives would be freed, the oppressed would be liberated, and the "year of favor of the Lord" would be promulgated (Isaiah 61:1–2). The Isaiah text suggests concrete ways of implementing the Jubilee laws expressed in Leviticus.

After he read from the Isaiah scroll, Jesus gave it back to the synagogue attendant and announced, "Today this scripture has been fulfilled while you were listening." With these words, Jesus declared two things: first, that he was the Messiah; second, that it was time for a Jubilee Year to be observed. Justice required its proclamation and promulgation. Centuries after the composition of the Leviticus and Isaiah texts, Jesus declared that the poor had been kept from their inheritance for too long. The "good news for the poor" was that it was time for the Jubilee that would give them a land base and a chance to begin their lives anew.

The Jubilee Year advocated by Jesus is indeed "good news for the poor." A person in the worst economic situation, in which they had lost the family farm, overworked it and gone into debt trying to save it, and finally had become a slave when unable to pay their debt or even to obtain food and shelter, would be extraordinarily exhilarated when the Jubilee was observed. They would get back the family homestead, it would rest for a year to be rejuvenated, debts that encumbered the land and burdened poor families would be canceled, and they could work the land as free people. Obviously, the poor of the land would be lifted up from their downtrodden position and be joyful, while the rich who would lose land, slaves, and debt repayments would be unhappy. Roman government officials, and many of the wealthy Jewish landowners of Jesus' time (and their political and religious supporters), would not have greeted kindly Jesus' proclamation of the Jubilee.

Today, similar political, economic class, and even religious resistance can be expected when Jews and Christians seek to revive Jubilee teachings and practices. But the times require a reconsideration and promotion of Jubilee-based laws and community projects that are relevant to new historical periods and social situations. A class war is being waged against the poor within the United States and other affluent nations, and by those dominant nations against "underdeveloped" countries whose economic "development" and social well-being are subordinate to ("under") the wants and control of affluent nations. Poor people and racial and ethnic groups lack employment, living wages, adequate health care, basic education, and a voice in their governance. The class war is waged internally without tanks and bombs, externally with those weapons and with political bribes and the overthrow of democratically elected majority governments. Populist songwriter and folk singer Woody Guthrie sang during the Great Depression of the twentieth century that "some people fight with a fountain pen, and some people fight with a gun."

Oppressed populations suffer from both types of control. It is time for a Jubilee consciousness. It is time for a new Jubilee.

THE JUBILEE

In his sermons during his travels, Jesus asked his followers to be like yeast in bread dough. Just as a small amount of leavening could influence a large mass of dough, Jesus' disciples, although few in number, were to impact the world at large by disseminating beyond their place and time Jesus' teachings about the "reign of God," a spiritually and socially relational community in communion with the Spirit. This integral relational community would seek to eliminate those aspects of human life and culture, those problems and injustices of the historical moment, which contradicted principles expressed in Jesus' social teachings.

Christians who relate to Earth as a sacramental commons, and to life as a biotic community, could participate in and extend the developing relational community by imagining and implementing a contemporary expression of the Jubilee Year. Complementary to the Leviticus text, and in the spirit of teachings from the prophet Isaiah and Jesus, they could offer a new Jubilee as a means of caring for the Earth commons, distributing commons goods as common goods, and promoting the common good of humankind integrated within biokind as a whole. They could help to effect local, regional, and national extensions of the relational community. In the third Christian millennium, the new Jubilee offers a dynamic vision, to be realized gradually even as it evolves and adapts to new crises and contexts.

Based on biblical Jubilee Year requirements, the Jubilee principles are as follows:

- Conserve the commons.
- Commit to the common good.
- Compart common goods.
- Commonize the commons.

The implementation of contemporary expressions of the Jubilee Year would enable conditions for the relational community to be realized. Engagement with the revelatory or sacramental commons suggests implementation of the Jubilee. People who envision a transformed commons are strengthened to strive to implement Jubilee provisions: to benefit Earth, future generations of humankind, and biokind as a whole.

Conserve the Commons

Conserve the commons is the Jubilee requirement that parallels and renews the biblical Jubilee Year prescription to rest the land. In a world of more than six billion people, agricultural land could not be taken out of production throughout Earth or even in multiple Earth regions. People could not refrain from harvesting produce for very practical, subsistence reasons: food production provides for international nutrition needs and provides wages for workers to support their families. Even a temporary pause in agriculture's role would harm people, especially the most vulnerable. But the underlying principles, that Earth should be conserved as a trust from God and that the biotic community as a whole has a right to subsistence food, can be observed in complementary ways. To conserve the commons means to care for the ecosystem—including its biotic and abiotic manifestations—responsibly.

With a Jubilee consciousness, people see their region as a commons, as their common dwelling, and as the provider of the natural goods needed by all members of the community of life. Natural habitats for members of the biotic community would be restored, as needed, and conserved. Communities would ensure that their citizens have clean air, potable water, and chemical-free soil. Mining operations would be carefully controlled, and prohibited where and when they would pollute the Earth solely to gain metals, such as gold, used primarily for adornment. Mined and forested lands would be restored. Agricultural lands, which should be cooperative enterprises or owner-operated family enterprises, would have appropriate crop rotations and periodic rest for regeneration on selected sections; many family farmers and ranchers today are actively engaged in such practices. Agriculturalists would use organic methods to the greatest extent possible. Free and domesticated animals, birds, and fish would have access to viable habitats and sustainable food sources not only during Jubilee years, but also in the years between their periodic observance. The biotic community, including its human members, has a right to a clean and healthful commons. If people conserve the commons that right will be restored and retained. The Jubilee would stimulate such conservation.

Commit to the Common Good

People who *commit to the common good* dedicate themselves to ensuring the well-being of the human community and the extended biotic community. In conduct that extends beyond the narrow Jubilee prescription of release for slaves, which freed only Israelite members of the Israelite ethnic group, people committed to the common good reject in every way subjugation or oppression of others. They do not enslave or otherwise exploit, nor do they merely "tolerate" human beings who are racially, ethnically, economically, religiously, sexually, and otherwise distinct from themselves; they accept them as diverse members of a single species and an extended family.

To be committed to the common good is to be involved in, or at least support, peoples' struggles for justice. It means working to free people who are economically enslaved because of their subsistence needs and the lack of available employment at living wages and with adequate family health care. It means ensuring a just, "living" wage and a consequent modicum of economic freedom for farmworkers—the "poor of the land"—and a fair return at parity level for farmers and ranchers. It means being especially conscious of a particular responsibility toward the poor, and willingness to promote policies and activities guided by the "preferential option for the poor" advocated in Christian churches' documents. Although slavery in the United States and other countries throughout the world has long been illegal, currently in all nations the unemployed and low-income working people have suffered economic deprivation and poverty parallel to that experienced by slaves in earlier times and places. The creating Spirit intends a universal destination—an equitable distribution—of Earth goods needed by humankind. Compassion for the most vulnerable in society, and government action to enable them to live with dignity and to secure the necessities of life, parallels the Jubilee concern for the well-being of slaves. An economic democracy would be fostered to complement political democracy and to counter the flaw in the latter where a minority possesses a substantial majority of national and international wealth. The common good of the biotic community, within the context of continuing evolution with its interspecies and intraspecies competition and collaboration, would be fostered.

Compart Common Goods

People with a Jubilee commitment will *compart common goods* personally and socially, to the extent that their financial means will permit. Remission of debts, the earlier Jubilee requirement, would be retained as a Jubilee requirement, and supplemented by economic restructuring based on the needs of the poor. This would require an analysis of the economic impacts of globalization, global capitalism, and such institutions as the World Bank, the International Money Fund, the World Trade Organization, and private transnational banking institutions on national populations in general (such as their ability to exercise their right to subsistence goods), and on working people in particular (such as their rights to a just, living wage; safe places of work; and health benefits). People would construct judicial systems and implement laws based on justice, not power, so that economic structures would benefit economically oppressed populations and eliminate residual prior economic oppression. Equitable financial arrangements among borrowers and lenders, just interest rates, fair renegotiation of onerous existing loans, and cancellation of some debts (e.g., of owner-operators of moderate-sized family farms in the United States, and of impoverished third world nations and their poorer citizens), as appropriate, would embody the cancellation of debts required in the biblical Jubilee Year. Citizens would develop an equitable, progressive tax structure so that those who most profit from social and natural wealth will fulfill their social and ecological responsibilities. Citizens would willingly pay their fair share of taxes and be compassionate toward people in need. Wealth would be distributed equitably and *re*distributed to the extent possible to eliminate advantages to a few; current wealth has resulted primarily from prior familial accumulations (which themselves might have resulted from unjust compensation for working people, in terms of their salary, health benefits, and retirement savings), and not personal inventiveness or industry. In any case, community need and community well-being take precedence over personal acquisitiveness, avarice, or pecuniosity.

Commonize the Commons

It is necessary to *commonize the commons* for the Jubilee to have its best opportunity to succeed. In the biblical Jubilee, land was redistributed periodically only every fifty years. The reason and the ideal that this Jubilee Year practice expressed were laudable: maintain land as a community good by restricting private accumulation of property in land. However, the practice was flawed in that not only was it hard to require the wealthy to return their acquisitions of property from other members of the community who had less productive lands, but also in that if it were redistributed back to the descendants of the original owners, then the farmers whose ancestral families had lost their homestead because it had poor soil and no viable water supply would receive back the same land in the Jubilee Year. Ongoing or periodic droughts would ensure that farmers who could not keep their land productive because of natural disasters would be locked into a never-ending cycle of exile from and return to their land. Alternatives to this system, with the same intent to have a widespread distribution of the benefits of property in land, would be either gradually to move people away from their original land and onto different land, so that all equally would have diverse experiences of wealth and poverty over time, a sense of community, and sympathy for those with the least desirable lands; or, cooperative ownership where people own their lands communally, and share its benefits together. The first option would be almost impossible to implement. The second option is feasible, as seen in some countries that have done so through their tax system, through expropriation (with fair compensation to the owners) and redistribution, or through revolution. To commonize the commons would be to complement the biblical idea of a periodic redistribution of land with a just, ongoing redistribution of the land into cooperative holdings, along with associated water sources and water rights, to benefit the common good. This would require a reevaluation of patterns and practices of land ownership, and laws and policies related to them, in the light of the common good and the needs of the commons.

Individual and corporate land ownership could be redistributed into cooperative holdings through a progressive land tax and progressive inheritance laws, and provision of low-interest loans to actual and potential owner-operators of family farms who would want to form a single cooperative from their individual properties. Naturally occurring essential goods ("resources") such as oil would become public property; their extraction would be licensed to responsible corporations and cooperatives, so that the community, and not a handful of investors, would benefit from the profits accruing to energy corporations and set just rates for residential, commercial, and industrial consumers. Agricultural, industrial, and commercial cooperatives would be initiated and maintained. Water, a natural right, human right, and common good, would be publicly owned, and conserved and retained for the common good. National, state, and local community parks, forests, and waterways would be retained in the public domain for public use and as reminders of ongoing divine presence, power, and providence.

People who prioritize private property over community needs and social responsibility object to the commonization of Earth's land. Their opposition often is based on present or potential financial insecurity, rooted in experience or fear; or a sense of entitlement for who they perceive themselves to be and for what they have accomplished personally; or greed and lack of compassion for others.

People in the first category worry about providing for themselves or their family, and they trust that the property and goods that they have acquired will help them get through trying times. This type of opposition to commonization can be overcome if a sufficiency of subsistence goods (food, clothing, shelter, medical care, energy, social interaction, recreation, rest) are ensured for all people, which should be an outcome if current corporate profits are redistributed and refocused into community coffers.

People in the second category have worked hard for what they possess and resent distribution or redistribution of property, money, goods, and savings that they have accumulated or expect to acquire. Such people are products of a culture of individualism and overconsumption, in which advertising propaganda proclaims "You earned it" and "Give something to yourself," reinforcing the (mis)education they have received, an indoctrination into values of individualism and competition rather than of community and cooperation. This type of objection can be overcome if people (re)learn compassion and a sense of community responsibility, if they experience a "conversion," in the best biblical sense, from selfishness or extreme self-interest, to regard for others and responsiveness to their needs, and a willingness to use their talents not only for personal gain but also for community well-being.

People in the third category, which is the most powerful foe of commonization and the greatest problem for community well-being, possess a hierarchical view not only of humankind above the rest of biokind and abiotic Earth but also of some privileged members of humankind over the rest of humanity. Possessions take precedence over people; consumption supercedes compassion. Their perspective contradicts fundamental religious, philosophical, and humanist teachings—even while some claim they are living according to "Christian values." This type of opposition, barring a conversion experience on the part of its advocates, often requires a change of conduct caused by enactment and enforcement of laws that prioritize the common good over individual greed, and the commons good over Earth's exploitation, such as through equitable progressive taxes on income and land.

Humans are part of the natural world and are responsible to God and to community to care for it and use it wisely and sparingly. Humans may use Earth's land and goods to meet their needs, but may not abuse Earth's land and goods to satisfy their wants; sufficiency should have primacy over satiety. Private property is a civil good that must be integrated with public property as a common good. Common needs take precedence over individual wants, and property holdings—whether in land, water, or any of Earth's goods, including energy sources—are all part of divine creation and are intended to meet community needs before their individual appropriation. When the community as a whole benefits from social structures and natural goods, then all individuals benefit, as members of the community. When an individual or a particular class or group benefits most both socially and materially, the community will suffer from their selfishness. Cooperative arrangements in a commonized commons will integrate the security of private ownership (in a dispersed manner) with the social consciousness of community orientation.

If the Jubilee were to be observed—and it need not be only every fifty years—people would take steps to restore relationships among themselves and among themselves, Earth, and all Earth's inhabitants. When people rest the land and invite free and domesticated animals to partake of its bounty, they are in some sense reenacting the idealized relationship of people, all creatures, to the Earth and the Spirit expressed in the story of the Garden of

Eden (Genesis 2). When people free economic slaves and forgive debts, they give priority to compassion over profit, and progress beyond individualism and financial practices focused on profits over people, which are characteristic of capitalism. When people redistribute land equitably in communal or private holdings, they acknowledge that Earth's Creator wills that all people have the opportunity to care for and live from the Earth's bounty. The practice of the New Jubilee, if its ideals were to be extended throughout the world and appropriately adapted to differences of culture and place, gradually would lead people toward providing a context for the creation commons to become realized in a renewed Earth.

In a commonized commons, people will have a greater sense of intergenerational and cross-generational responsibility. When working people retire or are prevented by accident or illness from earning their livelihood, younger workers with a communal community consciousness will not resent the lack of current input by those who were coworkers. They will acknowledge their prior and new, alternative contributions to community well-being. Similarly, people earning their livelihood in the present will acknowledge their debt to past generations and bear in mind the material needs of coming generations, and not consume excessively the goods Earth provides or human labor produces. A commons-sharing community will be attuned to communal needs in the present and future.

In the present historical moment, people are displaced from their lands throughout the world because political, economic, or religious injustices ensure that individual greed (for wealth or power) expressed nationally and globally is the primary factor in determining that Earth's land and goods are to be used to benefit the minority few rather than the majority many; and waste products pollute air, land, and water as emissions or effluents. Biblical teachings, and complementary ideas from contemporary environmental, ethical, and social thought, present alternative attitudes toward Earth and community, and alternative ways to work with Earth and safeguard community. It is time to promote and protect the sacramental commons by proclaiming a Jubilee, to be concretized regionally and nationally. It is time for a redistribution of the land from the few to the many for the benefit of all, and a time for Earth to be cared for, conserved for, and used for the benefit of present and future generations. It is time for people to "cultivate and care for" garden Earth in fulfillment of the ideal presented in Genesis (2:15).

JUBILEE AND PEOPLES OF THE LAND

For agriculturalists, the Jubilee prescriptions and the understandings of a sacramental universe and a sacramental commons come together in a unique way. Family farmers were especially singled out for recognition in the biblical Jubilee Year, not just because agriculture was the predominant occupation of the time but also because food for family and community was an essential need. No matter what technological developments might occur in a society, farming will remain the most important occupation; no one can survive without food. Agriculturalists (who, as Wendell Berry has pointed out, are distinct from agribusinesspeople) should be enabled to work well with the community commons that is mortgaged socially from the community as a whole, which conditionally grants to people engaged in agriculture both the right to provide for their own livelihood, and the responsibility to benefit their local and extended communities. The condition of the social mortgage (which applies to all property in land, intended by the Spirit to meet biotic community needs in the Earth commons) is that agriculturalists and other property owners use their land responsibly, and conserve it well for the community extended in time and place, Earth's present and future generations.

In order to be responsible for that part of creation entrusted to their care, owner-operator family farmers must receive, as should all people, a living wage for their work; they should receive prices for their goods that cover land and production costs, support their family, and offer modest security for the future. Moderate-sized family farms should be promoted. Organic food and production processes should be fostered, conservation techniques utilized, and diversified operations promoted. Transnational corporations should not dictate what farmers produce, nor how they produce it, nor what they pay their workers, nor what price they receive for their product. Government policies should promote family agriculture, particularly cooperative agriculture, and prohibit the nonfamily corporatization of agriculture.

If owner-operator family farms were to become the norm in the United States and abroad, then agricultural goods would be secure, healthier, and safer; rural communities and economies would be revitalized; the land would be conserved and restored; and the commons would bloom for all creatures.

In the United States and other parts of the world, physical and cultural genocide against native peoples has caused not only the disappearance or diminution of distinct human communities and cultures, but also a diminished respect for Earth. Native peoples have lost their traditional territories or had them significantly reduced in extent and controlled by governments external to their own community, resulting in ecological devastation of Earth and economic deprivation for native communities.

Native peoples would especially welcome the Jubilee Year, as its consciousness and practices reflect in many ways their own history. Native social and religious traditions embody a community orientation, communal sharing, and communally controlled territories. Native peoples' communities have a history of sharing the human goods they have derived from Earth goods, and of caring for their people and their land intergenerationally. The Acts ideal of the sharing community within Jerusalem is well paralleled by native peoples' sharing communities, which are not confined to one location but are embodied among the respective native peoples and their communities as a whole.

A SACRAMENTAL JUBILEE

In biblical teachings and the Christian tradition the Earth is a *commons*, a shared sacred space and a source of the goods required to meet living creatures' needs. The commons is neither created for nor oriented toward only humans; as part of nature, people live in a common Earth habitat and partake of common Earth goods. Earth is intended by the creating Creator Spirit to provide for all creatures as they live in ecological relation, in complex and at times distinct and diverse ecosystems. Scientific studies, for their part, have stimulated increased respect for natural forces and flows, and an enhanced appreciation for Earth's intricately related biotic community, which contains incredibly diverse and complex species living in collaborative and competitive relationships. Scientific data and spiritual awareness independently and conjointly stimulate people to foster sustainability to promote an Earth commons context of inherent ecosystemic integrity, and a socially organized and Earth-integrated system of community economic viability.

In the sacramental commons people not only observe the Spirit's loving creativity in its diversity of creatures, varied topography, distinct peoples, and ability to provide food and shelter for its inhabitants but also see how the Jubilee will renew and strengthen human community bonds, and human affinity for and kinship with the other members of the biotic community. Each Earth place is naturally a commons. It is home to all members of the community of life. It is the source of their respective food and habitat needs. It is the context in which their competitive needs are balanced and their collaborative relationships reinforced. In the Earth commons, the New Jubilee will promote relationships and projects that remind people of their relationships with Creator and creation, and their responsibilities toward both. The Jubilee imperatives—to conserve the commons, commit to the common good, compart common goods, and commonize the commons—when integrated together will guide humanity to walk with the Spirit, walk gently on Earth, and relate lovingly to their biotic relatives.

People are part of a community of life, a family of God's creatures. As such, they should enhance their relations not only with members of human communities from distinct ethnic groups, social classes, political ideologies and religious beliefs, but also with other lives and with the landscapes that all inhabit together and on which all depend for their needs. All species share a common origin in the creative acts of the Spirit that began in the primordial moment and continue to unfold among and around them, and all creatures share as well a common bond as participants in the dynamics of Earth. A Jubilee practiced in the commons will reinforce this relational consciousness, and enable its embodiment in projects dedicated to ensuring commons security as the context for species evolutionary sustainability.

People—like the Spirit who transcends and yet is present to creation—while recognizing that they are distinct beings, should be solicitous of and relate to the wondrous works of God: Earth and Earth's inhabitants. People should integrate the spiritual meaning of sacramental and the social meaning of commons with a relational consciousness within a relational community, a creation commons community.

Jubilee understandings and practices would help to restore and conserve ecologically integrated regions. They would express appreciation for and advocate consciousness of the sacramental commons, the locus of the Spirit's interactive presence. In this commons, they would care for God's creation, celebrate the diversity of life, earn their livelihood responsibly, and equitably share common goods. In the commons, they would act for the common good not only of human beings but of all God's creatures. They would care for the common good and the good of the commons. Jubilee consciousness and practices would enable and enhance commons well-being and sacramentality.

The Jubilee itself can be sacramental. If understood as a renewed presentation of traditional divine hopes for and expectations of humanity, it can be revelatory of divine regard for abiotic and biotic creation, an integrated and revelatory whole graced by divine presence and providence. The new Jubilee suggests concrete community expressions of the ideals of the sacramental commons.

VISIONS OF A COMMONS FUTURE

In the Jubilee, to some extent the past land would be present in the future. That is, people would recognize the divine origin of Earth and Earth's goods and respect Earth as a sacred provider of life. Consequently, people conscious of their responsibilities as trustees of a divine work—to care for Earth and respectfully work with Earth so that Earth might continue to be fruitful for all living beings—would incorporate Jubilee principles in their lives and work and commit themselves to make the principles visibly operative in local communities and bioregions. Earth's few remaining pristine or near-pristine places, which are remnants and reminders of divine creativity and loci of aesthetic and evolutionary beauty, would be conserved. Sun and stars would be visible in their turn, waters would be living and potable, and soil would be healthy and productive. People's *vision* today of a beautiful and bountiful future for Earth might become their children's *reality* tomorrow.

As a consequence of the Jubilee, places of natural beauty would be preserved: selected unique wilderness, forest, seashore, and other areas would be sheltered from industrial and commercial development. The national park system, which is a network of land for the people that is owned by the people, would be maintained in a manner that would preserve natural ecologies.

Need would replace greed as the criterion for the development and distribution of Earth's limited resources. People would come before profit in the organization of human economic structures. Economic justice would be linked to environmental justice in considerations of land ownership and use. Economic democracy would complement political democracy.

The Jubilee observation heightens humans' understanding that they dwell in a sacramental commons that is part of a sacramental universe. People engage the cosmic Spirit-transcendent as a loving, creating, Earth-related, and biotic community-related Spirit-immanent. The Jubilee promotes concern for the sacramental commons, and stimulates concrete efforts to ensure that it is conserved and provides for the needs of interrelated biokind.

The formulation of a new Christian ecological vision for the twenty-first century should be based on an assessment of individual and institutional attitudes toward Earth, all peoples, and all members of the biotic community. Such a vision would prompt dedication to providing a spiritual, intellectual, social, and ecological transformation of Earth and Earth's lives. Jubilee considerations provide a particular point of reference for peoples of the land, especially those involved in agriculture, to form this vision.

People who reflect on biblically based and community oriented ideals and images, and on similar understandings of human responsibility for the land in native peoples' traditions and practices, consider the relationship of these ideals to their present reality. They might consider also related ideas and ideals, and modes of conduct they suggest, in documents from diverse religious and humanist traditions. The disparity between current realities and commons ideals might then inspire people to commit to and to concretize a Jubilee in the Earth commons for the Earth community.

· 11 ·

Commons Commitments: Ecological Ethics

$\mathcal{O}$ver the centuries, individuals and communities have reflected on human-kind's responsibility for Earth. People from diverse perspectives developed ecological principles to guide human conduct so that humankind's relation-ship with its place and its biotic neighbors would fulfill its role as rulers over, stewards of, or relatives in creation. As new data, understandings, and theories became available, they have been incorporated into previous expressions of what was believed to constitute appropriate individual and community con-duct. The newer formulations were revised or reformulated in turn to express more clearly to a new generation or a new culture their Earth-related respon-sibilities. The period comprising the twentieth and early twenty-first centu-ries was a particularly fruitful time for the development and implementation of theoretical and contextual principles for Earth-friendly behavior. The impetus for these was people's greater awareness of the impacts of intrusive human interventions into abiotic and biotic nature. These had been made possible by the invention, availability, and use of more complex and powerful technologies and tools.

The commons reveals the creative and creating transcendent-immanent Spirit. In the commons, species and individuals live interdependent and interrelated lives in an evolutionary dynamic. Human pressures on and dra-matic alterations of the abiotic context of life have eliminated some species and individuals (and threaten or endanger others' survival). In local and global ecosystems, humankind has violated the natural flow of continuing creation.

If the commons is to be a place where life can have a habitable context, then humans, who have the greatest impacts—for better or for worse—on abiotic nature must take greater responsibility for the ways in which they affect Earth. People who are conscious of the sacramentality of creation, and committed to safeguarding creation's dual role for humans as mediator of the Spirit, means of subsistence, and setting for sociality, can become inspired and impelled to reflect on their ecosystemic context and commit to just

199

conduct in it. In other words, they will formulate ecological ethics and will live according to the values and principles that they propose as guides for right human conduct.

When people as individuals and communities concretize ecological ethics in local contexts, the sacramentality of creation will become evident in the Earth commons, bioregional commons, and human commons; the integrity of abiotic creation will be strengthened; and the evolutionary viability of the biotic community will be assured. The initial step to this stage of existence is the development of an integral social and spiritual relational consciousness in the commons.

RELATIONAL CONSCIOUSNESS, RELATIONAL COMMUNITY

The primary message of Jesus was that the "reign of God" was present and future. This state of Earth being ruled by the divine sovereign had begun with the ministry of Jesus, and it gradually was to spread throughout the world. In a patriarchal context, monarchical imagery was appropriate to express divine rule over Earth, to assert divine authority over human rulers, and to stimulate obedience to divine commands. It has served to counteract oppressive political, economic, and religious ideologies and social structures in diverse places and eras.

The age of monarchs is over throughout most of the world, with most remaining rulers having more of a symbolic role than actual power. Rather than advocate a return to an earlier autocratic monarchy as an image of divine rule or use the term *reign* in an age when the monarch has much more limited power and the image of limited power is inadequate to express divine power (except as it is self-contained because of divine *kenosis*), it would be appropriate also to describe the vision and reality expressed by Jesus in complementary terms that retain its essence but remove its cultural and historical biases and limitations.

The relational consciousness and the relational community together express a sense of communion among member individuals and species of biokind, between biokind and Earth, and between biokind and the Spirit. They express the meaning of the "reign of God" advocated by Jesus. The evolving social reality of Spirit-Earth-spirit engagement is the creation commons community, with its creation-centered consciousness.

A *relational consciousness* is an awareness that the Spirit, the biotic community, and Earth are intimately linked to each other. It integrates people and peoples; humanity and all biota; the biotic community and Earth; and all creation with the loving and creating Spirit who invites it and guides it toward being a continuous, progressively enhanced relational community.

An integral *relational community* is an association of people who are engaged with each other as extended family members concerned about the material, social, and spiritual well-being of each and all; engaged with their kin in the biotic community as interdependent and interrelated children of Earth and Spirit; and engaged with the Spirit-transcendent-immanent as participants simultaneously in the spiritual, social, and corporeal dimensions of reality. Spirituality in its varied expressions is an important part of a relational consciousness and influences interactions within the relational community. Spiritual dimensions of existence include the personal spiritual (individual engagement with the Spirit), social spiritual (community engagement with the Spirit, usually through rituals expressing a religion's beliefs and doctrines), and the universal spiritual (transculturally shared understandings or experiences of the Spirit that are not confined to a specific institutional religion, but contextually transcend and yet universally permeate the beliefs of people engaged with the Spirit).

The *creation commons community* is engaged with the Spirit-immanent, conscious of its biotic relationships, and integrated with its Earth context. It is Spirit related, conscious of divine presence, and conscientious in living in accord with divine expectations as it understands them in its time and place. It is spiritually related, as its members acknowledge dimensions of existence not constrained by material existence. It has a creation-centered consciousness, which means, as expressed earlier, a recognition that Creator and creatures live in concrete relationships and encounter each other in Earth settings. It sees the Earth commons as an aggregate of contiguous, interacting bioregions that require sustainable abiotic-biotic integration. It strives for continuing community evidence that individuals and species of the web of all life are interrelated, interdependent, and integrated, to safeguard the commons good and the common good. To Jesus' description of the reign of God, the creation commons community adds an ecological dimension and biotic community relationships. In this regard, it complements Jesus' teaching of a consciousness and an alternative way of life that opposes and seeks to transform oppressive human social structures and harmful human conduct toward commons and community. It strives to embody Jesus' prayerful hope that God's reign will continue to come and be ever more manifest in people living "on Earth as in heaven" in an Eden-envisioned and Eden-inspired new Earth. The creation commons community reveals the horizontal dimension of Spirit-spirits relationship taught by Jesus in his "Abba" prayer (while recognizing that biota defer to the Spirit-transcendent-immanent), rather than the vertical, hierarchical relationship expressed in patriarchal images of the divine and of divine-human interaction. The creation commons community is a creation-conscious community that, when faithful to its calling, is the seed planted in fertile soil, hoping to bear fruit not only for itself but for the extended biotic community and for Earth for generations to come.

NATURAL HUMAN ACTIONS

Humans are part of the natural world. This does not mean that all human alterations to the Earth environment, and all human eliminations of other species are "natural" acts and events in which humans fulfill their particular role in evolution. Nor does it mean that every "natural" act is a good act or a morally neutral act. A sociopathic serial killer, for example, might act "naturally" according to what is "natural" for a person with that psychological problem; that is, the person's behavior accords with what psychiatrists would expect from someone in that state of mind. However, the sociopath is not acting in a "good" or "natural" way according to socialized human behavior, community and cultural norms, socially acceptable means toward individual or species self-fulfillment and self-preservation, criteria concerning what promotes the common good, or customary religious teachings. Similarly, a rabid dog acts "naturally" when its conduct is consonant with what is expected of an animal with a rabies infection, even though it is not ordinarily "natural" for a dog to contract rabies. Similarly also, an entrepreneur who destroys virgin forest to build a luxury lodge, or a recreational enthusiast who drives an all-terrain vehicle through a fragile desert, or a mining executive who gives orders to blow the tops off mountains that are sacred to native peoples and are habitat for endangered species, in order to extract gold to be used for jewelry, cannot justify their actions (as some have tried to do) by asserting that since humans are part of nature, and they are human, then whatever they do is "natural," so they can exploit nature to satisfy their greed or their irresponsible self-centeredness in whatever way they choose.

A "natural" human act, as used in ethical considerations, is human conduct that is integrated with human biological-personal-social-psychological-spiritual identity and aspirations; is consonant with the integration of humans within the biotic community and with abiotic nature; is compatible with Earth's evolutionary flow of time, energies, elements, and events; and represents or complements generally accepted social values and conduct. Humans are most natural when they are social beings who live in and with nature, and relate to nature while they work to ensure the commons good and the common good through an equitable distribution of commons goods as common goods.

Earth's living creatures of any historical moment have resulted from life evolving over billions of years, and, more recently, from millennia of evolutionary interactions of species and individuals seeking to find and maintain an appropriate ecosystemic niche. Members of the biotic community other than humans do not ordinarily have tools that assist their survival or enable them to be dominant, preeminent, or collaborative in their niche; they must utilize their natural physical and mental abilities for these purposes. In their struggles for survival, they assert or insert themselves in their bioregion in ways that do minimal damage to abiotic nature, which is the setting of their life and interaction. When humans meet their own needs with minimal but necessary alterations of abiotic places, they, too, are living as part of nature and working with natural processes and Earth's rhythms. But when humans carelessly or deliberately use their tools—whether hammers or bulldozers or other extensions of human strength and skill—to do unnecessary violence to Earth, they are not living as part of nature but as agents who are paradoxically and simultaneously external to and internal in their context, dominating and exploiting their home and habitat. People must recognize that because of the greater power that tools and technology provide for them to manipulate the elements, energies, entities, and events of nature, they should use this power only to the extent necessary, without doing harm to the natural world intentionally and while trying to avoid harming the natural world unintentionally.

Environmental crises are extant throughout Earth. Environmental crises do not result when human activity is natural. Crises result when humans deny their place in creation as its integrating consciousness reflecting on itself and as its complexity evolving beyond itself. When humans lose their sense of place—their setting and their role—they lose a sense of the sacred, they reject intrinsic value in abiotic nature and in species and individuals of the biotic community, they deny natural rights to nature, and they reject humanity's situation in creation as one of the uncounted numbers of all species who have complementary roles in the community of life, and are related to each other as the common offspring of cosmic becoming. All creatures are, in a very real sense, related stardust: their common ancestry is traced to the original existents of the singularity; they are descendants of the subsequent elementary forms of being that have resulted from the birth of the universe in a burst of light from its primordial womb in cosmic darkness. All living creatures are children of the creating Spirit and of the evolving Earth community. All life is called to share in Earth goods of the Earth commons.

People aware of the sacredness of creation as a whole, and of Earth as common ground shared with all life, develop a relational consciousness respectful of all creatures (including all the diverse members of humankind). They help to promote and sustain their Earth home, and the lives of those with whom they share it. In Christian traditions, this becomes possible through regard for Earth, as a whole and in its bioregions, as a sacramental commons.

The sacramental commons is a place where the Spirit-transcendent, from whom creation originates, may be experienced as the Spirit-immanent, who permeates continuing creation. The sacramental commons is sacred space shared by Earth's resident communities of life, all of whom depend (directly or indirectly) on each other and on the air, water, soil, and sun that are their abiotic locus, the sources of their life, and the contexts of their interaction.

PRESERVATION, RESTORATION, AND CONSERVATION

The sacramental commons is being polluted by effluents and emissions and is literally being blown apart by mining operations, military exercises, and housing and highway construction. As people become aware of this devastation, they search for ways to retain the remaining places of natural beauty and their biota and to restore the places harmed unnecessarily by human interventions.

The *preservation* of the commons is the effort, through judicial processes and judicious projects, to sustain the natural terrain and dynamics of the abiotic setting that serves as home and habitat for the biotic community. Species preservation should not be a goal of these efforts, except insofar as a species is understood to be essential for bioregional needs and is in danger of extinction because of invasive new members of the biotic community or intrusive past and present members of the human community. Evolution (whether regarded as an autopoietic biological process in and of itself or as a process set in motion by the Spirit) includes species diversification, complexification, individual death, and even species extinction; indeed, the biotic community's very existence requires these interruptions of biological "business as usual" where that means static maintenance of the status quo. Efforts to preserve species because they have "exotic," "fashionable," or "designer" appeal might satisfy an aesthetic bias, but such efforts might interfere with creative evolutionary processes.

The *restoration* of the commons includes human work in the present to ameliorate harmful human actions of the past and present. Impacts of mining and other industrial processes and chemical wastes, erosive and habitat-destructive (and thereby life-impairing) clear-cutting of forests, urban effluent and agricultural chemical pollution of waters, for example, have residual impacts on the land not only when they occur but long afterward. Restoration includes projects such as reforestation; riparian mitigation; removal and safe storage of harmful chemical residues and radioactive waste; reclamation of mining areas; conversion of dump sites to parks and athletic fields; removal of dams that harm migratory fish or whose backed-up waters contain harmful sediments from mining and other industrial operations; elimination of water pollution, including by strict water quality standards and laws; improving air quality by the implementation of strict enforcement of air quality laws that eliminate airborne pollutants; and removal of vehicular pollution by stricter auto and truck emission standards. These and similar projects would help to restore air, land, and water quality.

The *conservation* of the commons is the effort to retain preserved and restored areas and to prevent future harmful human actions, to the extent possible—because they are foreseeable or projected, or because a precautionary approach is taken when considering potential Earth impacts. The *precautionary principle* states that if insufficient data or theories are available to know or foresee the result of the use of a particular product (such as a new chemical compound), a new process (the latest gold-mining technique that, once again, gold companies claim is safe for the environment) or the outcome of a particular action (such as the impacts of a production process, diversion of a river, or use of an explosive device), then reasonable caution requires nonuse until the data are complete. It is better to err on the side of health, safety, and environmental integrity than to alter dramatically and irreversibly Earth's rhythms, cycles, and geophysical or climatic integrity. Conservation means using sparingly Earth's land and Earth goods. It means retaining pristine places because of their intrinsic value, because they are most revelatory of Spirit-immanent, and because they have instrumental spiritual, aesthetic, and sustenance value for humankind. It means seeking alternative sources of needed and wanted goods when the amount of available and accessible Earth goods is diminishing; reducing overall consumption, and reusing and recycling currently available goods or their residual materials during or after their life cycle. It means changing the operative ideology and consciousness in which people define themselves and are defined by others in terms of the material things they possess. It means regarding others for who they are as neighbors (in Jesus' sense of *neighbor*) and what they do for the community; this would foster individual and cultural quests for relationships rather than things, for compassion rather than selfishness, and for collaboration rather than competition. Conservation expresses consciousness of, and exemplifies living within, the carrying capacity of Earth as a whole and in its bioregional ecosystems. Human populations, as with populations of free or domesticated animals, cannot long survive if their numbers exceed Earth's maximum capacity to provide for them sufficient good soil for their food, potable water to drink, clean air to breathe, and materials derived from biotic or abiotic origins that enable them to construct homes and businesses that are warmed and lit by clean, efficient, and sufficient energy. It means the consciousness and practice of intergenerational and transgenerational responsibility. Reasonable and equitable distribution and use of Earth's land and other goods globally today will enable people of all age groups in any moment of time and throughout the world, and their descendants through time and across places, to share in Earth's bounty to meet their needs, and to interact relationally and responsibly with Earth and the biotic community.

SACRALITY AND SUSTAINABILITY

When a sense of the sacred and commitment to community are integrated and operational, people care for the commons, justly and compassionately distribute among members of the human community the goods they need, and respectfully share commons benefits with members of the biotic community as a whole. When they are conscious of the sacramentality of creation, people relate to the Spirit and are nourished by a spirituality that enables them to discern and experience a familial bond among all creatures, a cross-species kinship. This spirituality incorporates essential understandings of the cosmos as creation and of creatures as kin. It flows from and returns to permeate the creation commons community.

People need sacred spaces and sacramental places because they need the opportunity to encounter the Creator in creation. Sacred spaces can be all places, from urban areas to wilderness areas. Sacramental places include the latter but also specially designated space dedicated to communion with the Spirit. Such space includes pristine or near-pristine nature revelatory of the Creator because of minimal human intrusions and impacts; and mosques, temples, synagogues, and churches—human-constructed edifices built for prayer and ritual observances. Spiritual, social, and corporal growth are incorporated in the integral human being and represent diverse but interrelated means of encountering and experiencing distinct but interwoven dimensions of existence. The holistic human person walks within all of these dimensions, sometimes becoming immersed primarily in one, but remaining conscious of and engaged with all.

Spirituality is a relationship with the Spirit, and a way of life that flows from that relationship and is expressed in thought, word, and deed, through formulaic, spontaneous, or implied prayer. Spiritual consciousness can be especially (but not solely) stimulated in dedicated sacred space. Some natural places should be conserved as sacred space not only for that reason, but to remind people of the Creator Spirit's imagination expressed evolutionarily, and to leave some space free of human control, thereby enabling free evolutionary developments. Conservation of sacred space demonstrates that people acknowledge that they should not dominate but be integrated within, interdependent with, and related to the Earth on which they live and the biotic community of which they are a part. The connection between sacrality and sustainability is evidenced by sustained sacred places. Respect for these places stimulates people to foster sustainability in other ways, and to appreciate that all creation is sacred.

In light of ever-deepening ecological crises, the relevance of spiritual consciousness in creation is ever more apparent. If people view Earth with anthropocentric eyes (whether from a religious or scientific perspective), then all creatures will be regarded as instrumental for human needs and wants because they will be understood to exist solely or primarily for human benefit. Creation will be viewed as imperfect until human work transforms it in whole or in part to serve humankind. Should this perspective prevail, exploitation of all of Earth's goods, including minerals, water, and land as well as Earth's living beings, will the more readily be justified, with potentially catastrophic consequences. Alternatively, if people view Earth with respectful eyes (whether from a scientific, religious, or humanist perspective, or combinations thereof), then they will appreciate the inherent worth of all creatures, and the inherent beauty of creation as the continuous concretization either of divine imagination or of cosmic dynamics and evolutionary processes. Should this perspective grow—and its seeds have been planted over millennia by diverse people from distinct places and traditions, such as Jesus of Nazareth, Hildegard von Bingen, Francis of Assisi, John Muir, Phillip Deere, David Sohappy, Thomas Berry, and the Ecumenical Patriarch Bartholomew I, and nourished by others—then the potential exists for Earth to be renewed and Earth's creatures to live in a balanced relationship with each other. Personal and communal spirituality; religious and ethical theory and practice; scientific data and theories; direct community engagement with ecological problems and projects—all are directly related to biotic and abiotic well-being and sustainability.

Spirituality can foster sustainability. In its *social concern* for the common good, it declares that human *need*, not human *greed*, should be the prevailing factor in considerations of the means and form to be utilized to effect economic development. In its *creation consciousness* and advocacy of the commons good, it expresses its understanding that environmental integrity should be a significant factor when determining the site and extent of economic development.

When social concern and care for creation are linked, impacts of product manufacture on citizens and communities are considered. Often, corporations do not internalize all of their social and environmental costs, including them in the cost of production; rather, they externalize some costs to increase their profits. For example, a coal-fired power plant can save money by not installing scrubbers on its smokestacks to capture sulfur (which can return to Earth as acid rain in near or distant locations, and kill fish and forests) or by not utilizing other pollution prevention devices to eliminate mercury release (which can especially harm the unborn, infants, and young children), expecting the wind to carry away emissions. The smoke is breathed by area residents, whose health is impacted and who must pay for medical visits and medicine, and, if employed, pay with lost work time (and therefore lost income), used sick leave or vacation leave, or increases in their health insurance premiums. People living or working near industrial facilities or biomedical facilities, for example, should ask important questions about the need, usefulness, development, impacts, and disposition of commercial and industrial products, and of the production processes used to make them; and the impacts of resource acquisition (such as coal mining or uranium mining and milling) and use, and of the means of generating electricity, of utility plants.

Considerations for technological development include the following:

1. Is there a present and projected *need* for this product that justifies the environmental and social impacts of its materials' extraction and its production plant's social and environmental impacts?

2. What are the social costs (boom and bust employment that affects working people and their families in terms of income, job and familial stability, personal security, and social relationships; increased infrastructural expenditures such as roads, schools, and local government salaries; facility construction and closure impacts on schools, the social welfare system, etc.); and environmental costs (geophysical alterations; loss of carbon sequestering trees, plants, and grasses; diminution of available water supplies for residential, commercial, agricultural, or recreational use) of producing this product?

3. Is this the only product that can meet that need, or would recycled products or residual ("waste") products, or other, more ecologically neutral products, meet the need with less environmental and social cost?

4. What Earth goods ("natural resources") will produce this product? Are these the only sources suitable for production, or are there available recycled resources from previously used products, or residual products from another production process?

5. Is this the only production process possible for this product?

6. What are the projected social and environmental impacts of the product and the process?

7. Are the costs of production internalized or externalized?
8. How will members of the biotic community benefit from or be harmed by the product and the process?
9. What by-products will result from the production process? What will be their recycling potential when used, and their final disposition?
10. What will be the final disposition of the product?
    • Can it have a recycled life, or must it be discarded? If it must be discarded, will that be done locally or elsewhere (must facilities for safe disposition be constructed or are there facilities already available, such as a landfill, hazardous waste facility, or incinerator; or will it be shipped elsewhere for disposal and, if so, at what cost in fuel, time, and potential spillage en route)? How will the results of the mode or process of disposition, such as burial, burning, or liquid release, and the consequent end product—ashes, pellets, liquids, smoke—impact nearby communities from its storage space (if in a landfill or similar site, will it have safeguards to prevent air, soil, or groundwater pollution?) or as emissions or effluents?[1]

When these questions are asked, the appropriateness of responses to them, the degree of apparent sincerity expressed in the responses, the record the enterprise has established in the past, and the extent of commitment to ensure that the commons good and the common good are not harmed, would assist people in determining whether or not to accept new products, production processes, or facilities. Careful community consideration, conscientious corporate commitments, and careful monitoring of ongoing production and its impacts together will help to ensure that bioregional benefits, and not harms to the community and the commons, will result from a new or expanded commercial or industrial enterprise.

Sustainability, from the perspective of spiritual consciousness, means the degree to which Earth is cared for consonant with several concerns: Earth's ability to exist as part of the Spirit's creation; and Earth's capability to maintain existential harmony among the natural laws of biology, chemistry, and physics that are operative in Earth and ensure its survivability and the survival of the biotic community residing on it. Earth's rhythms, inherent essence, interactive elements, and capacity to provide for the competing or complementary needs of living inhabitants should be secure.

Sustainability has a sense of the long-term relationships inherent in any context: relationships among different types of organisms and between those organisms and the soil, air, sunlight, climate, minerals, and water of their specific region.

In its most comprehensive sense *sustainability* might be defined as the capability of a bioregional commons and its biotic community to maintain the conditions and Earth goods necessary for the existential requirements of its various and diverse life forms and abiotic components in their particular existence-maintaining or existence-enhancing activities, and to integrate those particular activities in balance with the existence-maintaining or existence-enhancing activities of other abiotic components or biokind endemic to the area and biokind entering the area. The Earth commons as a whole will be sustained in its integrity of place, its biotic integrity, and its communities' integrity when each regional commons is sustainably integrated into it, and when commons sustainability and biotic integrity take precedence over merely economic considerations. Aldo Leopold's succinct expression of a "land ethic" is relevant here: "A thing is right when it tends to preserve the integrity, stability, and beauty of the biotic community. It is wrong when it tends otherwise."[2]

SOCIAL ETHICS: CONCERNS, CHOICES, AND COMMITMENTS

Christian *social ethics*, of which Christian ecological ethics is a part, is the reflective integration of *social experience* (contextual encounters with locally, regionally, or nationally operative political, economic, and religious institutions, and with their individual and community impacts); *social consciousness* (awareness of harms caused, and benefits provided, by societal structures and institutions); *social analysis* (critical evaluation of societal values, of the relationship between societal institutions and societal harms and benefits, and of the (mal)distribution of commons goods and common goods); *social theory* (dynamic contextual reflection on societal institutions and their impacts, and possible means of enhancing positive impacts and diminishing negative impacts); *social commitment* (dedication to using social theory to promote justice for and in communities); and *social projects* (practical efforts to express social commitment by eliminating harmful societal policies and practices and implementing beneficial policies and practices, and fostering equitable distributions of commons goods and common goods, to promote societal well-being).

Social ethics does not settle into abstract, armchair discussions of theory and principle; its theory becomes embodied in practical participatory projects for social transformation, for and with victims of social injustice. In practice, social ethics guides individuals and societies to work with those who suffer from human evil imposed by oppressive individuals and the sinful political, economic, and religious structures within which they wield their power. Social ethics stimulates support for and solidarity with people who are deprived of their just share of commons goods and common goods, and are separated from a community common good.

Social ethics should be informative, normative, and transformative. When ethics is *informative*, it suggests social values and provides data and principles that are sufficient, as far as is possible in a given culture and time, to guide right conduct (or at least to orient toward and stimulate toward right conduct) that leads to individual and social justice: for societies and for their individual members. When ethics is *normative*, its principles offer reasoned and reasonable bases for the social interaction of individuals and for the development and continuance of just political, economic, and religious social structures that are not founded on nor promotive of individual or social selfishness, individualism, and competition but that stimulate self-regard, social-regard, cooperativism, and collaboration; its norms are not absolute but reasonable and strongly affirmed. It guides just conduct toward effecting a new person in a new society on a renewed Earth. When ethics is *transformative*, its practitioners and those influenced by them have a vision of what Earth might come to be if justice were to be realized within human communities, if people were to recognize that interrelationship and interdependence should characterize humankind's integration within the biotic community, and if people were to respond as individuals and communities to the sacramental moments that they experience in the sacramental commons. When ethics is transformative, it links deontological and teleological perspectives as it provides a foundation for replacing the present topia by an envisioned utopia, and stimulates creative and effective projects to realize the new reality.

Complementarily, social ethics is reflective, adaptive, and transportive. When ethics is *reflective*, it periodically analyzes and reevaluates, in context, its informative dimension. It is open to understanding that new scientific, social scientific, and religious information, understandings, and beliefs might lead to and require ethical rethinking and reformulation in order to be faithful responses to newly recognized data. When ethics is *adaptive*, it embodies an openness to context and to dynamic process; it acknowledges that norms are enduring but not absolute and that just conduct in context might be complementary to, and consonant but not congruent with, previously accepted norms or rules for appropriate conduct. When ethics is *transportive*, it carries core values and norms through time and across cultures, in conversation with the transportive values and norms of cultures other than the one(s) in which the values and mores originated, and seeks collaborative and creative formulation of common values and norms that encompass diverse cultural and religious perspectives.

Informative-reflective, normative-adaptive, and transformative-transportive are dialectic and dialogic paired concepts that interact to inform social consciousness and conduct.

Ethics guides human conduct and holds people accountable for their conduct. It assumes that individuals are able freely to make choices, to distinguish between good and evil, and to foresee the consequences of their actions. Some philosophers, theologians, psychologists, and biologists, among others, contest the understanding that people have "free will." They believe that human choices and human acts result solely from the interaction of their genes and the environment(s) in which they have lived and now live. But ecological ethics and environmental law assume that human individuals (including transnational corporation shareholders and government officials) are biologically and personally constituted, socially situated, and have free will: the freedom to make voluntary choices (unless freedom of choice is impaired by pressing external coercive factors, or internal shortcomings) when several possible courses of action or inaction are available.

Biologically (as living organisms), individuals result from the interaction of nature and nurture, from their parental genes and the influences from places in which they live and people with whom they interact. They make choices in complex contexts, in the interplay of nature, nurture, time (this moment of choice; the moments that have led to this moment), and place (the context of this particular choice). Personally (as distinct but socially embedded, engaged, and interrelated organisms), individuals result from their biological being and their familial, social, cultural (including religion, if present), and educational environments.

Free will means that individuals prioritize and select from possible courses of action available to them, consciously or unconsciously integrating in their decision making the biological and personal components of who they are in this time (of human history, cultural history, and personal history) and place (psychological, social, physical, educational broadly conceived) where the choice is to be made.

No individual is ethically perfect; no one always makes the right choice. Human factors (such as genetic composition, temperament, familial origin, fear, insecurity, greed for wealth or power, poverty) and social pressures influence choices made. Conversely, no individual is completely unethical. A person who acts customarily in a despotic or autocratic manner might, for example, periodically provide some goods for people in need.

As they go through life and make decisions based on their understanding of right and wrong, people come to have a basic orientation toward choosing good and avoiding evil, or a basic orientation toward choosing evil and rejecting good. This basic orientation is their *consistent ethical commitment*.

Throughout their life, people make mundane choices (selecting clothing style and color); significant choices (choosing a career), ethical choices (to pay to employees living wages with health benefits, or minimal wages with no benefits), and significant ethical choices (tax assessments to provide assistance for the poor, or tax reductions to benefit the rich). When making a *significant ethical choice*, a person influences their consistent ethical commitment: they reaffirm and strengthen their prior values, commitments, and orientation; alter them; or at least strongly impact the direction of their life and the future choices that they will make. A person oriented toward the good (love of God and neighbor) might reaffirm and reinforce that commitment, or alter it significantly; a person oriented toward evil (oppression of the powerless for personal profit) might reaffirm and reinforce that commitment, or alter it significantly.

The significant ethical choice, then, impacts a person's consistent ethical commitment.

Social groups, from community organizations through social classes and on to nations, might also have a consistent ethical commitment and periodically make significant ethical choices. The commitment or the choices might be made by the people as a whole, by a majority controlling the whole, by a minority controlling the whole, or by a leader actually or supposedly representing the whole. The group's shift from an ethical to an unethical consistent ethical commitment, or vice versa, might result from internal changes in the one(s) who make decisions on behalf of the group, or from external pressures by others who are concerned about or have been impacted by the group.

The assumption in every presentation of ethical guidelines is that individuals have some degree of free will in order to make, and to be held accountable for, ethical decisions. Similarly, for groups: people as members of a group are responsible for its ethical commitments and choices, unless they are powerless within the group because of coercive control (including threats to life and family) by the group's leader(s). Otherwise, they would be expected to guide the group to make significant ethical choices for the individual and social good with, as described earlier, the prioritization of needs over wants, and the intention of providing for the commons good and the common good.

In the biblical and Christian tradition, principles expressed in laws have taken a variety of forms and been expressed in varied numbers of requirements. The biblical ten commandments expressed in Exodus and attributed to Yahweh's conversation with Moses (but that reflect, in part, the Code of Hammurabi enacted centuries before Moses) are embedded in the Torah's lengthier list of 613 commandments. In the gospels of Luke and Mark, Jesus affirms a single "Great Commandment," with two parts: love of God and love of neighbor. Augustine would later suggest a single commandment, which omitted specific mention of the neighbor: "Love God and do what you want." (For some people, this might seem very simple, parallel to how some view Christian faith: if one becomes a believer, they are "saved" for life, no matter their conduct; faith alone suffices. However, a careful analysis of Augustine's directive eliminates that: for if a person loves God, they will want to do what they believe *God* wants them to do.)

Ethics should be social and transformative. The intellectual formulation of ethics originates in a specific social setting. The practical application of ethics should take place in concrete settings. An ongoing dialogue should occur between what has been formulated, what has previously been implemented in comparable situations, and changing or changed social conditions. A continuous interaction and balancing of the content of ethics and the context of ethics utilization takes place, either theoretically or in practical situations. *Content-fidelity* (the use of previously formulated principles apparently appropriate to the situation under consideration) and *context-specificity* (the selection, prioritization, and application of principles related to the situation) become engaged by a conscientious person who is open to content transition (amendment of prior principles or formulation of new principles or subprinciples) and is committed to context transformation.

CHRISTIAN ECOLOGICAL ETHICS

Christian *ecological ethics* is the study of relationships in the Earth environment: among human communities, between humankind and the rest of the biotic community, and between life and its Earth habitat; and the formulation or development of principles and practices that would help to sustain or stimulate planetary and ecosystemic integrity and interdependence. Ecological ethics expresses and guides commitments to creation and community. Christian ecological ethics in the sacramental commons relates principles to context, applies principles in context, and reformulates principles, as necessary, for context. Its theological base is integrated with insights from the natural and social sciences, the humanities, diverse religious traditions, philosophy, and ideas from environmental thinkers of varied backgrounds. Its proposals for practical projects are developed from interactions with humanist ecological ethics, scientific studies and insights, and communities' experiences in context.

Christian ecological ethics, then, does not develop in a vacuum or even from within a single tradition isolated from insights external to its community. It emerges from the Earth commons, and responds to issues that need conscientious practical resolution. It seeks to anticipate concerns and injustices so that it might be ready to address them in a specific situation. Ecological ethics has been developed within Christian contexts for several decades. In the past few decades, Christian ethicists have advocated human responsibility within nature for the well-being of nature by proposing basic rights for nature or ethical principles to guide human interaction with nature.

James Nash in *Loving Nature* establishes love as the ground of Christian theology and ethics,[3] suggests seven "dimensions of love,"[4] proposes seven environmental rights focused on human needs,[5] and offers a "Bill of Biotic Rights" that suggests eight rights for nonhuman individuals and species.[6]

In *Earth Community Earth Ethics*, Larry Rasmussen offers six moral norms "of and for sustainability": *participation*, which is "the optimal inclusion of all involved voices in society's decisions" so that all those impacted by decisions to be made will assist in their formulation and implementation; *sufficiency*, which means "the commitment to meet the basic material needs of all life possible"; *equity*, which requires "distributive and procedural justice" to ensure balanced treatment among nations, throughout the biotic community, across generations, and between women and men; *accountability*, which is "the sense and structuring of responsibility toward one another and earth," and incorporates "transparency"; *material simplicity and spiritual richness* as indicators of a "quality of life" that includes but goes beyond providing "bread alone"; *responsibility*, which includes "actions commensurate with workable community" and use of appropriate technologies; and *subsidiarity*, which means that "problems should be resolved at the closest level" available to make decisions, and effectively implemented.[7] Rasmussen also proposes "according the full sweep of nature inherent moral value."[8]

Leaders of several Christian churches have issued environment-related statements since 1975. Among these documents, two regional Catholic bishops' statements offer principles for appropriate human relationships with the commons and for the common good. The midwestern bishops issued *Strangers and Guests: Toward Community in the Heartland* (1980),[9] which focused on issues of land ownership and use. They suggested ten principles in the document.

Principles of Land Stewardship

1. The land is God's;
2. People are God's stewards on the land;
3. The land's benefits are for everyone;
4. The land should be distributed equitably;
5. The land should be conserved and restored;
6. Land use planning must consider social and environmental impacts;
7. Land use should be appropriate to land quality;

8. The land should provide a moderate livelihood;
9. The land's workers should be able to become the land's owners; and
10. The land's mineral wealth should be shared.

The Western Canadian and U.S. bishops in their bioregional statement, *The Columbia River Watershed: Caring for Creation and the Common Good* (2001),[10] propose ten "considerations" that serve as principles.

Considerations for Community Caretaking

1. Consider the common good;
2. Conserve the watershed as a common good;
3. Conserve and protect species of wildlife;
4. Respect the dignity and traditions of the region's indigenous peoples;
5. Promote justice for the poor, linking economic justice and environmental justice;
6. Promote community resolution of economic and ecological issues;
7. Promote social and ecological responsibility among reductive and reproductive enterprises;
8. Conserve energy and establish environmentally integrated alternative energy sources;
9. Respect ethnic and racial cultures, citizens and communities; and
10. Integrate transportation and recreation needs with sustainable ecosystem requirements.

The proposals from ethicists and church leaders share in common a regard for the needs and rights of human communities; respect for the biotic community and abiotic creation; concern for an equitable distribution of commons goods and common goods to provide for the common good; and suggestions for right conduct to promote the good of the commons from which, directly or indirectly, needed goods are taken. The well-being of creation and of community are inextricably linked in these proposals. The liberation of each requires the liberation of both. The groans of nature and the cries of the poor and the racially and ethnically oppressed form an integrated plea for redress and a demand for justice.

Consideration of these perspectives leads toward a complementary and contemporary exposition of principles for Christian ecological ethics. Human reflection, whether from a scientific or spiritual base, uses current knowledge to build on a past foundation, and invites future revision over time as developing cultural history brings new data and theories. Ethics, no less than science or theology, or religious, political, and economic theories and practices, should be dynamic. The present should not be absolutized in either ideology or structure. Paradigms can shift, and seemingly irrefutable "truths" turn out to be best-developed understandings of a specific time and place, no matter the extent to which they have been incorporated into diverse contexts and historical moments, for however long, and with whatever confidence that they are universal in origin and application.

The biblical warning to Israel that if people do not remember and obey their covenant with the Creator-Liberator God, the land entrusted to them by Yahweh might become unproductive or taken away by Yahweh, is instructive today in the context of human-caused and human-exacerbated environmental devastation. Ecological ethics is needed to guide humanity as a whole and in its cultural and individual parts to be responsible for the sacred and sacramental Earth in order that as a sacramental commons it might continue to be the mediation of the Spirit, provide needed goods for all people, and nurture the biotic community.

Consciousness of the current crises confronting creation, and a consequent commitment to the commons good and the common good should lead to concrete community projects to foster preservation, restoration, and conservation of the sacramental commons. Within the Christian community, guides for social commitment and action to care for creation, expressed as principles in Christian ecological ethics, can catalyze a transformation of current attitudes and actions, and promote positive Christian conduct in commons and community.

Christian ecological ethics has its foundations in biblical ethics; diverse understandings (expressed or unexpressed) of some form of natural law ethics or natural relations ethics (whether or not expressed as such); situation ethics; and social ethics. It integrates be-ing ethics and do-ing ethics.

Basic values incorporated into ecological ethics are *solidarity* (consciousness of and actions for the shared interests and needs of the human species and all biota); *sociality* (interrelation with and regard for the human community and the broader biotic community); *sufficiency* (acknowledgment of, and efforts to provide for, the integrated needs and integrity of humankind, all biokind, and abiotic creation); *sustainability* (attention to the present and projected integral viability of life in its diverse forms, communities, and relationships, and of life's habitats, through biotic and geologic time); *subsidiarity* (responsible resolution of biotic conflicts—including human-human and human-otherkind—by local constituencies in local communities, using external consultation or more extended laws as necessary—for technical expertise not locally available, and for an objective complementary analysis—and more extended laws as necessary—where, for example, national laws would provide greater commons protection—to the greatest extent possible; this process would include special regard for local ecosystem conservation and, in the case of human communities, for local energy production and local economic development); *security* (safeguarding the integrity of individuals, species, and their habitat, to enable them to meet their respective requirements through time, as resolved in competitive and cooperative relationships in evolutionary Earth commons settings); and *spirituality* (consciousness of and relatedness to the Spirit from whose vision, creativity, and love the cosmos-chaos-cosmos and the commons emerged and are emerging).

Since what is here proposed is *Christian* ecological ethics, the Great Commandment affirmed by Jesus will be the foundation for the suggested principles. The commandment is expressed in the gospel of Luke as "You shall love the Lord your God with all your heart, and with all your soul, and with all your strength, and with all your mind; and your neighbor as yourself" (10:27).

Bearing in mind Augustine's idea that one loves God while trying to have one's will in accord with God's, and mindful of previous discussions about the Jubilee and divine engagement with creation and biblical teachings expressing this, the use of the Great Commandment for Christian ecological ethics requires exploration of its elements, most notably in terms of what might be the implications of loving one who is simultaneously Spirit-Transcendent, the creating Spirit, Spirit-Being; and Spirit-Immanent, the engaging Spirit, Spirit-Becoming. It is important to consider, too, who is the "neighbor" to be loved. Jesus' questioner in the gospel narratives wanted to limit human responsibility to the family next door, to friends and relatives, or to a reasonable handful of people. Rather, the understanding of "neighbor" might be expanded, as Jesus did, to include all people and peoples; and, in the spirit of Jesus, "neighbor" might be extended further: to the "birds of the air" and the "lilies of the field" mentioned by Jesus as creatures God cared for, and to the soaring eagles and swimming fish about whom God is solicitous in the book of Job.

In response to the query, "Who is my neighbor?" Jesus tells the story of the Good Samaritan. The parable is sometimes misinterpreted to mean that a person in need is the neighbor (thus, "Good Samaritan" laws in some states require people who have the training to do so to assist a person in an emergency situation), or that everyone is a neighbor. These interpretations are partly right: Jesus instructs people to help those in need. But he went beyond that, as evidenced by his question to the questioning lawyer: "Which of these three, do you think, was a neighbor to the man who fell into the hands of the robbers?" The lawyer correctly answers that the Samaritan (whom Jews regarded as an enemy) is the one who was a neighbor to the injured Jew. Jesus teaches that people should not await someone's cry for help to respond to a call to be a neighbor; they should make themselves neighbors to those who need them. From the parable might be drawn two ideas for ecological ethics:

first, assist those who are in need; second, choose to be consistently a neighbor to others.

Humans are not the only neighbors who are suffering and need help. Earth and the biotic community are in crisis and in need of assistance. People are called to make themselves neighbors to humankind, to Earth, and to extended biokind. In light of these ideas, it would not be inappropriate to suggest that states need a "Good Samaritan Law" regarding care for or assistance to the environment. Everyone would be responsible for alleviating environmental degradation, according to their abilities, from recycling aluminum cans to reporting instances of pollution. The law would enable also prosecution of *ecoterrorists*—those whose individual and corporate greed causes pollution of air, land, and water—by fining (at levels that are not a "slap on the wrist" and offer no incentive to stop polluting since it is less expensive to pay the fine than to eliminate the source of pollution) or jailing these ecoterrorists and demanding that they give restitution to Earth, to the impacted community, and to individuals harmed by their practices. Corporate and individual ecoterrorists would be required to develop alternative processes, products, and energy sources to replace those causing environmental degradation and harming the biotic community.

An ecological ethics interpretation of the Great Commandment means, then, that since the creating Creator Spirit loves creation and all creatures, and since people who love God should love what God loves: in the sacramental commons, those to be loved include Earth as an abiotic whole; humankind; and biota as a whole and in part. When this love is active for the Earth neighbor and Earth communities, bioregional integrity and viability are maintained, and the biotic community flourishes in the integrated and interdependent relational community.

PRINCIPLES OF CHRISTIAN ECOLOGICAL ETHICS

1. Care for the Earth commons, which is the revelation of the Spirit and home for the biotic community.
2. Respect the intrinsic value of creation; conserve the instrumental value of creation.
3. Respect the intrinsic value of the biotic community; be grateful for the instrumental value of its members.
4. Respect natural rights and acknowledge their authority over civil laws and customs.
5. Prioritize the community common good over the individual good.
6. Prioritize community and species needs over an individual's or another community's wants.

7. Integrate the commons good, the common good, and the individual good.
8. Regard the common good as both an instrumental good and an intrinsic good.
9. Ensure that human communities in all their ethnic and class diversity have a sufficiency of subsistence goods designated as common goods, and available for and accessible by individuals: through community ownership and cooperative enterprises, and equitable (re)distribution of land and Earth-related goods.
10. Promote the commons good, the common good and, as necessary, common goods: in Earth's land, Earth's other needed goods, and goods resulting from human labor on Earth goods.
11. Maintain human populations at intergenerational levels appropriate to the carrying capacity of the Earth commons and the bioregional commons.
12. Consume responsibly products and goods that are directly or indirectly derived from commons goods, in a manner consonant with abiotic integrity and intergenerational biotic community needs.

These principles express love of the Spirit, love of human neighbors, love of biokind neighbors, and love of the Earth neighbor, and they promote relational consciousness, relational community, and relational commitments. As just conduct increases, the relational community will extend over time to embrace all creation in its Creator. In the process, Earth commons goods will be equitably distributed to provide for the common good, to meet the needs of human individuals, communities, and biokind as a whole. Restorative justice (returning to people, to Earth and to biota what has been unjustly taken from them) and distributive justice (an equitable sharing of Earth goods) will be necessary in some contexts for this to occur.

Christians inspired by awareness of the Spirit's engaging presence in the universe and in the commons, and conscious of the commons as their shared spiritual, social, scientific, and spatial common ground, strive to fulfill a caregiving role in the Earth commons. Their dynamically developing creation care consciousness, and the practical projects in which they express it, enable people to be aware of the common ground they share and to be active in promoting the common good of those who share their local commons. People who understand what is meant by "sacramental universe" and "sacramental commons" act accordingly. They implement Christian ecological ethics to maintain their consistent ethical commitment through significant ethical choices that promote the well-being of Earth and the biotic community.

Human needs in that setting are met through interdependent relationships with the Earth commons and its living inhabitants.

Creation and Creator have a dynamic relationship in *integral being*. The Spirit-transcendent freely and creatively brings cosmos-chaos-cosmos into being; the Spirit-immanent permeates created being. All that exists flows from divine being, directly or indirectly. Integral being has integral natural rights, from which all natural rights are derived. Christian ecological ethics requires that a person of faith acknowledge integral being—the dynamic cosmos that exists in, is engaged with, emerges from, and is sacred because of, the creating transcendent-immanent, Being-Becoming Spirit—and respect, have regard for, and express responsibility toward, integral being. The humanist recognizes integral being as all-existent cosmic being, of unknown origin before it burst into existence; the spiritual person also acknowledge a divine presence in which and from which cosmic being emerges. Integral being requires ethical consideration. Atheist, agnostic, and theist share common ground when they acknowledge and fulfill their ethical responsibilities toward integral being.[11]

Creation weaves an intricate and beautiful tapestry of being. Creation-conscious practices will instill in communities an appreciation of that tapestry in all its complexity, and inspire a commitment to care for it in its continuous emergence from its primordial origin in the Spirit's vision and power. Eco-logical ethics that embody and stimulate care about, for, and within creation will sustain the commons, conserve common goods and commons goods, and promote the common good.

NOTES

1. These predevelopment questions are adapted and expanded from John Hart, *Ethics and Technology: Innovation and Transformation in Community Contexts* (Cleveland, Ohio: Pilgrim, 1997), 24.

2. Aldo Leopold, *A Sand County Almanac and Sketches Here and There* (New York: Oxford University Press, 1987), 225.

3. James A. Nash, *Loving Nature: Ecological Integrity and Christian Responsibility* (Nashville, Tenn.: Abingdon, 1992), 140.

4. Nash, *Loving Nature*, 152–59.

5. Nash, *Loving Nature*, 171.

6. Nash, *Loving Nature*, 186–89.

7. Larry Rasmussen, *Earth Community Earth Ethics* (Maryknoll, N.Y.: Orbis, 1996), 172.

8. Rasmussen, *Earth Community Earth Ethics*, 345.

9. The statement and related audiovisual aids are available from the National Catholic Rural Life Conference, Des Moines, Iowa.

10. The statement and related information are available on the Web site of the Columbia River Pastoral Letter Project, at www.columbiariver.org.

11. *Integral being*, as understood by the believer or humanist (and here the latter perspective includes the atheist and the agnostic), is the totality of being which has been both the origin of all being and beings, and the stuff from which all being has been and is being comprised since just before the singular initial explosive expansion of the cosmos, and throughout the eons thereafter. Integral being is the mother of all being, which emanates from it. Human beings are the reflective consciousness of *Earth*, and a part of reflective *cosmic* consciousness, which might include other evolved beings (and which includes—for the believer—the Spirit creating). The origin/mother of integrated beings should be acknowledged and protected, not violated by its member-beings, because of its inherent, originating, and necessary processes. *Integral being* originates all being through the interaction of cosmos (order) and chaos (apparently disorderly events, or events at least disorderly in terms of known orderly dynamic systems and beings). Integral being has natural rights by virtue of being the dynamic origin-being, which as such deserves respect and protection so that its processes might continue. "Natural rights" (as described in chapter 7) is a construct of human beings, who are part of nature and part of cosmic consciousness. Humans' acceptance of natural rights for integral being would prevent violation of cosmic systems similar to what humans have done to Earth processes, that is, alteration of weather patterns by global warming, endangering the integrity of multiple organisms through the irresponsible bioengineering of some, and so on.

· 12 ·

Spirit, Commons, and Community

$\mathcal{T}$he Earth commons shared by the biotic community mediates the creating Spirit. In diverse but integrated ecosystems, species and individuals live interdependent and integrated lives in an evolutionary and dynamic place. Humans have put stresses on the abiotic context of life, and in the biotic community, they have eliminated some species and individuals and threaten or endanger others' survival. Humans' extinction of biotic beings that otherwise would have participated in an integrated evolution has violated the natural ebb and flow of life on Earth. While some species disappear because they compete with humankind for the same Earth goods or habitat to meet their needs, others are "extincted" because human irresponsibility, carelessness, or greed exploits the commons far more than is necessary to obtain and sustain a good life and livelihood.

The common space shared by the human community is intended by Spirit to meet the needs of all people and peoples. Appropriation of Earth's land or goods for selfish reasons or purposes subverts this intention. Some members of the human family are deprived of nutritious food, potable water, and other necessities of life provided by Earth, while others live opulently.

Abiotic nature and the biotic community suffer from global warming that is caused or at least exacerbated by human action (e.g., carbon emissions) and inaction (denying that warming is occurring; refusing to diminish vehicular and smokestack emissions, as necessary). Abiotic nature and the biotic community suffer also from depletion of available and accessible potable water supplies, because of water pollution and privatization.

Human violence against the biotic community, the human community, and abiotic creation demonstrates that few people are conscious of and related to Spirit-transcendent-immanent present in Earth and revealed through Earth (a spiritual consciousness), a sense of the social bonds that relate people to each other and to all life (a social consciousness), a realization of the importance of place in their lives (a spatial consciousness), and a commitment

223

to act to meet communities' needs (a prophetic consciousness, concretely expressed).

The sacrament of creation—a visible sign of the immanence and loving solicitude of the creating Spirit—includes the sacramental universe and the sacramental commons. The wonders of the cosmos speak of divine creativity in the extensive and expanding sacramental universe. Spiritual and social consciousness and community commitment unite in human awareness of and relationship with Earth as an evolving sacramental commons.

The prophetic dimension complements the revelatory or sacramental dimension. Biblical passages require compassion for and responsibility toward the neighbor. Job and his adversaries agree that these are signs of a just person. Jesus as Son of Man identifies himself with and among the poor. Jesus teaches in the parable of the Good Samaritan that people should not only be responsive to a neighbor's request for assistance but be a neighbor who is alert to the needs of others and responds to them. A relational consciousness extends the understanding of "neighbor" beyond the human community, to all biota. Human responsibility to neighbors is fulfilled through a compassionate sharing of the goods of the Earth commons to provide for the human common good and the broader biotic good, in a relational community attuned to the presence of the Spirit-immanent.

COMMON GOOD AND PERSONAL GOOD

The priority of the community over the individual might be troubling to some. The understanding and advocacy of individual human rights emerged, and rightly so, in response to the laws and practices of oppressive governments that were controlled by a single despot or a tyrannical group. It should be noted that the community that has priority is not to be identified with a government or an unjust body within and controlling society, nor is it to be identified with the adherents of unjust laws that affect the citizenry or people as a whole. The community that has priority is the aggregate of people who strive to be just and to develop just institutions that promote love of neighbor, compassion for the oppressed neighbor and, eventually, a spirit- and spiritually related community, the creation commons community. In human social structures, the common good, the good of all the human community rather than just a part of it, is the goal.

In this understanding, then, the types of despotism, suppression of human rights, and oppression of actual or potential dissidents that have characterized numerous governments over millennia would not be operative. Those who controlled these systems have not represented the community as a whole. The integral relational community and its approximations in history stand in contradiction to the tyranny of a majority (ethnic, religious, or racial; the latter exemplified in slavery, toxic waste dump siting, and redlined neighborhoods in the United States); the tyranny of the minority (exemplified in apartheid in South Africa); and the tyranny of an individual (exemplified, almost universally in human consciousness, in Adolf Hitler).

Individual human rights are not negated when the community is prioritized; neither are individual goods negated, although they might be diminished in periods of scarcity so that at least the subsistence goods of all individuals might be provided in an aggregate manner. Earth has a sufficiency of goods, when properly gathered and equitably distributed, to meet the needs of all: currently, and in the future, if human populations increase within the constraints of Earth's carrying capacity, and if this and other principles of ecological ethics are observed. The personal good of all individuals will be enhanced if the common good of the aggregate of individuals is prioritized. In the envisioned integral relational community this will occur.

COMMONS GOODS FOR
THE COMMON GOOD

The story of Jesus' meeting with the Rich Young Man brings together in a particularly telling way elements of the sacred and the social, the sacramental and the prophetic. The encounter reveals the relationship among Spirit, commons, and community, and it offers thought-provoking insights into the integration of common good and common goods, the meaning of communion and community, and the nature of Nature as sacramental commons.

The Rich Young Man's wealth, the gospel relates, was in the form of "many possessions" or "landed property."[1] The latter translation would be more appropriate because Matthew positions the narrative just prior to where he places Jesus' parable of the workers in the vineyard. In the parable, a landowner parts with the goods of his land (by giving away their equivalent value in payment to his workers) but does not part with the land itself, when he pays all the workers equally whether they spent one or twelve hours in the hot sun picking his grape crop. He goes beyond the Torah requirement (to pay his workers a "fair day's wage") by paying most of his hired hands more than they had earned according to the terms of the contract the twelve-hour workers negotiated with the vineyard owner. Jesus invites the Rich Young Man to act in a way parallel to the conduct of the landowner in the parable. He invites him to go beyond Torah requirements and to part with his possessions. The vineyard owner had fulfilled his Torah responsibility to pay his workers fair wages and moreover had assisted the poor by giving them money as alms in the form of wages. It could be extrapolated, from his conduct as an employer toward the laborers who worked for him, that the vineyard owner helped the poor also by allowing them to be gleaners behind the paid workers as is their biblical right (Leviticus 19:9–10 and Deuteronomy 24:19–22). He paid the poor workers a full day's wages because although they worked for as little time as an hour, they would have twelve hours' worth of expenses to pay when the workday was over, since all workers needed the full fair day's wage to provide for themselves and their family.

The Rich Young Man probably fulfilled his Torah responsibility. But he did not go beyond it, even after asking Jesus how he might do so. He probably had received his property as an inheritance, and therefore is not among those condemned for adding "field to field" (Isaiah 5:8), or by the pseudepigraphal pre-Christian section of the apocalyptic 1 Enoch in which the Son of Man condemns landowners who have enriched themselves at the expense of the poor.[2] He obeys the Torah, except for its Jubilee provisions that had not been practiced for more than a millennium. Perhaps he is unaware of the justice requirement that the Jubilee be revived and that Jesus had proclaimed it in the Nazareth synagogue. He is not among those condemned for failing to abide by Jubilee provisions; this would be inferred by Jesus' acceptance of his claim that he had been obeying the Torah. Jesus notes his obedience to the Torah and his potential to go beyond Torah requirements; looks at him lovingly; and offers him a greater responsibility, an opportunity to express greater compassion than the Torah requires of him, and an invitation to be part of the traveling community of believers. It seems likely from the narrative's context that he was seeking to do more (perhaps he already went beyond the Torah requirements to assist those in need) and to be more. The major stumbling block might have been the invitation to part with his land.

COMMONS LAND AS COMMON LAND

In the Jubilee Year, as seen previously, lands were to be returned to their original owners or their descendants. Families that had acquired extensive holdings in land were to redistribute the sections that were not their ancestral holdings to the landless people who had a biblical claim on them. This land redistribution, joined with other Jubilee provisions that required rest for the land, remission of debts, and release of slaves, comprised the "good news to the poor" that Isaiah proclaimed and Jesus tried to promulgate.

Jesus invites the Rich Young Man to go from being landed to landless, not just by meeting a Jubilee requirement of restorative justice but also by relinquishing his own land and giving up his right to any claim on it in the future; it would become the ancestral land of the poor to whom he gave it. Whether he relinquished part of his land that was others' rightful inheritance in fidelity to the Jubilee requirement or gave away all of his land to honor the Jubilee and follow Jesus, the Rich Young Man's land would be (re)distributed to others, in whole or in part.

Jesus offers the Rich Young Man an enhanced Jubilee perspective, consciousness, and practice. The Son of Man says, effectively, "Redistribute your property and give it to the poor, even though in your case you have not acquired it unjustly from them; and live as they have been living, without land and the security it and other forms of property provide." But the Rich Young Man keeps his possessions—*for* himself and *from* the poor.

The encounter with the Son of Man takes place in a very visible and striking way for the Rich Young Man in the gospel narratives. It exemplifies the type of encounter that other people have had over the centuries with the Spirit, in creation and in the Bible.

The Christian hope for land, or at least for goods of Earth to meet everyone's needs, is sometimes overlooked even by biblical scholars. In *The Gospel and the Land*, W. D. Davies states that in the New Testament "the notion of 'entering the land' had been spiritualized,"[3] asserting that "the doctrine of the land was very alive in first-century Judaism, whereas the land does not occupy writers of the New Testament to any comparable, serious degree"[4] and that Jesus "broke . . . the bonds of the land" for early Christians.[5] The spiritualization of the land that Davies sees in the New Testament might rather be a sublimation of land ownership in two senses: a rejection of land as national territory; and a recollection that land is primordially community property—the community shares the land and its goods prior to private distributions, and any property holdings are to be productive to help meet community needs. The ideal and practice passed on through Christian generations ordinarily will not be land, then, but the goods of the land transformed into the goods of the community for the common good. Davies rightly notes that early Christianity rejected Jewish territorial doctrine, but he overextends this perspective by declaring that Christians spiritualized the land. He does not discuss the Jubilee proclamation of Jesus (Luke 4:16–21), which indicates the time is at hand to have a redistribution of land. In an oblique reference to Davies, Walter Brueggemann declares that "spiritual Christianity, by refusing to face the land question, has served to sanction existing inequities."[6]

In its context of political oppression in its early centuries, the Christian community prudently would not advocate acquiring territorial land (thereby angering the Romans or exacerbating Herod's fears), nor would it oppose

Jubilee redistribution (thereby alienating its Jewish brethren). As with any oppressed group, Christians would not publicly express their radical hope—in this instance for (communal) land holdings. But traces of their hope can be seen in their actions and teachings. The distribution of land from the rich to the poor would be a practical step toward inviting the landless poor to remain *personally* landless (as to individual or familial legal title and entitlement), but *communally* landholders. Common property in land would overcome the Jubilee distribution flaw that those whose ancestors had received poorer soil and no access to water would always get back this same land, while those who began with rich soil and access to flowing waters would always retain that same land. Brueggemann notes that "in both Testaments the land possessed or promised concerns the whole people. . . . The unit of decision-making is the community and that always with reference to the land."[7]

While Davies rightly notes that early Christians rejected Jewish "territorial doctrine" insofar as this expressed ethnic nationalism, they seemed to live with a sense, as Davies also notes, that every place is sacred space because of Jesus' journeys and Jesus' presence with them. Therefore, they reject a monarchical territory, but probably envision community holdings or community property of some type, or at least community sharing of Earth's goods, any and all of which would provide for the common good. Peter and the Apostles in Acts redistribute, to those in their Christian community who are in need, the money received from land and houses sold by devout Christians. A gospel example of redistributing the land's goods to those in need occurs when Jesus' hungry disciples take and eat wheat grain as they pass through a farmer's field on the sabbath (Luke 6:1): satisfying their hunger in this way is permitted (Deuteronomy 23:25) and that is itself an indication of the right of the poor to food, even on private property, when they are hungry. Similarly, Christians might replace possession of land as national territory, and possession of land as individual property, with possession of the land's goods (and, later, even of land itself) as common property.

In creation, the pristine and the prophetic, the sacramental and the social, intertwine in the sacramental commons. In this place, community commitments maintain the integrity of creation and sustain the viability of human life and work, and they meet human needs in a manner integrated with the needs of other creatures and of creation as a whole.

SACRAMENTS IN THE COMMONS

In Christian traditions whose religious practice includes *sacraments*—signs of God's granting of grace to their recipients—creation itself can be viewed as *sacramental.* The beauty, diversity, and complexity of the created world can stimulate people who are open to an encounter with the Spirit to become aware of the divine presence immanent in Earth. It is helpful to recall here the distinction between *ecclesial* sacraments, which are particular rituals ordinarily mediated by a member of the clergy or by a designated church representative, and *universal* sacraments, which are mediated by creation in whole or in part. The idea of universal sacraments was suggested biblically: "From the greatness and beauty of created things their original author, by analogy, is seen" (Wisdom 13:5).

The *universal sacrament of creation*, then, offers moments of grace, of personal or communal engagement with the Spirit. No religious representative is needed at such times to mediate the divine presence or to facilitate praise of or gratitude toward the Spirit: the experience is direct and, at times, mystical. It is a moment of engaging the Spirit who is *transcendent* to creation (distinct from creation) and *immanent* in creation (present in creation).

There is a danger that creation might be seen as divine in itself, rather than a sign of the Spirit who gave it being and in whom it exists: "[People] from the good things seen did not succeed in knowing him who is, and from studying the works did not discern the artisan" (Wisdom 13:1). People with a creation-centered consciousness, who are members of an integral relational community, do not succumb to this temptation.

Consciousness of the sacramental commons can provide a deeper appreciation of the sacred in all aspects of the Christian life, linking liturgy in church with the life of people in all creation. For the Christian, just as wheat from the fields provides bread both for the priest or minister to bless and distribute from the altar table for spiritual nourishment, and for the family to eat at the dinner table for bodily nourishment, so, too, must the commons be enabled to mediate both spiritual nourishment as a sacrament of creation, and provide bodily nourishment to sustain human life. To provide both spiritual and physical nourishment for the holistic well-being of their recipient, the sacramental commons must have clean soil, living water, and pure air, conserved intergenerationally.

COMMITMENT TO CREATION
AND COMMUNITY

When sacred and social consciousness are integrated, commitment to community flows into concrete actions. People care for the commons, justly and compassionately distribute among members of the human community the goods its members need for their subsistence, and respectfully share the commons goods as common goods in the *human* community and as shared goods with members of the *biotic* community as a whole.

Christians concerned about conserving and sustaining the sacramental commons for present and future generations go beyond justice to compassion and commitment. They accept the invitation that Jesus extends today just as he extended it to the Rich Young Man two millennia ago. Earth's goods are sufficient to provide for the common good—the needs of all communities and their individual members—but will not satisfy excessive aggregate individual wants—the greed of the few whose avarice deprives the poor of their subsistence needs. A just distribution and an equitable use of Earth's goods characterize the sacramental commons.

Sustaining the sacramental commons is an endeavor that requires relating faith and good works. A sacramental consciousness enables Christians to encounter the Creator in creation and to respect the Creator's work and creatures. It inspires Christians to conserve and restore the commons so that it might meet the needs of human communities and the broader biotic community. It stimulates efforts to promote the commons good (the well-being of place as home and habitat), the common good (of humankind and other living creatures), and common goods (the sharing of the benefits the Spirit and Earth provide for all).

THE COMMONS TO COME

All humans are nomads in space and time, transient inhabitants of Earth. Although their individual traces might disappear, people leave behind, and thus for the future, some mark of their passing and past presence. Each individual has a particular biological, social, intellectual, emotional, sexual, and spiritual history. Each culture has its ethnic, economic, and contextual history. Cultural history outlasts most individual histories, extends into the consciousness of people and peoples beyond its point and place of origin, and lasts through generations. People as individuals and as cultures inhabit Earth (and perhaps eventually will inhabit other places in the universe) in the present moment between the lives of their ancestors and the lives of their children, between the past that was bequeathed to them and the future that they will leave for the generations to come—of their own and other species. As individuals and as a species, humans living in any present moment bridge the past and the future in distinctive ways. They are genetic, social, and ecological bridges. Their children and future generations of human beings will carry their DNA and combine it with that of others' offspring. The societies they envision and activate will affect currently present and creatively potential societal constructs and future regional, national, and international relationships, stimulating collaboration or competition, concord or conflict. The way people work with or against their Earth habitat and the needs of other species (and whether they respect the latter's natural rights and intrinsic value or regard them solely as instrumental) will influence, and at times determine, future social structures, governing ideas, biotic relationships, and Earth's viability. People can construct a bridge to any of several distinct distant shores depending on their creativity, the choices they make of materials, the responsible crafting of their product, and their careful consideration of what they would want their offspring to inherit.

People live in particular places and times only for a short period in cosmic or geologic time, but they must still care for Earth, carefully construct social systems, and compassionately relate to each other and to the rest of the biotic community. They must be concerned not just about their present moment and locale but about what is yet to come and how they will impact it through their actions and their inaction, through their traditional ideologies and through their utopian visions.

When people analyze the world around them, they see both the beauty and the blight that they have inherited and that they have caused. If they listen, they might hear the voices of those who are gone who plead on behalf of creation and community. If they listen even more attentively, they might hear the voices of those yet to come who plead for a livable future, which will be their own present. When people reflect carefully and considerately on their world, they see around them that the teachings of the past and the pleas of the future often are being ignored in the name of an ephemeral "progress" for all or "national security" for some. They hear also promises of positive benefits from "globalization" and from adherence to a particular belief system that has its own form of "salvation" in conflict with distinct rival faiths, each of which affirms its exclusive and excluding religious "truth."

When people consider the evident dissonance between past visions and present realities, and between present visions and developing future realities, they are called—as people of faith (however delineated, and whether religion or humanist based) and as children of Earth—to reflect on their responsibilities for their own time and for others' future time. They are challenged to make the reality yet to come congruent with the best visions of the past and present. They are prompted to ask, in their historical moment between the past and future commons, between the realities that are and the realities that might emerge from either their finest dreams or their worst nightmares, how they will be responsible caretakers of their individual and species niches in the commons, and coevolve with their place and their living neighbors in the cosmos.

People seek today to experience kinship with Earth and biota, find it increasingly rare, and wonder what has brought drastic changes to the natural world. They begin to realize that traditional spiritual insights, more than transient economic ideologies, present enduring values of care for creation and concern for community that are needed to renew Earth. Concrete embodiment of these values would promote the commons good and common good, and ensure a just distribution of commons goods and common goods.

In order to get from present peril to envisioned future, from conflictive ideologies and conflicted institutions to an integral relational community, people must make some serious and difficult changes in attitudes toward and relationships with Earth, all life, and each other. Humankind's attitude must change from domination over and destruction of creation to respect for and relatedness to creation. People must once again learn that prayerful sense of awe before the wonders of the cosmos of which they are a part, and a sense of kinship with the cosmos through which they recognize that each cosmic being is related to every other and to the Spirit within a web of primordial and expanding stardust. They must regain their lost role as caretakers of a place, Earth's garden, and as citizens of cosmic space. Thomas Berry calls people to be part of a "Great Work": to be integrated with the dynamics of the cosmos and the commons, to recognize that there is a single community of life, and, as a result, to be part of a movement that gives "shape and meaning to life."[8]

To be called by the Spirit is to be called to service in the commons and for the common good and, indeed, because all is interconnected and interdependent, in some way for the cosmos good. It is a call to be engaged in and with the human and biotic communities, on Earth and in the cosmos where the Spirit-immanent lives and is revealed, not an invitation to be attached to an individualistic, transient, euphoric transcendent moment. It is a call to communal relation, not to individual self-absorption and selfishness. It is a call to be a child of the universe and of the creating, loving Spirit. The mountaintop is tempting as a permanent place of rest. The call of the Spirit, however, is an invitation to be immersed in, not separated from, creation and community. It is a call to share the insights and visions received and to seek their realization.

The Creator is encountered and engaged in and through the creation community. The physical or spiritual mountain is a place of divine commission, not of permanent personal residence. People who engage the Spirit there must depart while not departing and descend from the mountain while yet remaining in union with the Spirit and being strengthened by the memory of and a continuing engagement with the relational experience.

The present is the child of the future; the future is the child of the present.

People's visions of the future guide their actions in the present; their actions in the present form the future that they will develop for the generations to come. If people live as an integral relational community in a sacramental commons, responsibly caring for their Earth home, conscious of their relationship to the Spirit, to each other, to Earth, and to all life, and are thereby a sign in their community and a sign with their commons of the Spirit's creating presence and their openness to it and engagement with it, the future will be bright and blessed. When people promote the commons good on Earth, they will enable Earth to be a sacramental commons in itself and in its bioregional parts, where living water will flow for all: as a common good, and for the common good. People must plant in the sacramental commons the seeds of trees of life, nourished by living water, that will begin to bear good fruit for their children and for the generations to come.

NOTES

1. Walter Brueggemann suggests that "landed property" would be the better translation of the Greek *ktemata*. *Dialog* (Summer 1980): 172.

2. The Son of Man, who "was concealed in the presence of the (Lord of the Spirits) prior to the creation of the world," will come with great power, and "In those days, the kings of the earth and the mighty landowners shall be humiliated on account of the deeds of their hands." 1 Enoch in *The Old Testament Pseudepigrapha, Volume 1: Apocalyptic Literature and Testaments*, ed. James H. Charlesworth (New York: Doubleday, 1983), 35–36.

3. W. D. Davies, *The Gospel and the Land: Early Christianity and Jewish Territorial Doctrine* (Berkeley: University of California Press, 1974), 362.

4. Davies, *The Gospel and the Land*, 370.

5. Davies, *The Gospel and the Land*, 375.

6. Walter Brueggemann, *The Land: Place as Gift, Promise, and Challenge in Biblical Faith* (Minneapolis: Augsburg Fortress, 1977), 193.

7. Brueggemann, *The Land*, 186.

8. Thomas Berry, *The Great Work: Our Way into the Future* (New York: Bell Tower, 1999), 7.

Afterword

*J*ohn Hart has taken a leadership role in bringing Western religious traditions to support a more integral human-Earth presence to each other. A central aspect of his work is the presentation of a sense of the sacred throughout the natural world as a primary inspiration for preserving Earth from destructive use by humans.

John Hart does amazing work. In his latest presentation he has gone more extensively into the rituals of the natural world and of human society, as well as those formally referred to as sacraments. His finest contribution is in the clarification of words and terms referring to divine presence in the universe; these are important distinctions since there are different modes of the same reality. A key understanding of the book is the sacramental nature of the universe as a whole, and of planet Earth in all its modalities.

When I think of indigenous peoples, I note that they consistently held a certain sense of the mystery and the wonder of the natural world. They suffered because of natural catastrophes, but at the same time they recognized that the benefits of the natural world fulfilled ultimate relationships. In *Sacramental Commons* indigenous peoples' relationships to planet Earth are described particularly in chapter 3, "Native Spirits," which discusses the life and teachings of Phillip Deere (whom I knew from our encounters at various conferences, and by whom I was very impressed); and in chapter 6, "Species Survival," which relates the life and social activism of David Sohappy Sr.

Next year, two important events will be commemorated: the publication forty years ago of Lynn White Jr.'s "The Historical Roots of Our Ecologic Crisis" in the journal *Science* in 1967; and the United Nations General Assembly's promulgation twenty-five years ago of the *World Charter for Nature* in 1982.

White noted rightly that Christianity in recent centuries has been alienating its followers from the natural world. Originally, however, Christianity had two sources revelatory of divine presence: the universe and the Bible. The

235

Bible exalts the natural world as a magnificent presentation of the deepest meaning of our existence; *Sacramental Commons* illustrates this belief very well. The natural world is a manifestation of the world of the sacred. Today many people think of the natural world and the universe as "out there," separate from the human, as if the human were looking at it from outside rather than from inside. The universe is the cause of the human; the human is not the cause of the universe. The two are, in a sense, mutually related and mutually fulfilling. The primacy in divine intention is the total community, and not any single member of the community, not even the human. The work of the religious community is to enter into this process in every possible way. The natural world has to be seen as part of the revelatory presence of divine being.

The *World Charter for Nature* is one of the basic documents of the United Nations and the finest thing the United Nations has ever done in regard to human-Earth relationships. It had only a negative response from the United States, the only country to cast a negative vote in the General Assembly when the document was put to a vote; considerably more than one hundred countries approved the Charter. That Charter sought to draw all phases of the human project into a more profound appreciation of the human-Earth relationship, to a more profound understanding of the significance of the natural world. It is one of the best statements of what should be our sense of our place in the natural world and the universe.

Planet Earth is in crisis because of humans' actions and inactions. We have to get people to focus on the problem of how we relate to this planet Earth, and to accept the fact that the human is subordinate to planet Earth. Some religious people think that Earth is made for the human, or is in service to the human; they do not realize that the human is part of Earth. Humans and Earth serve each other, in a certain sense. Earth is a community and is part of a larger community. Humans have a role in the Earth community. The human is that being in whom the universe reflects on and celebrates itself in a special mode of conscious self-awareness. The universe celebrates its origin and meaning in a special mode of consciousness, so the human is more a mode of being of the universe than an individual being in the universe. The human is not the universe, but the universe could not be itself without the human. The universe would not be a universe without the human, because the human is its consciousness; an unconscious universe would be meaningless.

There is an ecological crisis because of the human exploitation of planet Earth and its threat to Earth's sustainability. A Great Work is needed to confront the Earth crisis and to begin a process whereby consciousness of an integrated human-Earth relationship is restored, and humans live in harmony with each other, with all life, and with Earth. All people have a responsibility to engage in this Great Work, to move humans from their destructive relationship with Earth to a more benign relationship. The difficulty throughout the human order is turning into a difficulty in the functioning of the planet. A dysfunctioning planet is a disfunctioning of everything on the planet. The Great Work is simply restoring some integral relationship between humans and the planet Earth.

As we find our way into the new world of the twenty-first century, these considerations help us become increasingly conscious of the infinite wonder, beauty, and fulfillment possible in the sacred world enfolding us. In *Sacramental Commons*, John Hart provides a substantial contribution to the Great Work.

Thomas Berry
Greensboro, North Carolina
April 11, 2006

Thomas Berry (1914–) is a Passionist priest and an internationally recognized historian of cultures who has taught in several universities before founding the Riverdale Center for Religious Research, where scholars explore the place of humans on Earth and in the cosmos. His most influential books include *The Dream of the Earth* (1988), *The Universe Story: From the Primordial Flaring Forth to the Ecozoic Era* (1992), in collaboration with mathematical-cosmologist Brian Swimme, and *The Great Work: Our Way Into the Future* (1999).

Selected Bibliography

Armstrong, Regis J., O.F.M. Cap., J. A. Wayne Hellmann, O.F.M. Conv., and William J. Short, O.F.M. *Francis of Assisi: The Saint.* Vol. 1 of *Francis of Assisi: Early Documents.* New York: New City Press, 1999.

————. *Francis of Assisi: The Founder.* Vol. 2 of *Francis of Assisi: Early Documents.* New York: New City Press, 1999.

————. *Francis of Assisi: The Prophet.* Vol. 3 of *Francis of Assisi: Early Documents.* New York: New City Press, 1999.

Berry, Thomas. *The Great Work: Our Way into the Future.* New York: Bell Tower, 2000.

————. *The Dream of the Earth.* San Francisco: Sierra Club Books, 1988.

Berry, Wendell. *The Unsettling of America: Culture and Agriculture.* New York: Avon Books, 1978.

Black Elk. *Black Elk Speaks: Being the Life Story of a Holy Man of the Oglala Sioux.* Recorded and ed. John G. Neihardt. New York: Pocket Books, 1972.

————. *The Sacred Pipe: Black Elk's Account of the Seven Rites of the Oglala Sioux.* Recorded and ed. Joseph Epes Brown. New York: Penguin, 1976.

Boff, Leonardo. *Cry of the Earth, Cry of the Poor.* Maryknoll, N.Y.: Orbis, 1997.

————. *Ecology and Liberation: A New Paradigm.* Trans. John Cumming. Maryknoll, N.Y.: Orbis, 1996.

Brown, Raymond E., S.S., Joseph A. Fitzmyer, S.J., and Roland E. Murphy, O.P. *The New Jerome Biblical Commentary.* Englewood Cliffs, N.J.: Prentice-Hall, 1990.

Brueggemann, Walter. *The Land: Place as Gift, Promise, and Challenge in Biblical Faith.* Minneapolis: Augsburg Fortress, 1977.

Caprettini, Gian Paolo. *San Francesco, il Lupo, i segni.* Turin: Einaudi, 1974.

Carreira Das Neves, Manuel. *Francesco Profeta di Pace e di Ecologia.* Trans. Enzo De Marchi. Padova: Messaggero Padova, 1993.

Chryssavgis, John, ed. *Cosmic Grace, Humble Prayer: The Ecological Vision of the Green Patriarch Bartholomew I.* Grand Rapids, Mich.: Eerdmans, 2003.

Clark, Robert. *River of the West: A Chronicle of the Columbia.* New York: Picador, 1997.

Commission on Theological Concerns of the Christian Conference of Asia, ed. *Minjung Theology: People as the Subjects of History.* Maryknoll, N.Y.: Orbis, 1981.

Cone, Joseph. *A Common Fate: Endangered Salmon and the People of the Pacific Northwest.* Corvallis: Oregon State University Press, 1996.

Coogan, Michael D., ed. *The New Oxford Annotated Bible: New Revised Standard Version with the Apocrypha*. 3rd ed. New York: Oxford University Press, 2001.

Davies, W. D. *The Gospel and the Land: Early Christianity and Jewish Territorial Doctrine*. Berkeley: University of California Press, 1974.

Deloria, Vine, Jr. *The World We Used to Live In: Remembering the Powers of the Medicine Men*. Golden, Col.: Fulcrum Publishing, 2006.

Fortini, Arnaldo. *Francis of Assisi*. Trans. Helen Moak. New York: Crossroad, 1981.

Gottlieb, Roger S., ed. *This Sacred Earth: Religion, Nature, Environment*. New York: Routledge, 1996.

Hart, John. *What Are They Saying about Environmental Theology?* Mahwah, N.J.: Paulist, 2004.

———. *Ethics and Technology: Innovation and Transformation in Community Contexts*. Cleveland, Ohio: Pilgrim, 1997.

———. *The Spirit of the Earth: A Theology of the Land*. Mahwah, N.J.: Paulist, 1984.

———."Sustaining the Sacramental Commons." *Dialog: A Journal of Theology* 42, no. 3 (September 2003): 235–41, "Saving the Planet" issue.

———. "Living Water: A Sacramental Commons." *Catholic Rural Life* 45, no. 2 (Spring 2003): 4–11.

———. "Salmon and Social Ethics: Relational Consciousness in the Web of Life." *Journal of the Society of Christian Ethics* 22 (Fall 2002): 67–93.

———. "A Jubilee for a New Millennium: Justice for Earth and for Peoples of the Land." *Catholic Rural Life* 43, no. 2 (Spring 2001): 23–31.

Heschel, Abraham J. *The Prophets: An Introduction*. 2 vols. New York: Harper Torchbooks, 1969.

Hildegard of Bingen. *Hildegard of Bingen's Book of Divine Works*. Ed. Matthew Fox. Santa Fe, N.M.: Bear, 1987.

House, Adrian. *Francis of Assisi: A Revolutionary Life*. Foreword by Karen Armstrong. Mahwah, N.J.: Paulist, 2001.

John Paul II, Pope. *The Ecological Crisis: A Common Responsibility*. Washington, D.C.: United States Catholic Conference, 1990.

Johnson, Elizabeth A. *Women, Earth, and Creator Spirit*. New York: Paulist, 1993.

Leopold, Aldo. *A Sand County Almanac and Sketches Here and There*. New York: Oxford University Press, 1987.

Louth, Andrew. *Maximus the Confessor*. London: Routledge, 1996.

Maximus. *Maximus Confessor: Selected Writings*. Trans. George C. Berthold. Classics of Western Spirituality. New York: Paulist, 1985.

McFague, Sallie. *The Body of God: An Ecological Theology*. Minneapolis: Fortress, 1993.

McGrath, Alister. *The Reenchantment of Nature: The Denial by Religion and the Ecological Crisis*. New York: Doubleday, 2002.

Nash, James A. *Loving Nature: Ecological Integrity and Christian Responsibility*. Nashville, Tenn.: Abingdon, 1991.

Peacocke, Arthur. *Paths from Science towards God: The End of All Our Exploring*. Oxford: OneWorld, 2001.

———. *Theology for a Scientific Age: Being and Becoming—Natural, Divine and Human*. London: SCM, 1993.

Rasmussen, Larry L. *Earth Community Earth Ethics*. Maryknoll, N.Y.: Orbis, 1996.

Relander, Click. *Drummers and Dreamers*. Seattle: Northwest Interpretive Association, 1986.

Robb, Carol S., and Carl J. Casebolt. *Covenant for a New Creation: Ethics, Religion, and Public Policy*. Maryknoll, N.Y.: Orbis, 1991.

Rolston, Holmes, III. *Environmental Ethics: Duties to and Values in the Natural World*. Philadelphia: Temple University Press, 1988.

———. *Conserving Natural Value*. New York: Columbia University Press, 1994.

Ruether, Rosemary Radford. *Integrating Ecofeminism, Globalization, and World Religions*. Lanham, Md.: Rowman & Littlefield, 2005.

———. *Gaia and God*. San Francisco: Harper, 1992.

Sorrell, Roger D. *St. Francis of Assisi and Nature: Tradition and Innovation in Western Christian Attitudes toward the Environment*. New York: Oxford University Press, 1988.

Teale, Edwin Way. *The Wilderness World of John Muir*. Boston: Houghton Mifflin, 1954.

Tinker, George. *Spirit and Resistance: Political Theology and American Indian Liberation*. Minneapolis: Fortress Press, 2004.

U.S. Catholic Bishops. *Renewing the Earth: An Invitation to Reflection and Action on Environment in Light of Catholic Social Teaching* (1991). In *Renewing the Face of the Earth: A Resource for Parishes*. Washington, D.C.: Department of Social Development and World Peace, United States Catholic Conference, 1994.

U.S. and Canadian Columbia River Watershed Catholic Bishops. *The Columbia River Watershed: Caring for Creation and the Common Good*. Seattle: Columbia River Pastoral Letter Project/Roman Catholic Archdiocese of Seattle, 2001.

U.S. Midwestern Catholic Bishops. *Strangers and Guests: Toward Community in the Heartland*. Des Moines, Iowa: National Catholic Rural Life Conference, 1980.

Wilson, Edward O. *The Diversity of Life*. New York: Norton, 1992.

———. *Biophilia*. Cambridge, Mass.: Harvard University Press, 1984.

Wolfe, Linnie Marsh. *Son of the Wilderness: The Life of John Muir*. Madison: University of Wisconsin Press, 1980.

Index

About the Author

John Hart is a professor of Christian ethics at the Boston University School of Theology. Previously, he served as a professor of theology and founding director of Environmental Studies at Carroll College, Helena, Montana. He has authored three books: *What Are They Saying About Environmental Theology?* (2004); *Ethics and Technology: Innovation and Transformation in Community Contexts* (1997); and *The Spirit of the Earth: A Theology of the Land* (1984). He has written chapters for five edited books and has more than forty published articles and essays, including seven in the *Encyclopedia of Religion and Nature* (2005). His doctorate (1978) is from the Union Theological Seminary, New York, where he was a tutor in Christian ethics (1974–1976) and a tutor in liberation theology for Gustavo Gutiérrez (1976). He received his B.A. from Marist College in New York (1966), and studied Latin American literature at the Universidad Nacional Autónoma de México (1966). He was director of the midwestern Catholic bishops' twelve-state Heartland Project, and editor and principal writer of their land pastoral, *Strangers and Guests: Toward Community in the Heartland* (1980). He wrote the draft of Pope John Paul II's homily on land stewardship presented at the Living History Farms near Des Moines, Iowa (1979). He has worked with native spiritual leaders and human rights activists, has been a member of the Delegation of the International Indian Treaty Council (a nongovernmental organization accredited to the United Nations) to the UN International Human Rights Commission, Geneva (1987, 1990), and was an invited observer at the World Conference of Indigenous Peoples, Rio de Janeiro, while participating in the United Nations Earth Summit (1992). He has been selected for three National Endowment for the Humanities programs: a summer stipend for research into Native American spirituality (1985), a summer seminar grant for postdoctoral study at the Harvard Divinity School (1986), and a summer seminar grant to participate in "St. Francis in the Thirteenth Century" in Siena, Rome, and Assisi (2003). He received an international

Science-Religion Course Award (1995) from the John Templeton foundation for his course "Spirit, Science, and Nature." Carroll College faculty recognized him as an Outstanding Faculty Member (1995) and as a Distinguished Scholar (2002). He coauthored the "Declaration on Distortions of the Gospel" issued by the Montana Association of Churches (1996) to affirm God's love for all peoples and wrote the draft for the MAC document "Caring in Creation" (1998) on Christianity and ecology. He was selected as a Lilly Teaching Scholar in Religion (1997–1998) and for the Templeton Oxford Seminars in Science and Christianity (University of Oxford, summers, 1999–2001). He was the project writer and a member of the Steering Committee for the Western U.S. and Canada Catholic bishops' bioregional pastoral letter, *The Columbia River Watershed: Caring for Creation and the Common Good* (2001), on the ethics, economics, and ecology of the region. On behalf of this project, he received a Sacred Gift for a Living Planet Award (2000) in Bhaktapur, Nepal, from the Alliance of Religions and Conservation and the World Wide Fund for Nature. He is associated with the Center for Maximum Potential Building Systems (Texas) and served as vice president of the board of the Wild Divide Chapter of the Montana Wilderness Association, a member of the Board of the Montana Association of Churches, and a member of the board of the Montana Environmental Information Center. He is a member of the American Academy of Religion and the Society of Christian Ethics, is listed in *Who's Who in the World* and in other biographical publications, and served as the local secretary of Montana Mensa. He has been involved with the *Earth Charter* as a participant in the World Council of Churches Ecumenical Center meeting on Benchmark II (Geneva, 1999); in the "*Earth Charter* Ethics Seminar" as one of twenty-five invited scholars from four continents (New York, 2002); as a member of the delegation to Urbino, Italy, for implementation planning meetings (2002); and as a participant in the "Earth Charter + 5" Conference (Amsterdam, 2005). Internationally known for his work in social ethics and environmental ethics, he has given almost two hundred presentations on four continents. He enjoys hiking, skiing, and snowshoeing; and singing and playing guitar and Native American flute. He and his wife, Jane, have two children, Shanti and Daniel, pursuing professional careers.